HARDPRESS.NET
HOME OF HARD-TO-FIND BOOKS

The Poetical Works of Beattie, Blair, and Falconer
by James Beattie

Address:
HardPress
8345 NW 66TH ST #2561
MIAMI FL 33166-2626
USA
Email: info@hardpress.net

Lewis Henry Corkran
from
Edward P. Rawnsley
On his leaving Eton
Election 1866

THE

POETICAL WORKS

OF

BEATTIE, BLAIR, AND FALCONER.

BALLANTYNE, PRINTER, EDINBURGH.

THE

POETICAL WORKS

OF

BEATTIE, BLAIR,

AND

FALCONER.

With Lives, Critical Dissertations, and
Explanatory Notes,

BY THE
REV. GEORGE GILFILLAN.

EDINBURGH: JAMES NICHOL.
LONDON: JAMES NISBET & CO.   DUBLIN: W. ROBERTSON.
M.DCCC.LIV.

CONTENTS.

BEATTIE'S POETICAL WORKS.

BLAIR'S POETICAL WORKS.

FALCONER'S POETICAL WORKS.

POETICAL WORKS

OF

JAMES BEATTIE.

BEATTIE'S POEMS.

THE MINSTREL;

OR,

THE PROGRESS OF GENIUS.

PREFACE.

The design was, to trace the progress of a Poetical Genius, born in a rude age, from the first dawning of fancy and reason, till that period at which he may be supposed capable of appearing in the world as a MINSTREL, that is, as an itinerant poet and musician :—a character which, according to the notions of our forefathers, was not only respectable, but sacred.

I have endeavoured to imitate Spenser in the measure of his verse, and in the harmony, simplicity, and variety of his composition. Antique expressions I have avoided; admitting, however, some old words, where they seemed to suit the subject : but I hope none will be found that are now obsolete, or in any degree not intelligible to a reader of English poetry.

To those who may be disposed to ask what could induce me to write in so difficult a measure, I can only answer, that it pleases my ear, and seems, from its Gothic structure and original, to bear some relation to the subject and spirit of the poem. It admits both simplicity and magnificence of sound and of language, beyond any other stanza I am acquainted with. It allows the sententiousness of the couplet, as well as the more complex modulation of blank verse. What some critics have remarked, of its uniformity growing at last tiresome to the ear, will be found to hold true only when the poetry is faulty in other respects.

A

BOOK I.

Me vero primum dulces ante omnia Musæ,
Quarum sacra fero, ingenti perculsus amore,
Accipiant——   VIRG.

1 AH! who can tell how hard it is to climb
The steep where Fame's proud temple shines afar?
Ah! who can tell how many a soul sublime
Has felt the influence of malignant star,
And waged with Fortune an eternal war—
Check'd by the scoff of Pride, by Envy's frown,
And Poverty's unconquerable bar—
In life's low vale remote has pined alone,
Then dropp'd into the grave, unpitied and unknown?

2 And yet the languor of inglorious days,
Not equally oppressive is to all;
Him who ne'er listen'd to the voice of praise,
The silence of neglect can ne'er appal.
There are, who, deaf to mad Ambition's call,
Would shrink to hear the obstreperous trump of Fame
Supremely blest, if to their portion fall
Health, competence, and peace.   Nor higher aim
Had he whose simple tale these artless lines proclaim.

3 The rolls of fame I will not now explore;
Nor need I here describe, in learned lay,
How forth the Minstrel fared in days of yore,
Right glad of heart, though homely in array;
His waving locks and beard all hoary gray;
While from his bending shoulder, decent hung
His harp, the sole companion of his way,
Which to the whistling wild responsive rung:
And ever as he went some merry lay he sung.

4 Fret not thyself, thou glittering child of pride,
  That a poor villager inspires my strain ;
  With thee let Pageantry and Power abide :
  The gentle Muses haunt the sylvan reign ;
  Where through wild groves at eve the lonely swain
  Enraptured roams, to gaze on Nature's charms :
  They hate the sensual and scorn the vain,
  The parasite their influence never warms,
Nor him whose sordid soul the love of gold alarms.

5 Though richest hues the peacock's plumes adorn,
  Yet horror screams from his discordant throat.
  Rise, sons of harmony, and hail the morn,
  While warbling larks on russet pinions float :
  Or seek at noon the woodland scene remote,
  Where the grey linnets carol from the hill.
  Oh, let them ne'er, with artificial note,
  To please a tyrant, strain the little bill,
But sing what Heaven inspires, and wander where they will

6 Liberal, not lavish, is kind Nature's hand ;
  Nor was perfection made for man below ;
  Yet all her schemes with nicest art are plann'd ;
  Good counteracting ill, and gladness woe.
  With gold and gems if Chilian mountains glow ;
  If bleak and barren Scotia's hills arise ;
  There plague and poison, lust and rapine grow ;
  Here, peaceful are the vales, and pure the skies,
And Freedom fires the soul, and sparkles in the eyes.

7 Then grieve not, thou, to whom the indulgent Muse
  Vouchsafes a portion of celestial fire ;
  Nor blame the partial Fates, if they refuse
  The imperial banquet and the rich attire.

Know thine own worth, and reverence the lyre.
Wilt thou debase the heart which God refined ?
No ; let thy heaven-taught soul to Heaven aspire,
To fancy, freedom, harmony resign'd ;
Ambition's grovelling crew for ever left behind.

8 Canst thou forego the pure ethereal soul
In each fine sense so exquisitely keen,
On the dull couch of Luxury to loll,
Stung with disease, and stupified with spleen ;
Fain to implore the aid of Flattery's screen,
Even from thyself thy loathsome heart to hide
(The mansion then no more of joy serene),
Where fear, distrust, malevolence abide,
And impotent desire, and disappointed pride ?

9 Oh, how canst thou renounce the boundless store
Of charms which Nature to her votary yields ?
The warbling woodland, the resounding shore,
The pomp of groves, and garniture of fields ;
All that the genial ray of morning gilds,
And all that echoes to the song of even,
All that the mountain's sheltering bosom shields,
And all the dread magnificence of heaven,
Oh, how canst thou renounce, and hope to be forgiven ?

10 These charms shall work thy soul's eternal health,
And love, and gentleness, and joy impart.
But these thou must renounce, if lust of wealth
E'er win its way to thy corrupted heart :
For, ah ! it poisons like a scorpion's dart ;
Prompting the ungenerous wish, the selfish scheme,
The stern resolve, unmoved by pity's smart,
The troublous day, and long distressful dream.
Return, my roving Muse, resume thy purposed theme.

11 There lived in Gothic days, as legends tell,
   A shepherd-swain, a man of low degree ;
   Whose sires, perchance, in Fairyland might dwell,
   Sicilian groves, or vales of Arcady ;
   But he, I ween, was of the north countrie ; [1]
   A nation famed for song and beauty's charms ;
   Zealous, yet modest ; innocent, though free ;
   Patient of toil ; serene amidst alarms ;
Inflexible in faith ; invincible in arms.

12 The shepherd swain of whom I mention made,
   On Scotia's mountains fed his little flock ;
   The sickle, scythe, or plough he never sway'd :
   An honest heart was almost all his stock ;
   His drink the living water from the rock :
   The milky dams supplied his board, and lent
   Their kindly fleece to baffle winter's shock ;
   And he, though oft with dust and sweat besprent,
Did guide and guard their wanderings, wheresoe'er they
      went.

13 From labour, health, from health, contentment, springs
   Contentment opes the source of every joy.
· He envied not, he never thought of kings ;
   Nor from those appetites sustain'd annoy,
   That chance may frustrate, or indulgence cloy ;
   Nor Fate his calm and humble hopes beguiled ;
   He mourn'd no recreant friend, nor mistress coy,
   For on his vows the blameless Phœbe smiled,
And her alone he loved, and loved her from a child.

[1] There is hardly an ancient ballad, or romance, wherein a minstrel or a
harper appears, but he is characterized, by way of eminence, to have been
' of the north countrie.' It is probable, that under this appellation were for-
merly comprehended all the provinces to the north of the Trent.—See *Percy's
Essay on the English Minstrels.*

14 No jealousy their dawn of love o'ercast,
      Nor blasted were their wedded days with strife ;
    Each season look'd delightful, as it pass'd,
      To the fond husband, and the faithful wife.
      Beyond the lowly vale of shepherd life
    They never roam'd : secure beneath the storm
      Which in Ambition's lofty hand is rife,
    Where peace and love are canker'd by the worm
  Of pride, each bud of joy industrious to deform.

15 The wight whose tale these artless lines unfold,
      Was all the offspring of this humble pair :
    His birth no oracle or seer foretold ;
      No prodigy appear'd in earth or air,
      Nor aught that might a strange event declare.
    You guess each circumstance of Edwin's birth ;
      The parent's transport, and the parent's care ;
    The gossip's prayer for wealth, and wit, and worth ;
  And one long summer day of indolence and mirth.

16 And yet poor Edwin was no vulgar boy ;
      Deep thought oft seem'd to fix his infant eye.
    Dainties he heeded not, nor gaude, nor toy,
      Save one short pipe of rudest minstrelsy :
      Silent when glad ; affectionate, though shy ;
    And now his look was most demurely sad ;
      And now he laugh'd aloud, yet none knew why.
    The neighbours stared and sigh'd, yet bless'd the lad :
  Some deem'd him wondrous wise, and some believed him
        mad.

17 But why should I his childish feats display ?
      Concourse, and noise, and toil he ever fled ;
    Nor cared to mingle in the clamorous fray
      Of squabbling imps ; but to the forest sped,

Or roam'd at large the lonely mountain's head,
Or, where the maze of some bewilder'd stream
To deep untrodden groves his footsteps led,
There would he wander wild, till Phœbus' beam,
Shot from the western cliff, released the weary team.

18 The exploit of strength, dexterity, or speed,
To him nor vanity nor joy could bring.
His heart, from cruel sport estranged, would bleed
To work the woe of any living thing,
By trap, or net ; by arrow, or by sling :
These he detested ; those he scorn'd to wield ;
He wish'd to be the guardian, not the king,
Tyrant far less, or traitor of the field.
And sure the sylvan reign unbloody joy might yield.

19 Lo ! where the stripling, wrapt in wonder, roves
Beneath the precipice o'erhung with pine ;
And sees, on high, amidst the encircling groves,
From cliff to cliff the foaming torrents shine :
While waters, woods, and winds in concert join,
And Echo swells the chorus to the skies.
Would Edwin this majestic scene resign
For aught the huntsman's puny craft supplies ?
Ah ! no ; he better knows great Nature's charms to prize.

20 And oft he traced the uplands, to survey,
When o'er the sky advanced the kindling dawn,
The crimson cloud, blue main, and mountain gray,
And lake, dim-gleaming on the smoky lawn :
Far to the west the long long vale withdrawn,
Where twilight loves to linger for a while ;
And now he faintly kens the bounding fawn,
And villager abroad at early toil.
But, lo ! the Sun appears, and heaven, earth, ocean smile

21 And oft the craggy cliff he loved to climb,
    When all in mist the world below was lost.
    What dreadful pleasure! there to stand sublime,
    Like shipwreck'd mariner on desert coast,
    And view the enormous waste of vapour toss'd
    In billows, lengthening to the horizon round,
    Now scoop'd in gulfs, with mountains now emboss'd!
    And hear the voice of mirth and song rebound,
Flocks, herds, and waterfalls, along the hoar profound!

22 In truth he was a strange and wayward wight,
    Fond of each gentle, and each dreadful scene.
    In darkness, and in storm, he found delight:
    Nor less than when on ocean-wave serene
    The southern Sun diffused his dazzling sheen,[1]
    Even sad vicissitude amused his soul:
    And if a sigh would sometimes intervene,   .
    And down his cheek a tear of pity roll,
  A sigh, a tear, so sweet, he wish'd not to control.

23 "O ye wild groves! O where is now your bloom?"
    (The Muse interprets thus his tender thought)
    "Your flowers, your verdure, and your balmy gloom,
    Of late so grateful in the hour of drought?
    Why do the birds, that song and rapture brought
    To all your bowers, their mansions now forsake?
    Ah! why has fickle chance this ruin wrought?
    For now the storm howls mournful through the brake,
And the dead foliage flies in many a shapeless flake.

24 "Where now the rill, melodious, pure, and cool,
    And meads, with life and mirth and beauty crown'd?

---

    [1] 'Dazzling sheen:' Brightness, splendour.   The word is used by some
late writers, as well as by Milton.

Ah ! see, the unsightly slime and sluggish pool,
Have all the solitary vale imbrown'd ;
Fled each fair form, and mute each melting sound,
The raven croaks forlorn on naked spray :
And, hark ! the river, bursting every mound,
Down the vale thunders, and with wasteful sway
Uproots the grove, and rolls the shatter'd rocks away.

25 " Yet such the destiny of all on earth !
So flourishes and fades majestic Man.
Fair is the bud his vernal morn brings forth,
And fostering gales awhile the nursling fan.
Oh, smile, ye heavens serene ! ye mildews wan,
Ye blighting whirlwinds, spare his balmy prime,
Nor lessen of his life the little span !
Borne on the swift, though silent wings of Time,
Old age comes on apace to ravage all the clime.

26 " And be it so.   Let those deplore their doom,
Whose hope still grovels in this dark sojourn :
But lofty souls, who look beyond the tomb,
Can smile at Fate, and wonder how they mourn.
Shall Spring to these sad scenes no more return ?
Is yonder wave the Sun's eternal bed ?
Soon shall the orient with new lustre burn,
And Spring shall soon her vital influence shed,
Again attune the grove, again adorn the mead.

27 " Shall I be left forgotten in the dust,
When Fate, relenting, lets the flower revive ?
Shall Nature's voice, to man alone unjust,
Bid him, though doom'd to perish, hope to live ?
Is it for this fair Virtue oft must strive
With disappointment, penury, and pain ?

No! Heaven's immortal springs shall yet arrive,
And man's majestic beauty bloom again,
Bright through the eternal year of Love's triumphant
    reign."

28 This truth sublime his simple sire had taught :
In sooth, 'twas almost all the shepherd knew.
No subtle nor superfluous lore he sought,
Nor ever wish'd his Edwin to pursue.
" Let man's own sphere," said he, " confine his view ;
Be man's peculiar work his sole delight."
And much, and oft, he warn'd him to eschew
Falsehood and guile, and aye maintain the right,
By pleasure unseduced, unawed by lawless might.

29 " And from the prayer of Want, and plaint of Woe,
O never, never turn away thine ear !
Forlorn, in this bleak wilderness below,
Ah ! what were man, should Heaven refuse to hear !
To others do (the law is not severe)
What to thyself thou wishest to be done.
Forgive thy foes ; and love thy parents dear,
And friends, and native land ; nor those alone :
All human weal and woe learn thou to make thine own."

30 See, in the rear of the warm sunny shower
The visionary boy from shelter fly ;
For now the storm of summer rain is o'er,
And cool, and fresh, and fragrant is the sky.
And, lo ! in the dark east, expanded high,
The rainbow brightens to the setting Sun !
Fond fool, that deem'st the streaming glory nigh,
How vain the chase thine ardour has begun !
'Tis fled afar, ere half thy purposed race be run.

31 Yet couldst thou learn that thus it fares with age,
  When pleasure, wealth, or power the bosom warm;
  This baffled hope might tame thy manhood's rage,
  And disappointment of her sting disarm.
  But why should foresight thy fond heart alarm?
  Perish the lore that deadens young desire!
  Pursue, poor imp, the imaginary charm,
  Indulge gay hope, and fancy's pleasing fire:
Fancy and hope too soon shall of themselves expire.

32 When the long-sounding curfew from afar
  Loaded with loud lament the lonely gale,
  Young Edwin, lighted by the evening star,
  Lingering and listening, wander'd down the vale.
  There would he dream of graves, and corses pale,
  And ghosts that to the charnel-dungeon throng,
  And drag a length of clanking chain, and wail,
  Till silenced by the owl's terrific song,
Or blast that shrieks by fits the shuddering aisles along.

33 Or, when the setting Moon, in crimson dyed,
  Hung o'er the dark and melancholy deep,
  To haunted stream, remote from man, he hied,
  Where fays of yore their revels wont to keep;
  And there let Fancy rove at large, till sleep
  A vision brought to his entrancèd sight.
  And first, a wildly murmuring wind 'gan creep
  Shrill to his ringing ear; then tapers bright,
With instantaneous gleam, illumed the vault of night.

34 Anon in view a portal's blazon'd arch
  Arose; the trumpet bids the valves unfold;
  And forth a host of little warriors march,
  Grasping the diamond lance, and targe of gold.

Their look was gentle, their demeanour bold,
And green their helms, and green their silk attire;
And here and there, right venerably old,
The long-robed minstrels wake the warbling wire,
And some with mellow breath the martial pipe in
     spire.

35 With merriment, and song, and timbrels clear,
A troop of dames from myrtle bowers advance;
The little warriors doff the targe and spear,
And loud enlivening strains provoke the dance.
They meet, they dart away, they wheel askance;
To right, to left, they thread the flying maze;
Now bound aloft with vigorous spring, then glance
Rapid along: with many-colour'd rays
Of tapers, gems, and gold, the echoing forests blaze.

36 The dream is fled. Proud harbinger of day,
Who scar'dst the vision with thy clarion shrill,
Fell chanticleer; who oft hath reft away
My fancied good, and brought substantial ill!
Oh, to thy cursed scream, discordant still,
Let harmony aye shut her gentle ear:
Thy boastful mirth let jealous rivals spill,
Insult thy crest, and glossy pinions tear,
And ever in thy dreams the ruthless fox appear!

37 Forbear, my Muse. Let Love attune thy line.
Revoke the spell. Thine Edwin frets not so.
For how should he at wicked chance repine,
Who feels from every change amusement flow?
Even now his eyes with smiles of rapture glow,
As on he wanders through the scenes of morn,

Where the fresh flowers in living lustre blow,
Where thousand pearls the dewy lawns adorn,
A thousand notes of joy in every breeze are borne.

38 But who the melodies of morn can tell?
The wild brook babbling down the mountain side;
The lowing herd; the sheepfold's simple bell;
The pipe of early shepherd dim descried
In the lone valley; echoing far and wide
The clamorous horn along the cliffs above;
The hollow murmur of the ocean-tide;
The hum of bees, the linnet's lay of love,
And the full choir that wakes the universal grove.

39 The cottage curs at early pilgrim bark;
Crown'd with her pail the tripping milkmaid sings;
The whistling ploughman stalks afield; and, hark!
Down the rough slope the ponderous waggon rings;
Through rustling corn the hare astonish'd springs;
Slow tolls the village clock the drowsy hour;
The partridge bursts away on whirring wings;
Deep mourns the turtle in sequester'd bower,
And shrill lark carols clear from her aërial tour.

40 O Nature, how in every charm supreme!
Whose votaries feast on raptures ever new!
O for the voice and fire of seraphim,
To sing thy glories with devotion due!
Blest be the day I 'scaped the wrangling crew,
From Pyrrho's maze, and Epicurus' sty;
And held high converse with the godlike few,
Who to the enraptured heart, and ear, and eye,
Teach beauty, virtue, truth, and love, and melody.

41   Hence! ye, who snare and stupify the mind,
     Sophists! of beauty, virtue, joy, the bane!
     Greedy and fell, though impotent and blind,
     Who spread your filthy nets in Truth's fair fane,
     And ever ply your venom'd fangs amain!
     Hence to dark Error's den, whose rankling slime
     First gave you form! Hence! lest the Muse should deign
     (Though loth on theme so mean to waste a rhyme),
  With vengeance to pursue your sacrilegious crime.

42   But hail, ye mighty masters of the lay,
     Nature's true sons, the friends of man and truth!
     Whose song, sublimely sweet, serenely gay,
     Amused my childhood, and inform'd my youth.
     O let your spirit still my bosom soothe,
     Inspire my dreams, and my wild wanderings guide;
     Your voice each rugged path of life can smooth,
     For well I know, wherever ye reside,
  There harmony, and peace, and innocence abide.

43   Ah me! neglected on the lonesome plain,
     As yet poor Edwin never knew your lore,
     Save when against the winter's drenching rain,
     And driving snow, the cottage shut the door.
     Then, as instructed by tradition hoar,
     Her legend when the beldam 'gan impart,
     Or chant the old heroic ditty o'er,
     Wonder and joy ran thrilling to his heart;
  Much he the tale admired, but more the tuneful art.

44   Various and strange was the long-winded tale;
     And halls, and knights, and feats of arms display'd;
     Or merry swains, who quaff the nut-brown ale,
     And sing enamour'd of the nut-brown maid;

The moonlight revel of the fairy glade ;
Or hags, that suckle an infernal brood,
And ply in caves the unutterable trade,[1]
'Midst fiends and spectres quench the Moon in blood,
Yell in the midnight storm, or ride the infuriate flood.

45 But when to horror his amazement rose,
   A gentler strain the beldam would rehearse,
   A tale of rural life, a tale of woes,
   The orphan babes, and guardian uncle fierce.
   O cruel ! will no pang of pity pierce
   That heart, by lust of lucre sear'd to stone ?
   For sure, if aught of virtue last, or verse,
   To latest times shall tender souls bemoan
Those hopeless orphan babes by thy fell arts undone.

46 Behold, with berries smear'd, with brambles torn,[2]
   The babes, now famish'd, lay them down to die :
   Amidst the howl of darksome woods forlorn,
   Folded in one another's arms they lie ;
   Nor friend, nor stranger, hears their dying cry :
   " For from the town the man returns no more."
   But thou, who Heaven's just vengeance dar'st defy,
   This deed with fruitless tears shalt soon deplore,
When Death lays waste thy house, and flames consume thy
       store.

47 A stifled smile of stern vindictive joy
   Brighten'd one moment Edwin's starting tear,—

[1] Allusion to Shakspeare :—
        Mac. How now, ye secret, black, and midnight hags,
            What is't ye do ?
        Wit. A deed without a name.
                            —MACBETH, Act 4, Scene 1.
[2] See the fine old ballad called, ' The Children in the Wood.'

" But why should gold man's feeble mind decoy,
And innocence thus die by doom severe ?"
O Edwin ! while thy heart is yet sincere,
The assaults of discontent and doubt repel :
Dark even at noontide is our mortal sphere ;
But let us hope ; to doubt is to rebel :
Let us exult in hope, that all shall yet be well.

48 Nor be thy generous indignation check'd,
Nor check'd the tender tear to Misery given;
From Guilt's contagious power shall *that* protect,
This soften and refine the soul for Heaven.
But dreadful is their doom whom doubt has driven
To censure Fate, and pious Hope forego:
Like yonder blasted boughs by lightning riven,
Perfection, beauty, life, they never know,
But frown on all that pass, a monument of woe.

49 Shall he whose birth, maturity, and age
Scarce fill the circle of one summer day,
Shall the poor gnat, with discontent and rage,
Exclaim that Nature hastens to decay,
If but a cloud obstruct the solar ray,
If but a momentary shower descend ?
Or shall frail man Heaven's dread decree gainsay,
Which bade the series of events extend
Wide through unnumber'd worlds, and ages without end '

50 One part, one little part, we dimly scan
Through the dark medium of life's feverish dream ;
Yet dare arraign the whole stupendous plan,
If but that little part incongruous seem.
Nor is that part perhaps what mortals deem ;
Oft from apparent ill our blessings rise.

O, then, renounce that impious self-esteem,
That aims to trace the secrets of the skies:
For thou art but of dust ; be humble, and be wise.

51 Thus Heaven enlarged his soul in riper years.
    For Nature gave him strength and fire, to soar
    On Fancy's wing above this vale of tears ;
    Where dark cold-hearted sceptics, creeping, pore
    Through microscope of metaphysic lore ;
    And much they grope for Truth, but never hit.
    For why ? Their powers, inadequate before,
    This idle art makes more and more unfit ;
Yet deem they darkness light, and their vain blunders
        wit.

52 Nor was this ancient dame a foe to mirth.
    Her ballad, jest, and riddle's quaint device
    Oft cheer'd the shepherds round their social hearth ;
    Whom levity or spleen could ne'er entice
    To purchase chat or laughter, at the price
    Of decency.   Nor let it faith exceed,
    That Nature forms a rustic taste so nice.
    Ah ! had they been of court or city breed,
Such delicacy were right marvellous indeed.

53 Oft when the winter storm had ceased to rave,
    He roam'd the snowy waste at even, to view
    The cloud stupendous, from the Atlantic wave
    High-towering, sail along the horizon blue ;
    Where, 'midst the changeful scenery, ever new,
    Fancy a thousand wondrous forms descries,
    More wildly great than ever pencil drew,
    Rocks, torrents, gulfs, and shapes of giant size,
And glittering cliffs on cliffs, and fiery ramparts rise.

B

54   Thence musing onward to the sounding shore,
     The lone enthusiast oft would take his way,
     Listening, with pleasing dread, to the deep roar
     Of the wide-weltering waves.   In black array,
     When sulphurous clouds roll'd on the autumnal day,
     Even then he hasten'd from the haunt of man,
     Along the trembling wilderness to stray,
     What time the lightning's fierce career began,
   And o'er heaven's rending arch the rattling thunder ran.

55   Responsive to the lively pipe, when all
     In sprightly dance the village youth were join'd,
     Edwin, of melody aye held in thrall,
     From the rude gambol far remote reclined,
     Soothed with the soft notes warbling in the wind,
     Ah! then all jollity seem'd noise and folly,
     To the pure soul by Fancy's fire refined;
     Ah! what is mirth but turbulence unholy,
   When with the charm compared of heavenly melancholy?

56   Is there a heart that music cannot melt?
     Alas! how is that rugged heart forlorn!
     Is there, who ne'er those mystic transports felt
     Of solitude and melancholy born?
     He needs not woo the Muse; he is her scorn.
     The sophist's rope of cobweb he shall twine;
     Mope o'er the schoolman's peevish page; or mourn,
     And delve for life in Mammon's dirty mine;
   Sneak with the scoundrel fox, or grunt with glutton swine.

57   For Edwin, Fate a nobler doom had plann'd;
     Song was his favourite and first pursuit.
     The wild harp rang to his adventurous hand,
     And languish'd to his breath the plaintive flute.

His infant Muse, though artless, was not mute :
Of elegance as yet he took no care ;
For this of time and culture is the fruit ;
And Edwin gain'd at last this fruit so rare :
As in some future verse I purpose to declare.

58 Meanwhile, whate'er of beautiful or new,
Sublime, or dreadful, in earth, sea, or sky,
By chance or search, was offer'd to his view,
He scann'd with curious and romantic eye.
Whate'er of lore tradition could supply
From Gothic tale, or song, or fable old,
Roused him, still keen to listen and to pry.
At last, though long by penury controll'd
And solitude, his soul her graces 'gan unfold.

59 Thus on the chill Lapponian's dreary land,
For many a long month lost in snow profound,
When Sol from Cancer sends the season bland,
And in their northern caves the storms are bound ;
From silent mountains, straight, with startling sound,
Torrents are hurl'd ; green hills emerge ; and, lo !
The trees with foliage, cliffs with flowers are crown'd ;
Pure rills through vales of verdure warbling go ;
And wonder, love, and joy, the peasant's heart o'erflow.[1]

60 Here pause, my Gothic lyre, a little while,
The leisure hour is all that thou canst claim.
But on this verse if Montagu should smile,
New strains ere long shall animate thy frame.

[1] Spring and autumn are hardly known to the Laplanders.   About the time
the sun enters Cancer, their fields, which a week before were covered with
snow, appear on a sudden full of grass and flowers.—Scheffer's *History of
Lapland.*

And her applause to me is more than fame ;
For still with truth accords her taste refined.
At lucre or renown let others aim,
I only wish to please the gentle mind,
Whom Nature's charms inspire, and love of humankind.

BOOK II.

Doctrina sed vim promovet insitam,
Rectique cultus pectora roborant.—HORAT.

1 OF chance or change, O let not man complain,
Else shall he never, never cease to wail ;
For, from the imperial dome, to where the swain
Rears the lone cottage in the silent dale,
All feel the assault of Fortune's fickle gale ;
Art, empire, earth itself, to change are doom'd ;
Earthquakes have raised to Heaven the humble vale,
And gulfs the mountain's mighty mass entomb'd ;
And where the Atlantic rolls wide continents have bloom'd.[1]

2 But sure to foreign climes we need not range,
Nor search the ancient records of our race,
To learn the dire effects of time and change,
Which in ourselves, alas ! we daily trace.
Yet at the darken'd eye, the wither'd face,
Or hoary hair, I never will repine :
But spare, O Time, whate'er of mental grace,
Of candour, love, or sympathy divine,
Whate'er of fancy's ray, or friendship's flame is mine.

[1] See Plato's ' Timæus.'

3 So I, obsequious to Truth's dread command,
   Shall here without reluctance change my lay,
   And smite the Gothic lyre with harsher hand ;
   Now when I leave that flowery path, for aye,
   Of childhood, where I sported many a day,
   Warbling and sauntering carelessly along ;
   Where every face was innocent and gay,
   Each vale romantic, tuneful every tongue,
Sweet, wild, and artless all, as Edwin's infant song.

4 " Perish the lore that deadens young desire,"
   Is the soft tenor of my song no more.
   Edwin, though loved of Heaven, must not aspire
   To bliss, which mortals never knew before.
   On trembling wings let youthful fancy soar,
   Nor always haunt the sunny realms of joy :
   But now and then the shades of life explore ;
   Though many a sound and sight of woe annoy,
And many a qualm of care his rising hopes destroy.

5 Vigour from toil, from trouble patience grows :
   The weakly blossom, warm in summer bower,
   Some tints of transient beauty may disclose ;
   But soon it withers in the chilling hour.
   Mark yonder oaks !   Superior to the power
   Of all the warring winds of heaven they rise,
   And from the stormy promontory tower,
   And toss their giant arms amid the skies,
While each assailing blast increase of strength supplies.

6 And now the downy cheek and deepen'd voice
   Gave dignity to Edwin's blooming prime ;
   And walks of wider circuit were his choice,
   And vales more wild, and mountains more sublime.

One evening, as he framed the careless rhyme,
It was his chance to wander far abroad,
And o'er a lonely eminence to climb,
Which heretofore his foot had never trod ;
A vale appear'd below, a deep retired abode.

7 Thither he hied, enamour'd of the scene ;
For rocks on rocks piled, as by magic spell,
Here scorch'd with lightning, there with ivy green,
Fenced from the north and east this savage dell.
Southward a mountain rose with easy swell,
Whose long long groves eternal murmur made :
And toward the western sun a streamlet fell,
Where, through the cliffs, the eye remote survey'd
Blue hills, and glittering waves, and skies in gold array'd.

8 Along this narrow valley you might see
The wild deer sporting on the meadow ground,
And, here and there, a solitary tree,
Or mossy stone, or rock with woodbine crown'd.
Oft did the cliffs reverberate the sound
Of parted fragments tumbling from on high ;
And from the summit of that craggy mound
The perching eagle oft was heard to cry,
Or on resounding wings to shoot athwart the sky.

9 One cultivated spot there was, that spread
Its flowery bosom to the noonday beam,
Where many a rosebud rears its blushing head,
And herbs for food with future plenty teem.
Soothed by the lulling sound of grove and stream,
Romantic visions swarm on Edwin's soul :
He minded not the sun's last trembling gleam,
Nor heard from far the twilight curfew toll ;
When slowly on his ear these moving accents stole :

10 " Hail, awful scenes, that calm the troubled breast,
     And woo the weary to profound repose !
     Can passion's wildest uproar lay to rest,
     And whisper comfort to the man of woes ?
     Here Innocence may wander, safe from foes,
     And Contemplation soar on seraph wings.
     O Solitude ! the man who thee foregoes,
     When lucre lures him, or ambition stings,
  Shall never know the source whence real grandeur springs.

11 " Vain man ! is grandeur given to gay attire ?
     Then let the butterfly thy pride upbraid :
     To friends, attendants, armies bought with hire ?
     It is thy weakness that requires their aid :
     To palaces, with gold and gems inlaid ?
     They fear the thief, and tremble in the storm :
     To hosts, through carnage who to conquest wade ?
     Behold the victor vanquish'd by the worm !
  Behold what deeds of woe the locust can perform !

12 " True dignity is his, whose tranquil mind
     Virtue has raised above the things below ;
     Who, every hope and fear to Heaven resign'd,
     Shrinks not, though Fortune aim her deadliest blow."
     This strain from 'midst the rocks was heard to flow
     In solemn sounds.   Now beam'd the evening star ;
     And from embattled clouds emerging slow,
     Cynthia came riding on her silver car ;
  And hoary mountain-cliffs shone faintly from afar.

13 Soon did the solemn voice its theme renew
     (While Edwin, wrapt in wonder, listening stood) :
     " Ye tools and toys of tyranny, adieu.
     Scorn'd by the wise, and hated by the good !

Ye only can engage the servile brood
Of Levity and Lust, who all their days,
Ashamed of truth and liberty, have woo'd
And hugg'd the chain that, glittering on their gaze,
Seems to outshine the pomp of Heaven's empyreal blaze.

14 " Like them, abandon'd to Ambition's sway,
I sought for glory in the paths of guile ;
And fawn'd and smiled, to plunder and betray,
Myself betray'd and plunder'd all the while ;
So gnaw'd the viper the corroding file ;
But now with pangs of keen remorse, I rue
Those years of trouble and debasement vile.
Yet why should I this cruel theme pursue ?
Fly, fly, detested thoughts, for ever from my view !

15 " The gusts of appetite, the clouds of care,
And storms of disappointment, all o'erpast,
Henceforth no earthly hope with Heaven shall share
This heart, where peace serenely shines at last.
And if for me no treasure be amass'd,
And if no future age shall hear my name,
I lurk the more secure from fortune's blast,
And with more leisure feed this pious flame,
Whose rapture far transcends the fairest hopes of fame.

16 " The end and the reward of toil is rest.
Be all my prayer for virtue and for peace.
Of wealth and fame, of pomp and power possess'd,
Who ever felt his weight of woe decrease ?
Ah ! what avails the lore of Rome and Greece,
The lay heaven-prompted, and harmonious string,
The dust of Ophir, or the Tyrian fleece,
All that art, fortune, enterprise can bring,
If envy, scorn, remorse, or pride the bosom wring ?

17 " Let Vanity adorn the marble tomb
    With trophies, rhymes, and 'scutcheons of renown,
    In the deep dungeon of some Gothic dome,
    Where night and desolation ever frown.
    Mine be the breezy hill that skirts the down,
    Where a green, grassy turf is all I crave,
    With here and there a violet bestrown,
    Fast by a brook, or fountain's murmuring wave ;
  And many an evening sun shine sweetly on my grave.

18 " And thither let the village swain repair ;
    And, light of heart, the village maiden gay,
    To deck with flowers her half-dishevell'd hair,
    And celebrate the merry morn of May.
    There let the shepherd's pipe the livelong day
    Fill all the grove with love's bewitching woe ;
    And when mild Evening comes in mantle gray,
    Let not the blooming band make haste to go ;
  No ghost, nor spell, my long and last abode shall know.

19 " For though I fly to 'scape from Fortune's rage,
    And bear the scars of envy, spite, and scorn,
    Yet with mankind no horrid war I wage,
    Yet with no impious spleen my breast is torn :
    For virtue lost, and ruin'd man I mourn.
    O man ! creation's pride, Heaven's darling child,
    Whom Nature's best divinest gifts adorn,
    Why from thy home are truth and joy exiled,
  And all thy favourite haunts with blood and tears defiled '

20 " Along yon glittering sky what glory streams !
    What majesty attends Night's lovely queen !
    Fair laugh our valleys in the vernal beams ;
    And mountains rise, and oceans roll between,

And all conspire to beautify the scene.
But, in the mental world, what chaos drear!
What forms of mournful, loathsome, furious mien!
O when shall that Eternal Morn appear,
These dreadful forms to chase, this chaos dark to clear?

21 "O Thou, at whose creative smile, yon Heaven,
In all the pomp of beauty, life, and light,
Rose from the abyss; when dark Confusion, driven
Down, down the bottomless profound of night,
Fled, where he ever flies thy piercing sight!
O glance on these sad shades one pitying ray,
To blast the fury of oppressive might,
Melt the hard heart to love and mercy's sway,
And cheer the wandering soul, and light him on the way!'

22 Silence ensued; and Edwin raised his eyes
In tears, for grief lay heavy at his heart.
"And is it thus in courtly life," he cries,
"That man to man acts a betrayer's part?
And dares he thus the gifts of Heaven pervert,
Each social instinct, and sublime desire?
Hail, Poverty! if honour, wealth, and art,
If what the great pursue and learn'd admire,
Thus dissipate and quench the soul's ethereal fire!"

23 He said, and turn'd away; nor did the Sage
O'erhear, in silent orisons employ'd.
The Youth, his rising sorrow to assuage,
Home, as he hied, the evening scene enjoy'd:
For now no cloud obscures the starry void;
The yellow moonlight sleeps on all the hills;[1]

---

[1] ' How sweet the moonlight sleeps upon this bank.'—*Shakspeare.*

Nor is the mind with startling sounds annoy'd ;
A soothing murmur the lone region fills
Of groves, and dying gales, and melancholy rills.

24 But he from day to day more anxious grew,
The voice still seem'd to vibrate on his ear.
Nor durst he hope the hermit's tale untrue ;
For man he seem'd to love, and Heaven to fear ;
And none speaks false, where there is none to hear.
" Yet, can man's gentle heart become so fell ?
No more in vain conjecture let me wear
My hours away, but seek the hermit's cell ;
'Tis he my doubt can clear, perhaps my care dispel."

25 At early dawn the Youth his journey took,
And many a mountain pass'd and valley wide,
Then reach'd the wild ; where, in a flowery nook,
And seated on a mossy stone, he spied
An ancient man : his harp lay him beside.
A stag sprang from the pasture at his call,
And, kneeling, lick'd the wither'd hand that tied
A wreath of woodbine round his antlers tall,
And hung his lofty neck with many a floweret small.

26 And now the hoary Sage arose, and saw
The wanderer approaching : innocence
Smiled on his glowing cheek, but modest awe
Depress'd his eye, that fear'd to give offence.
" Who art thou, courteous stranger ? and from whence ?
Why roam thy steps to this sequester'd dale ?"
" A shepherd boy," the Youth replied, "far hence
My habitation ; hear my artless tale ;
Nor levity nor falsehood shall thine ear assail

27 " Late as I roam'd, intent on Nature's charms,
      I reach'd at eve this wilderness profound ;
      And, leaning where yon oak expands her arms,
      Heard these rude cliffs thine awful voice rebound
      (For in thy speech I recognise the sound).
      You mourn'd for ruin'd man, and virtue lost,
      And seem'd to feel of keen remorse the wound,
      Pondering on former days, by guilt engross'd,
  Or in the giddy storm of dissipation toss'd.

28 " But say, in courtly life can craft be learn'd,
      Where knowledge opens and exalts the soul ?
      Where Fortune lavishes her gifts unearn'd,
      Can selfishness the liberal heart control ?
      Is glory there achieved by arts as foul
      As those that felons, fiends, and furies plan ?
      Spiders ensnare, snakes poison, tigers prowl :
      Love is the godlike attribute of man.
  O teach a simple youth this mystery to scan.

29 " Or else the lamentable strain disclaim,
      And give me back the calm, contented mind,
      Which, late exulting, view'd in Nature's frame
      Goodness untainted, wisdom unconfined,
      Grace, grandeur, and utility combined.
      Restore those tranquil days that saw me still
      Well pleased with all, but most with humankind ;
      When Fancy roam'd through Nature's works at will,
  Uncheck'd by cold distrust, and uninform'd by ill."

30 " Wouldst thou," the Sage replied, " in peace return
      To the gay dreams of fond romantic youth,
      Leave me to hide, in this remote sojourn,
      From every gentle ear the dreadful truth :

For if my desultory strain with ruth
And indignation make thine eyes o'erflow,
Alas ! what comfort could thy anguish soothe,
Shouldst thou the extent of human folly know ?
Be ignorance thy choice, where knowledge leads to woe.

31 " But let untender thoughts afar be driven ;
Nor venture to arraign the dread decree.
For know, to man, as candidate for heaven,
The voice of the Eternal said, Be free :
And this divine prerogative to thee
Does virtue, happiness, and heaven convey ;
For virtue is the child of liberty,
And happiness of virtue ; nor can they
Be free to keep the path, who are not free to stray.

32 " Yet leave me not. I would allay that grief,
Which else might thy young virtue overpower ;
And in thy converse I shall find relief,
When the dark shades of melancholy lower ;
For solitude has many a dreary hour,
Even when exempt from grief, remorse, and pain :
Come often then ; for haply, in my bower,
Amusement, knowledge, wisdom thou mayst gain :
If I one soul improve, I have not lived in vain."

33 And now, at length, to Edwin's ardent gaze
The Muse of history unrolls her page.
But few, alas ! the scenes her art displays,
To charm his fancy, or his heart engage.
Here chiefs their thirst of power in blood assuage,
And straight their flames with tenfold fierceness burn
Here smiling Virtue prompts the patriot's rage,
But, lo ! ere long, is left alone to mourn,
And languish in the dust, and clasp the abandon'd urn.

34 " Ambition's slippery verge shall mortals tread,
  Where ruin's gulf, unfathom'd, yawns beneath ?
  Shall life, shall liberty be lost," he said,
  " For the vain toys that Pomp and Power bequeath ?
  The car of victory, the plume, the wreath
  Defend not from the bolt of fate the brave :
  No note the clarion of Renown can breathe,
  To alarm the long night of the lonely grave,
Or check the headlong haste of time's o'erwhelming wave.

35 " Ah, what avails it to have traced the springs,
  That whirl of empire the stupendous wheel ?
  Ah, what have I to do with conquering kings,
  Hands drench'd in blood, and breasts begirt with steel ?
  To those, whom Nature taught to think and feel,
  Heroes, alas ! are things of small concern ;
  Could History man's secret heart reveal,
  And what imports a heaven-born mind to learn,
Her transcripts to explore what bosom would not yearn ?

36 " This praise, O Cheronean sage[1] is thine !
  (Why should this praise to thee alone belong ?)
  All else from Nature's moral path decline,
  Lured by the toys that captivate the throng ;
  To herd in cabinets and camps, among
  Spoil, carnage, and the cruel pomp of pride ;
  Or chant of heraldry the drowsy song,
  How tyrant blood o'er many a region wide,
Rolls to a thousand thrones its execrable tide.

37 " Oh, who of man the story will unfold,
  Ere victory and empire wrought annoy,
  In that Elysian age (misnamed of gold),
  The age of love, and innocence and joy,

------

[1] ' Cheronean sage : ' Plutarch.

When all were great and free ! man's sole employ
To deck the bosom of his parent earth ;
Or toward his bower the murmuring stream decoy,
To aid the floweret's long-expected birth,
And lull the bed of peace, and crown the board of mirth ?

38 " Sweet were your shades, O ye primeval groves !
Whose boughs to man his food and shelter lent,
Pure in his pleasures, happy in his loves,
His eye still smiling, and his heart content.
Then, hand in hand, Health, Sport, and Labour went.
Nature supplied the wish she taught to crave.
None prowl'd for prey, none watch'd to circumvent ;
To all an equal lot Heaven's bounty gave :
No vassal fear'd his lord, no tyrant fear'd his slave.

39 " But ah ! the Historic Muse has never dared
To pierce those hallow'd bowers : 'tis Fancy's beam
Pour'd on the vision of the enraptured bard,
That paints the charms of that delicious theme.
Then hail, sweet Fancy's ray ! and hail, the dream
That weans the weary soul from guilt and woe !
Careless what others of my choice may deem,
I long, where Love and Fancy lead, to go
And meditate on Heaven ; enough of Earth I know."

40 " I cannot blame thy choice," the Sage replied,
" For soft and smooth are Fancy's flowery ways.
And yet even there, if left without a guide,
The young adventurer unsafely plays.
Eyes dazzled long by fiction's gaudy rays,
In modest truth no light nor beauty find.
And who, my child, would trust the meteor blaze,
That soon must fail, and leave the wanderer blind,
More dark and helpless far, than if it ne'er had shined ?

41 " Fancy enervates, while it soothes the heart;
    And while it dazzles, wounds the mental sight :
    To joy each heightening charm it can impart,
    But wraps the hour of woe in tenfold night.
    And often, where no real ills affright,
    Its visionary fiends, an endless train,
    Assail with equal or superior might,
    And through the throbbing heart, and dizzy brain,
  And shivering nerves, shoot stings of more than mortal pain.

42 " And yet, alas ! the real ills of life
    Claim the full vigour of a mind prepared,
    Prepared for patient, long, laborious strife,
    Its guide experience, and truth its guard.
    We fare on earth as other men have fared.
    Were they successful ?   Let us not despair.
    Was disappointment oft their sole reward ?
    Yet shall their tale instruct, if it declare
  How they have borne the load ourselves are doom'd to bear.

43 " What charms the Historic Muse adorn, from spoils,
    And blood, and tyrants, when she wings her flight,
    To hail the patriot prince, whose pious toils,
    Sacred to science, liberty, and right,
    And peace, through every age divinely bright
    Shall shine the boast and wonder of mankind !
    Sees yonder sun, from his meridian height,
    A lovelier scene than virtue thus enshrined
  In power, and man with man for mutual aid combined ?

44 " Hail, sacred Polity, by Freedom rear'd !
    Hail, sacred Freedom, when by law restrain'd !
    Without you, what were man ?   A grovelling herd,
    In darkness, wretchedness, and want enchain'd.

Sublimed by you, the Greek and Roman reign'd
In arts unrivall'd !   O, to latest days,
In Albion may your influence unprofaned
To godlike worth the generous bosom raise,
And prompt the sage's lore, and fire the poet's lays !

45 " But now let other themes our care engage.
For, lo, with modest yet majestic grace,
To curb Imagination's lawless rage,
And from within the cherish'd heart to brace,
Philosophy appears !   The gloomy race
By Indolence and moping Fancy bred,
Fear, Discontent, Solicitude, give place ;
And Hope and Courage brighten in their stead,
While on the kindling soul her vital beams are shed !

46 " Then waken from long lethargy to life [1]
The seeds of happiness, and powers of thought ;
Then jarring appetites forego their strife,
A strife by ignorance to madness wrought.
Pleasure by savage man is dearly bought
With fell revenge ; lust that defies control,
With gluttony and death.   The mind untaught
Is a dark waste, where fiends and tempests howl ;
As Phœbus to the world, is science to the soul.

47 " And Reason now through number, time, and space,
Darts the keen lustre of her serious eye,
And learns, from facts compared, the laws to trace,
Whose long progression leads to Deity.
Can mortal strength presume to soar so high ?
Can mortal sight, so oft bedimm'd with tears,

[1] The influence of the philosophic spirit, in humanizing the mind, and pre-
paring it for intellectual exertion and delicate pleasure ;—in exploring, by
the help of geometry, the system of the universe ;—in banishing superstition ;
— in promoting navigation, agriculture, medicine, and moral and political
science.

C

Such glory bear?—for, lo! the shadows fly
From Nature's face ; confusion disappears,
And order charms the eye, and harmony the ears!

48 " In the deep windings of the grove, no more
The hag obscene and grisly phantom dwell ;
Nor in the fall of mountain-stream, or roar
Of winds, is heard the angry spirit's yell ;
No wizard mutters the tremendous spell,
Nor sinks convulsive in prophetic swoon ;
Nor bids the noise of drums and trumpets swell,
To ease of fancied pangs the labouring moon,
Or chase the shade that blots the blazing orb of noon.

49 " Many a long lingering year, in lonely isle,
Stunn'd with the eternal turbulence of waves,
Lo! with dim eyes, that never learn'd to smile,
And trembling hands, the famish'd native craves
Of Heaven his wretched fare ; shivering in caves,
Or scorch'd on rocks, he pines from day to day;
But Science gives the word ; and, lo! he braves
The surge and tempest, lighted by her ray,
And to a happier land wafts merrily away!

50 " And even where Nature loads the teeming plain
With the full pomp of vegetable store,
Her bounty, unimproved, is deadly bane :
Dark woods and rankling wilds, from shore to shore,
Stretch their enormous gloom ; which to explore[1]
Even Fancy trembles, in her sprightliest mood :
For there each eyeball gleams with lust of gore,
Nestles each murderous and each monstrous brood,
Plague lurks in every shade, and steams from every flood

[1] ' To explore : ' this, from Thomson, who says in his ' Summer '—
' Which even imagination fears to tread.'

51   " 'Twas from Philosophy man learn'd to tame
    The soil, by plenty to intemperance fed.
    Lo ! from the echoing axe and thundering flame,
    Poison and plague and yelling rage are fled.
    The waters, bursting from their slimy bed,
    Bring health and melody to every vale :
    And, from the breezy main, and mountain's head,
    Ceres and Flora, to the sunny dale,
To fan their glowing charms, invite the fluttering gale.

52   " What dire necessities on every hand
    Our art, our strength, our fortitude require!
    Of foes intestine what a numerous band
    Against this little throb of life conspire!
    Yet Science can elude their fatal ire
    A while, and turn aside Death's levell'd dart,
    Soothe the sharp pang, allay the fever's fire,
    And brace the nerves once more, and cheer the heart,
 And yet a few soft nights and balmy days impart.

53   " Nor less to regulate man's moral frame
    Science exerts her all-composing sway.
    Flutters thy breast with fear, or pants for fame,
    Or pines, to indolence and spleen a prey,
    Or avarice, a fiend more fierce than they ?
    Flee to the shade of Academus' grove ;
    Where cares molest not, discord melts away
    In harmony, and the pure passions prove
How sweet the words of Truth, breathed from the lips of Love.

54   " What cannot Art and Industry perform,
    When Science plans the progress of their toil?
    They smile at penury, disease, and storm ;
    And oceans from their mighty mounds recoil.

When tyrants scourge, or demagogues embroil
A land, or when the rabble's headlong rage
Order transforms to anarchy and spoil,
Deep-versed in man the philosophic sage
Prepares with lenient hand their frenzy to assuage.

55 " 'Tis he alone, whose comprehensive mind,
From situation, temper, soil, and clime
Explored, a nation's various powers can bind,
And various orders in one Form sublime
Of policy, that 'midst the wrecks of time,
Secure shall lift its head on high, nor fear
The assault of foreign or domestic crime,
While public faith, and public love sincere,
And industry and law, maintain their sway severe."

56 Enraptured by the hermit's strain, the youth
Proceeds the path of Science to explore.
And now, expanded to the beams of truth,
New energies, and charms unknown before,
His mind discloses: Fancy now no more
Wantons on fickle pinion through the skies;
But, fix'd in aim, and conscious of her power,
Aloft from cause to cause exults to rise,
Creation's blended stores arranging as she flies.

57 Nor love of novelty alone inspires,
Their laws and nice dependencies to scan;
For, mindful of the aids that life requires,
And of the services man owes to man,
He meditates new arts on Nature's plan;
The cold desponding breast of sloth to warm,
The flame of industry and genius fan,
And emulation's noble rage alarm,
And the long hours of toil and solitude to charm.

58 But she, who set on fire his infant heart,
    And all his dreams, and all his wanderings shared
    And bless'd, the Muse, and her celestial art,
    Still claim the enthusiast's fond and first regard.
    From Nature's beauties, variously compared
    And variously combined, he learns to frame
    Those forms of bright perfection,[1] which the bard,
    While boundless hopes and boundless views inflame,
  Enamour'd, consecrates to never-dying fame.

59 Of late, with cumbersome, though pompous show,
    Edwin would oft his flowery rhyme deface,
    Through ardour to adorn ; but Nature now
    To his experienced eye a modest grace
    Presents, where ornament the second place
    Holds, to intrinsic worth and just design
    Subservient still. | Simplicity apace
    Tempers his rage : /he owns her charm divine,
  And clears the ambiguous phrase, and lops the un-
        wieldy line.

60 Fain would I sing (much yet unsung remains)
    What sweet delirium o'er his bosom stole,
    When the great shepherd of the Mantuan plains [2]
    His deep majestic melody 'gan roll :
    Fain would I sing what transport storm'd his soul,
    How the red current throbb'd his veins along,
    When, like Pelides, bold beyond control,
    Without art graceful, without effort strong,
  Homer raised high to heaven the loud, the impetuous song.

---

[1] General ideas of excellence, the immediate archetypes of sublime imita-
tion, both in painting and in poetry.   See Aristotle's ' Poetics,' and the ' Dis-
courses of Sir Joshua Reynolds.' — [2] ' Great shepherd of the Mantuan plains : '
Virgil.

61 And how his lyre, though rude her first essays,
   Now skill'd to soothe, to triumph, to complain,
   Warbling at will through each harmonious maze,
   Was taught to modulate the artful strain,
   I fain would sing :——But ah ! I strive in vain.
   Sighs from a breaking heart my voice confound.
   With trembling step, to join yon weeping train,
   I haste, where gleams funereal glare around,
 And, mix'd with shrieks of woe, the knells of death
     resound.

62 Adieu, ye lays that Fancy's flowers adorn,
   The soft amusement of the vacant mind !
   He sleeps in dust, and all the Muses mourn,
   He, whom each virtue fired, each grace refined.
   Friend, teacher, pattern, darling of mankind !
   He sleeps in dust.[1]   Ah, how shall I pursue   .
   My theme ?   To heart-consuming grief resign'd,
   Here on his recent grave I fix my view,
 And pour my bitter tears.   Ye flowery lays, adieu !

63 Art thou, my GREGORY, for ever fled ?
   And am I left to unavailing woe ?
   When fortune's storms assail this weary head,
   Where cares long since have shed untimely snow,
   Ah, now for comfort whither shall I go ?
   No more thy soothing voice my anguish cheers :
   Thy placid eyes with smiles no longer glow,
   My hopes to cherish, and allay my fears.
 'Tis meet that I should mourn : flow forth afresh, my tears.

[1] This excellent person died suddenly on the 10th of February 1773.   The
conclusion of the poem was written a few days after.

MISCELLANEOUS POEMS.

ODE TO HOPE.

I. 1.

O THOU, who gladd'st the pensive soul,
More than Aurora's smile the swain forlorn,
Left all night long to mourn
Where desolation frowns, and tempests howl,
And shrieks of woe, as intermits the storm,
Far o'er the monstrous wilderness resound,
And 'cross the gloom darts many a shapeless form,
And many a fire-eyed visage glares around!
O come, and be once more my guest :
Come, for thou oft thy suppliant's vow hast heard,
And oft with smiles indulgent cheer'd
And soothed him into rest.

I. 2.

Smit by thy rapture-beaming eye
Deep flashing through the midnight of their mind,
The sable bands combined,
Where Fear's black banner bloats the troubled sky,

Appall'd retire.   Suspicion hides her head,
Nor dares the obliquely gleaming eyeball raise ;
Despair, with gorgon-figured veil o'erspread,
Speeds to dark Phlegethon's detested maze.
Lo ! startled at the heavenly ray,
With speed unwonted Indolence upsprings,
And, heaving, lifts her leaden wings,
And sullen glides away :

I. 3.

Ten thousand forms, by pining Fancy view'd,
Dissolve.——Above the sparkling flood,
When Phœbus rears his awful brow,
From lengthening lawn and valley low
The troops of fen-born mists retire.
Along the plain
The joyous swain
Eyes the gay villages again,
And gold-illumined spire ;
While on the billowy ether borne
Floats the loose lay's jovial measure ;
And light along the fairy Pleasure,
Her green robes glittering to the morn,
Wantons on silken wing.   And goblins all
To the damp dungeon shrink, or hoary hall,
Or westward, with impetuous flight,
Shoot to the desert realms of their congenial night.

II. 1.

When first on childhood's eager gaze
Life's varied landscape, stretch'd immense around,   .
Starts out of night profound,
Thy voice incites to tempt the untrodden maze.
Fond he surveys thy mild maternal face,

His bashful eye still kindling as he views,
And, while thy lenient arm supports his pace,
With beating heart the upland path pursues :
The path that leads, where, hung sublime,
And seen afar, youth's gallant trophies, bright
In Fancy's rainbow ray, invite
His wingy nerves to climb.

II. 2.

Pursue thy pleasurable way,
Safe in the guidance of thy heavenly guard,
While melting airs are heard,
And soft-eyed cherub-forms around thee play :
Simplicity, in careless flowers array'd,
Prattling amusive in his accent meek ;
And Modesty, half turning as afraid,
The smile just dimpling on his glowing cheek !
Content and Leisure, hand in hand
With Innocence and Peace, advance and sing ;
And Mirth, in many a mazy ring,
Frisks o'er the flowery land.

II. 3.

Frail man, how various is thy lot below !
To-day though gales propitious blow,
And Peace soft gliding down the sky
Lead Love along and Harmony,
To-morrow the gay scene deforms !
Then all around
The Thunder's sound
Rolls rattling on through Heaven's profound,
And down rush all the storms.
Ye days that balmy influence shed,
When sweet childhood, ever sprightly,

In paths of pleasure sported lightly,
Whither, ah ! whither are ye fled ?
Ye cherub train, that brought him on his way,
O leave him not 'midst tumult and dismay ;
For now youth's eminence he gains ;
But what a weary length of lingering toil remains !

III. 1.

They shrink, they vanish into air,
Now slander taints with pestilence the gale ;
And mingling cries assail,
The wail of Woe, and groan of grim Despair.
Lo ! wizard Envy from his serpent eye
Darts quick destruction in each baleful glance ;
Pride smiling stern, and yellow Jealousy,
Frowning Disdain, and haggard Hate advance.
Behold, amidst the dire array,
Pale wither'd Care his giant stature rears,
And, lo ! his iron hand prepares
To grasp its feeble prey.

III. 2.

Who now will guard bewilder'd youth
Safe from the fierce assault of hostile rage ?
Such war can Virtue wage,
Virtue, that bears the sacred shield of Truth ?
Alas ! full oft on Guilt's victorious car
The spoils of Virtue are in triumph borne ;
While the fair captive, mark'd with many a scar,
In lone obscurity, oppress'd, forlorn,
Resigns to tears her angel form.
Ill-fated youth, then whither wilt thou fly ?
No friend, no shelter now is nigh,
And onward rolls the storm.

III. 3.

But whence the sudden beam that shoots along ?
Why shrink aghast the hostile throng ?
Lo ! from amidst affliction's night
Hope bursts all radiant on the sight :
Her words the troubled bosom soothe.
" Why thus dismay'd ?
Though foes invade,
Hope ne'er is wanting to their aid
Who tread the path of truth.
'Tis I, who smoothe the rugged way,
I, who close the eyes of Sorrow,
And with glad visions of to-morrow
Repair the weary soul's decay.
When Death's cold touch thrills to the freezing heart,
Dreams of Heaven's opening glories I impart,
Till the freed spirit springs on high
In rapture too severe for weak mortality."

ODE TO PEACE.

I. 1.

PEACE, heaven-descended maid! whose powerful voice
From ancient darkness call'd the morn,
Of jarring elements composed the noise ;
When Chaos, from his old dominion torn,
With all his bellowing throng,
Far, far was hurl'd the void abyss along ;
And all the bright angelic choir
To loftiest raptures tune the heavenly lyre,
Pour'd in loud symphony the impetuous strain ;
And every fiery orb and planet sung,

And wide through night's dark desolate domain
Rebounding long and deep the lays triumphant rung.

I. 2.

Oh, whither art thou fled, Saturnian reign ?
Roll round again, majestic Years !
To break fell Tyranny's corroding chain,
From Woe's wan cheek to wipe the bitter tears,
Ye Years, again roll round !
Hark, from afar what loud tumultuous sound,
While echoes sweep the winding vales,
Swells full along the plains, and loads the gales !
Murder deep-roused, with the wild whirlwind's haste
And roar of tempest, from her cavern springs ;
Her tangled serpents girds around her waist,
Smiles ghastly stern, and shakes her gore-distilling wings.

I. 3.

Fierce up the yielding skies
The shouts redoubling rise :
Earth shudders at the dreadful sound,
And all is listening, trembling round.
Torrents, that from yon promontory's head
Dash'd furious down in desperate cascade,
Heard from afar amid the lonely night,
That oft have led the wanderer right,
Are silent at the noise.
The mighty ocean's more majestic voice,
Drown'd in superior din, is heard no more ;
The surge in silence sweeps along the foamy shore.

II. 1.

The bloody banner streaming in the air,
Seen on yon sky-mix'd mountain's brow,

The mingling multitudes, the madding car,
Pouring impetuous on the plain below,
War's dreadful lord proclaim.
Bursts out by frequent fits the expansive flame.
Whirl'd in tempestuous eddies flies
The surging smoke o'er all the darken'd skies.
The cheerful face of heaven no more is seen,
Fades the morn's vivid blush to deadly pale :
The bat flits transient o'er the dusky green,
Night's shrieking birds along the sullen twilight sail.

II. 2.

Involved in fire-streak'd gloom the car comes on.
The mangled steeds grim Terror guides.
His forehead writhed to a relentless frown,
Aloft the angry Power of Battles rides :
Grasp'd in his mighty hand
A mace tremendous desolates the land ;
Thunders the turret down the steep,
The mountain shrinks before its wasteful sweep ;
Chill horror the dissolving limbs invades,
Smit by the blasting lightning of his eyes ;
A bloated paleness beauty's bloom o'erspreads,
Fades every flowery field, and every verdure dies.

II. 3.

How startled Frenzy stares,
Bristling her ragged hairs !
Revenge the gory fragment gnaws ;
See, with her griping vulture-claws
Imprinted deep, she rends the opening wound !
Hatred her torch blue-streaming tosses round ;
The shrieks of agony and clang of arms
Re-echo to the fierce alarms

Her trump terrific blows.
Disparting from behind, the clouds disclose
Of kingly gesture a gigantic form,
That with his scourge sublime directs the whirling storm.

III. 1.

Ambition, outside fair ! within more foul
Than fellest fiend from Tartarus sprung,
In caverns hatch'd, where the fierce torrents roll
Of Phlegethon, the burning banks along,
Yon naked waste survey :
Where late was heard the flute's mellifluous lay ;
Where late the rosy-bosom'd Hours
In loose array danced lightly o'er the flowers ;
Where late the shepherd told his tender tale ;
And, waked by the soft-murmuring breeze of morn,
The voice of cheerful labour fill'd the dale ;
And dove-eyed Plenty smiled, and waved her liberal horn.

III. 2.

Yon ruins sable from the wasting flame
But mark the once resplendent dome ;
The frequent corse obstructs the sullen stream,
And ghosts glare horrid from the sylvan gloom.
How sadly silent all !
Save where outstretch'd beneath yon hanging wall
Pale Famine moans with feeble breath,
And Torture yells, and grinds her bloody teeth—
Though vain the muse, and every melting lay,
To touch thy heart, unconscious of remorse !
Know, monster, know, thy hour is on the way,
I see, I see the Years begin their mighty course.

III. 3.

What scenes of glory rise
Before my dazzled eyes !
Young Zephyrs wave their wanton wings,
And melody celestial rings :
Along the lilied lawn the nymphs advance,
Flush'd with love's bloom, and range the sprightly dance
The gladsome shepherds on the mountain-side,
Array'd in all their rural pride,
Exalt the festive note,
Inviting Echo from her inmost grot—
But ah ! the landscape glows with fainter light,
It darkens, swims, and flies for ever from my sight.

IV. 1.

Illusions vain !   Can sacred Peace reside,
Where sordid gold the breast alarms,
Where cruelty inflames the eye of Pride,
And Grandeur wantons in soft Pleasure's arms ?
Ambition ! these are thine ;
These from the soul erase the form divine ;
These quench the animating fire
That warms the bosom with sublime desire.
Thence the relentless heart forgets to feel,
Hate rides tremendous on the o'erwhelming brow,
And midnight Rancour grasps the cruel steel,
Blaze the funereal flames, and sound the shrieks of Woe.

IV. 2.

From Albion fled, thy once beloved retreat,
What region brightens in thy smile,
Creative Peace, and underneath thy feet
Sees sullen flowers adorn the rugged soil ?

In bleak Siberia blows,
Waked by thy genial breath, the balmy rose?
Waved over by thy magic wand,
Does life inform fell Libya's burning sand?
Or does some isle thy parting flight detain,
Where roves the Indian through primeval shades,
Haunts the pure pleasures of the woodland reign,
And led by Reason's ray the path of Nature treads?

IV. 3.

On Cuba's utmost steep,[1]
Far leaning o'er the deep,
The Goddess' pensive form was seen.
Her robe of Nature's varied green
Waved on the gale; grief dimm'd her radiant eyes,
Her swelling bosom heaved with boding sighs:
She eyed the main; where, gaining on the view,
Emerging from the ethereal blue,
'Midst the dread pomp of war
Gleam'd the Iberian streamer from afar.
She saw; and, on refulgent pinions borne,
Slow wing'd her way sublime, and mingled with the morn.

ODE ON LORD HAY'S BIRTHDAY.

1 A muse, unskill'd in venal praise,
  Unstain'd with flattery's art;
Who loves simplicity of lays
  Breathed ardent from the heart;

---

[1] This alludes to the discovery of America by the Spaniards under Columbus. These ravagers are said to have made their first descent on the islands in the Gulf of Florida, of which Cuba is one.

While gratitude and joy inspire,
Resumes the long unpractised lyre,
To hail, O HAY, thy natal morn:
No gaudy wreath of flowers she weaves,
But twines with oak the laurel leaves,
Thy cradle to adorn.

2 For not on beds of gaudy flowers
Thine ancestors reclined,
Where sloth dissolves, and spleen devours
All energy of mind.
To hurl the dart, to ride the car,
To stem the deluges of war,
And snatch from fate a sinking land;
Trample the invader's lofty crest,
And from his grasp the dagger wrest,
And desolating brand:

3 'Twas this that raised th' illustrious line
To match the first in fame!
A thousand years have seen it shine
With unabated flame;
Have seen thy mighty sires appear
Foremost in glory's high career,
The pride and pattern of the brave.
Yet pure from lust of blood their fire,
And from ambition's wild desire,
They triumph'd but to save.

4 The Muse with joy attends their way
The vale of peace along:
There to its lord the village gay
Renews the grateful song.

D

Yon castle's glittering towers contain
No pit of woe, nor clanking chain,
Nor to the suppliant's wail resound:
The open doors the needy bless,
The unfriended hail their calm recess,
And gladness smiles around.

5 There to the sympathetic heart
Life's best delights belong,
To mitigate the mourner's smart,
To guard the weak from wrong.
Ye sons of luxury be wise:
Know happiness for ever flies
The cold and solitary breast;
Then let the social instinct glow,
And learn to feel another's woe,
And in his joy be blest.

6 O yet, ere Pleasure plant her snare
For unsuspecting youth;
Ere Flattery her song prepare
To check the voice of Truth;
O may his country's guardian power
Attend the slumbering infant's bower,
And bright inspiring dreams impart;
To rouse the hereditary fire,
To kindle each sublime desire,
Exalt and warm the heart.

7 Swift to reward a parent's fears,
A parent's hopes to crown,
Roll on in peace, ye blooming years,
That rear him to renown;
When in his finish'd form and face
Admiring multitudes shall trace

Each patrimonial charm combined,
The courteous yet majestic mien,
The liberal smile, the look serene,
The great and gentle mind.

8 Yet, though thou draw a nation's eyes,
And win a nation's love,
Let not thy towering mind despise
The village and the grove.
No slander there shall wound thy fame,
No ruffian take his deadly aim,
No rival weave the secret snare:
For innocence with angel smile,
Simplicity that knows no guile,
And Love and Peace are there.

9 When winds the mountain oak assail,
And lay its glories waste,
Content may slumber in the vale,
Unconscious of the blast.
Through scenes of tumult while we roam,
The heart, alas! is ne'er at home,
It hopes in time to roam no more;
The mariner, not vainly brave,
Combats the storm and rides the wave,
To rest at last on shore.

10 Ye proud, ye selfish, ye severe,
How vain your mask of state!
The good alone have joy sincere;
The good alone are great:
Great, when, amid the vale of peace,
They bid the plaint of sorrow cease,

And hear the voice of artless praise;
As when along the trophied plain
Sublime they lead the victor train,
While shouting nations gaze.

THE JUDGMENT OF PARIS.

1 FAR in the depth of Ida's inmost grove,
    A scene for love and solitude design'd;
Where flowery woodbines wild, by Nature wove,
    Form'd the lone bower, the royal swain reclined.

2 All up the craggy cliffs, that tower'd to heaven,
    Green waved the murmuring pines on every side;
Save where, fair opening to the beam of even,
    A dale sloped gradual to the valley wide.

3 Echo'd the vale with many a cheerful note;
    The lowing of the herds resounding long,
The shrilling pipe, and mellow horn remote,
    And social clamours of the festive throng.

4 For now, low hovering o'er the western main,
    Where amber clouds begirt his dazzling throne,
The Sun with ruddier verdure deck'd the plain;
    And lakes and streams and spires triumphal shone.

5 And many a band of ardent youths were seen;
    Some into rapture fired by glory's charms,
Or hurl'd the thundering car along the green,
    Or march'd embattled on in glittering arms.

6 Others more mild, in happy leisure gay,
    The darkening forest's lonely gloom explore,
Or by Scamander's flowery margin stray,
    Or the blue Hellespont's resounding shore.

7 But chief the eye to Ilion's glories turn'd,
    That gleam'd along the extended champaign far,
And bulwarks in terrific pomp adorn'd,
    Where Peace sat smiling at the frowns of War.

8 Rich in the spoils of many a subject clime.
    In pride luxurious blazed the imperial dome;
Tower'd 'mid the encircling grove the fane sublime,
    And dread memorials mark'd the hero's tomb

9 Who from the black and bloody cavern led
    The savage stern, and soothed his boisterous breast;
Who spoke, and Science rear'd her radiant head,
    And brighten'd o'er the long benighted waste :

10 Or, greatly daring in his country's cause,
    Whose heaven-taught soul the awful plan design'd,
Whence Power stood trembling at the voice of laws;
    Whence soar'd on Freedom's wing the ethereal mind.

11 But not the pomp that royalty displays,
    Nor all the imperial pride of lofty Troy,
Nor Virtue's triumph of immortal praise
    Could rouse the langour of the lingering boy.

12 Abandon'd all to soft Enone's charms,
    He to oblivion doom'd the listless day;
Inglorious lull'd in Love's dissolving arms,
    While flutes lascivious breathed the enfeebling lay.

13 To trim the ringlets of his scented hair :
    To aim, insidious, Love's bewitching glance;
Or cull fresh garlands for the gaudy fair,
    Or wanton loose in the voluptuous dance :

14 These were his arts; these won Enone's love,
    Nor sought his fetter'd soul a nobler aim.
Ah, why should beauty's smile those arts approve
    Which taint with infamy the lover's flame ?

15 Now laid at large beside a murmuring spring,
    Melting he listen'd to the vernal song,
And Echo, listening, waved her airy wing,
    While the deep winding dales the lays prolong ;

16 When, slowly floating down the azure skies,
    A crimson cloud flash'd on his startled sight,
Whose skirts gay-sparkling with unnumber'd dyes
    Launch'd the long billowy trails of flickery light.

17 That instant, hush'd was all the vocal grove,
    Hush'd was the gale, and every ruder sound ;
And strains aërial, warbling far above,
    Rung in the ear a magic peal profound.

18 Near and more near the swimming radiance roll'd;
    Along the mountains stream the lingering fires ;
Sublime the groves of Ida blaze with gold,
    And all the Heaven resounds with louder lyres.

19 The trumpet breathed a note : and all in air,
    The glories vanish'd from the dazzled eye;
And three ethereal forms, divinely fair,
    Down the steep glade were seen advancing nigh.

20 The flowering glade fell level where they moved;
    O'erarching high the clustering roses hung;
And gales from heaven on balmy pinion roved,
    And hill and dale with gratulation rung.

21 The FIRST with slow and stately step drew near,
    Fix'd was her lofty eye, erect her mien :
Sublime in grace, in majesty severe,
    She look'd and moved a goddess and a queen.

22 Her robe along the gale profusely stream'd,
    Light lean'd the sceptre on her bending arm;
And round her brow a starry circlet gleam'd,
    Heightening the pride of each commanding charm.

23 Milder the NEXT came on with artless grace,
    And on a javelin's quivering length reclined :
To exalt her mien she bade no splendour blaze,
    Nor pomp of vesture fluctuate on the wind.

24 Serene, though awful, on her brow the light
    Of heavenly wisdom shone ; nor roved her eyes,
Save to the shadowy cliff's majestic height,
    Or the blue concave of the involving skies.

25 Keen were her eyes to search the inmost soul :
    Yet virtue triumph'd in their beams benign,
And impious Pride oft felt their dread control,
    When in fierce lightning flash'd the wrath divine.[1]

26 With awe and wonder gazed the adoring swain ;
    His kindling cheeks great Virtue's power confess'd;
But soon 'twas o'er ; for Virtue prompts in vain,
    When Pleasure's influence numbs the nerveless breast.

[1] This is agreeable to the theology of Homer, who often represents Pallas
as the executioner of divine vengeance.

27 And now advanced the QUEEN of melting JOY,
        Smiling supreme in unresisted charms :
    Ah, then, what transports fired the trembling boy !
        How throbb'd his sickening frame with fierce alarms!

28 Her eyes in liquid light luxurious swim,
        And languish with unutterable love.
    Heaven's warm bloom glows along each brightening limb,
        Where fluttering bland the veil's thin mantlings rove.

29 Quick, blushing as abash'd, she half withdrew :
        One hand a bough of flowering myrtle waved.
    One graceful spread, where, scarce conceal'd from view,
        Soft through the parting robe her bosom heaved.

30 "Offspring of Jove supreme! beloved of Heaven!
        ⁻Attend."   Thus spoke the Empress of the Skies.
    "For know, to thee, high-fated prince, 'tis given
        Through the bright realms of Fame sublime to rise,

31 " Beyond man's boldest hope ; if nor the wiles
        Of Pallas triumph o'er the ennobling thought ;
    Nor Pleasure lure with artificial smiles
        To quaff the poison of her luscious draught.

32 " When Juno's charms the prize of beauty claim,
        Shall aught on earth, shall aught in heaven contend ?
    Whom Juno calls to high triumphant fame,
        Shall he to meaner sway inglorious bend?

33 " Yet lingering comfortless in lonesome wild,
        Where Echo sleeps 'mid cavern'd vales profound,
    The pride of Troy, Dominion's darling child,
        Pines while the slow hour stalks in sullen round.

34 " Hear thou, of Heaven unconscious !   From the blaze
  Of glory, stream'd from Jove's eternal throne,
Thy soul, O mortal, caught the inspiring rays
  That to a god exalt Earth's raptured son.

35 " Hence the bold wish, on boundless pinion borne,
  That fires, alarms, impels the maddening soul;
The hero's eye, hence, kindling into scorn,
  Blasts the proud menace, and defies control.

36 " But, unimproved, Heaven's noblest boons are vain,
  No sun with plenty crowns the uncultured vale :
Where green lakes languish on the silent plain,
  Death rides the billows of the western gale.

37 " Deep in yon mountain's womb, where the dark cave
  Howls to the torrent's everlasting roar,
Does the rich gem its flashy radiance wave ?
  Or flames with steady ray the imperial ore ?

38 " Toil deck'd with glittering domes yon champaign wide,
  And wakes yon grove-embosom'd lawns to joy,
And rends the rough ore from the mountain's side,
  Spangling with starry pomp the thrones of Troy.

39 " Fly these soft scenes.   Even now, with playful art,
  Love wreathes the flowery ways with fatal snare ;
And nurse the ethereal fire that warms thy heart,
  That fire ethereal lives but by thy care.

40 " Lo ! hovering near on dark and dampy wing,
  Sloth with stern patience waits the hour assign'd,
From her chill plume the deadly dews to fling,
   That quench Heaven's beam, and freeze the cheerless
    mind.

41 " Vain, then, the enlivening sound of Fame's alarms,
       For Hope's exulting impulse prompts no more :
   Vain even the joys that lure to Pleasure's arms,
       The throb of transport is for ever o'er.

42 O who shall then to Fancy's darkening eyes
       Recall the Elysian dreams of joy and light ?
   Dim through the gloom the formless visions rise,
       Snatch'd instantaneous down the gulf of night.

43 " Thou who, securely lull'd in youth's warm ray,
       Mark'st not the desolations wrought by Time,
   Be roused or perish.   Ardent for its prey,
       Speeds the fell hour that ravages thy prime.

44 " And, 'midst the horrors shrined of midnight storm,
       The fiend Oblivion eyes thee from afar,
   Black with intolerable frowns her form,
       Beckoning the embattled whirlwinds into war.

45 " Fanes, bulwarks, mountains, worlds, their tempest
           whelms ;
       Yet glory braves unmoved the impetuous sweep.
   Fly then, ere, hurl'd from life's delightful realms,
       Thou sink to Oblivion's dark and boundless deep.

46 " Fly, then, where Glory points the path sublime,
       See her crown dazzling with eternal light !
   'Tis Juno prompts thy daring steps to climb,
       And girds thy bounding heart with matchless might.

47 " Warm in the raptures of divine desire,
       Burst the soft chain that curbs the aspiring mind ;
   And fly where Victory, borne on wings of fire,
       Waves her red banner to the rattling wind.

48 " Ascend the car : indulge the pride of arms,
        Where clarions roll their kindling strains on high,
    Where the eye maddens to the dread alarms,
        And the long shout tumultuous rends the sky.

49 " Plunged in the uproar of the thundering field,
        I see thy lofty arm the tempest guide :
    Fate scatters lightning from thy meteor-shield,
        And Ruin spreads around the sanguine tide.

50 " Go, urge the terrors of thy headlong car
        On prostrate Pride, and Grandeur's spoils o'erthrown,
    While all amazed even heroes shrink afar,
        And hosts embattled vanish at thy frown.

51 " When glory crowns thy godlike toils, and all
        The triumph's lengthening pomp exalts thy soul,
    When lowly at thy feet the mighty fall,
        And tyrants tremble at thy stern control :

52 " When conquering millions hail thy sovereign might,
        And tribes unknown dread acclamation join ;
    How wilt thou spurn the forms of low delight !
        For all the ecstasies of heaven are thine :

53 " For thine the joys, that fear no length of days,
        Whose wide effulgence scorns all mortal bound :
    Fame's trump in thunder shall announce thy praise,
        Nor bursting worlds her clarion's blast confound."

54 The Goddess ceased, not dubious of the prize :
        Elate she mark'd his wild and rolling eye,
    Mark'd his lip quiver, and his bosom rise,
        And his warm cheek suffused with crimson dye.

55 But Pallas now drew near.   Sublime, serene,
     In conscious dignity she view'd the swain :
  Then, love and pity softening all her mien,
     Thus breathed with accents mild the solemn strain :

56 " Let those whose arts to fatal paths betray,
     The soul with passion's gloom tempestuous blind,
  And snatch from Reason's ken the auspicious ray
     Truth darts from heaven to guide the exploring mind.

57 " But Wisdom loves the calm and serious hour,
     When heaven's pure emanation beams confess'd :
  Rage, ecstasy, alike disclaim her power,
     She woo's each gentler impulse of the breast.

58 " Sincere the unalter'd bliss her charms impart,
     Sedate the enlivening ardours they inspire :
  She bids no transient rapture thrill the heart,
     She wakes no feverish gust of fierce desire.

59 " Unwise, who, tossing on the watery way,
     All to the storm the unfetter'd sail devolve :
  Man more unwise resigns the mental sway,
     Borne headlong on by passion's keen resolve.

60 " While storms remote but murmur on thine ear,
     Nor waves in ruinous uproar round thee roll,
  Yet, yet a moment check thy prone career,
     And curb the keen resolve that prompts thy soul.

61 " Explore thy heart, that, roused by Glory's name,
     Pants all enraptured with the mighty charm—
  And does Ambition quench each milder flame ?
     And is it conquest that alone can warm ?

62 " To indulge fell Rapine's desolating lust,
   To drench the balmy lawn in streaming gore,
To spurn the hero's cold and silent dust—
   Are these thy joys ?   Nor throbs thy heart for more ?

63 " Pleased canst thou listen to the patriot's groan,
   And the wild wail of Innocence forlorn ?
And hear the abandon'd maid's last frantic. moan,
   Her love for ever from her bosom torn ?

64 " Nor wilt thou shrink, when Virtue's fainting breath
   Pours the dread curse of vengeance on thy head?
Nor when the pale ghost bursts the cave of death,
   To glare distraction on thy midnight bed ?

65 " Was it for this, though born to regal power,
   Kind Heaven to thee did nobler gifts consign,
Bade Fancy's influence gild thy natal hour,
   And bade Philanthropy's applause be thine ?

66 " Theirs be the dreadful glory to destroy,
   And theirs the pride of pomp, and praise suborn'd,
Whose eye ne'er lighten'd at the smile of Joy,
   Whose cheek the tear of Pity ne'er adorn'd :

67 " Whose soul, each finer sense instinctive quell'd,
   The lyre's mellifluous ravishment defies :
Nor marks where Beauty roves the flowery field,
   Or Grandeur's pinion sweeps the unbounded skies.

68 " Hail to sweet Fancy's unexpressive charm !
   Hail to the pure delights of social love!
Hail, pleasures mild, that fire not while ye warm,
   Nor rack the exulting frame, but gently move !

69 " But Fancy soothes no more, if stern remorse
        With iron grasp the tortured bosom wring.
    Ah then ! even Fancy speeds the venom's course,
        Even Fancy points with rage the maddening sting.

70 " Her wrath a thousand gnashing fiends attend,
        And roll the snakes, and toss the brands of hell ;
    The beam of Beauty blasts : dark heavens impend
        Tottering : and Music thrills with startling yell.

71 " What then avails, that with exhaustless store
        Obsequious Luxury loads thy glittering shrine ?
    What then avails, that prostrate slaves adore,
        And Fame proclaims thee matchless and divine ?

72 " What though bland Flattery all her arts apply ?—
        Will these avail to calm the infuriate brain ?
    Or will the roaring surge, when heaved on high,
        Headlong hang, hush'd, to hear the piping swain ?

73 " In health how fair, how ghastly in decay
        Man's lofty form ! how heavenly fair the mind
    Sublimed by Virtue's sweet enlivening sway !
        But ah ! to guilt's outrageous rule resign'd.

74 " How hideous and forlorn ! when ruthless Care
        With cankering tooth corrodes the seeds of life,
    And deaf with passion's storms when pines Despair,
        And howling furies rouse the eternal strife.

75 " Oh, by thy hopes of joy that restless glow,
        Pledges of Heaven ! be taught by Wisdom's lore ;
    With anxious haste each doubtful path forego,
        And life's wild ways with cautious fear explore.

76 "Straight be thy course : nor tempt the maze that leads
    Where fell Remorse his shapeless strength conceals,
And oft Ambition's dizzy cliff he treads,
    And slumbers oft in Pleasure's flowery vales.

77 "Nor linger unresolved : Heaven prompts the choice,
    Save when Presumption shuts the ear of Pride :
With grateful awe attend to Nature's voice,
    The voice of Nature Heaven ordain'd thy guide.

78 " Warn'd by her voice the arduous path pursue,
    That leads to Virtue's fane a hardy band :
What though no gaudy scenes decoy their view,
    Nor clouds of fragrance roll along the land ?

79 " What though rude mountains heave the flinty way ?
    Yet there the soul drinks light and life divine,
And pure aërial gales of gladness play,
    . Brace every nerve, and every sense refine.

80 "Go, prince, be virtuous and be blest.   The throne
    Rears not its state to swell the couch of Lust :
Nor dignify Corruption's daring son,
    'To o'erwhelm his humbler brethren of the dust.

81 " But yield an ampler scene to Bounty's eye,
    An ampler range to Mercy's ear expand :
And, 'midst admiring nations, set on high
    Virtue's fair model, framed by Wisdom's hand.

82 " Go then : the moan of Woe demands thine aid :
    Pride's licensed outrage claims thy slumbering ire :
Pale Genius roams the bleak neglected shade,
    And battening Avarice mocks his tuneless lyre.

83 " Even Nature pines, by vilest chains oppress'd:
    The astonish'd kingdoms crouch to Fashion's nod.
O ye pure inmates of the gentle breast,
    Truth, Freedom, Love, O where is your abode?

84 " O yet once more shall Peace from heaven return,
    And young Simplicity with mortals dwell !
Nor Innocence the august pavilion scorn,
    Nor meek Contentment fly the humble cell !

85 " Wilt thou, my prince, the beauteous train implore
    'Midst earth's forsaken scenes once more to bide ?
Then shall the shepherd sing in every bower,
    And Love with garlands wreathe the domes of Pride.

86 " The bright tear starting in the impassion'd eyes
    Of silent Gratitude: the smiling gaze
Of Gratulation, faltering while he tries
    With voice of transport to proclaim thy praise :

87 " The ethereal glow that stimulates thy frame,
    When all the according powers harmonious move,
And wake to energy each social aim,
    Attuned spontaneous to the will of Jove:

88 " Be these, O man, the triumphs of thy soul;
    And all the conqueror's dazzling glories slight,
That meteor-like o'er trembling nations roll,
    To sink at once in deep and dreadful night.

89 " Like thine, yon orb's stupendous glories burn
    With genial beam ; nor, at the approach of even,
In shades of horror leave the world to mourn,
    But gild with lingering light the empurpled heaven."

90 Thus while she spoke, her eye, sedately meek,
    Look'd the pure fervour of maternal love.
No rival zeal intemperate flush'd her cheek—
    Can Beauty's boast the soul of Wisdom move ?

91 Worth's noble pride, can Envy's leer appal,
    Or staring Folly's vain applauses soothe ?
Can jealous Fear Truth's dauntless heart enthrall ?
    Suspicion lurks not in the heart of Truth.

92 And now the shepherd raised his pensive head :
    Yet unresolved and fearful roved his eyes,
Scared at the glances of the awful maid ;
    For young unpractised Guilt distrusts the guise

93 Of shameless Arrogance.——His wavering breast,
    Though warm'd by Wisdom, own'd no constant fire
While lawless Fancy roam'd afar, unblest
    Save in the oblivious lap of soft Desire.

94 When thus the queen of soul-dissolving smiles :
    " Let gentler fate my darling prince attend,
Joyless and cruel are the warrior's spoils,
    Dreary the path stern Virtue's sons ascend.

95 " Of human joy full short is the career,
    And the dread verge still gains upon your sight ;
While idly gazing far beyond your sphere,
    Ye scan the dream of unapproach'd delight :

96 " Till every sprightly hour and blooming scene
    Of life's gay morn unheeded glides away,
And clouds of tempests mount the blue serene,
    And storms and ruin close the troublous day.

E

97   " Then still exult to hail the present joy,
     Thine be the boon that comes unearn'd by toil ;
No forward vain desire thy bliss annoy,
     No flattering hope thy longing hours beguile.

98   " Ah ! why should man pursue the charms of Fame,
     For ever luring, yet for ever coy ?
Light as the gaudy rainbow's pillar'd gleam,
     That melts illusive from the wondering boy !

99   " What though her throne irradiate many a clime,
     If hung loose-tottering o'er the unfathom'd tomb ?
What though her mighty clarion, rear'd sublime,
     Display the imperial wreath and glittering plume '

100   " Can glittering plume, or can the imperial wreath
     Redeem from unrelenting fate the brave ?
What note of triumph can her clarion breathe,
     To alarm the eternal midnight of the grave ?

101   " That night draws on : nor will the vacant hour
     Of expectation linger as it flies :
Nor fate one moment unenjoy'd restore :
     Each moment's flight how precious to the wise !

102   " O shun the annoyance of the bustling throng,
     That haunt with zealous turbulence the great :
There coward Office boasts the unpunish'd wrong,
     And sneaks secure in insolence of state.

103   " O'er fancied injury Suspicion pines,
     And in grim silence gnaws the festering wound ;
Deceit the rage-embitter'd smile refines,
     And Censure spreads the viperous hiss around.

104 " Hope not, fond prince, though Wisdom guard thy throne,
　　　Though Truth and Bounty prompt each generous aim,
　　Though thine the palm of peace, the victor's crown,
　　　The Muse's rapture, and the patriot's flame :

105 " Hope not, though all that captivates the wise,
　　　All that endears the good exalt thy praise :
　　Hope not to taste repose : for Envy's eyes
　　　At fairest worth still point their deadly rays.

106 " Envy, stern tyrant of the flinty heart,
　　　Can aught of Virtue, Truth, or Beauty charm ?
　　Can soft Compassion thrill with pleasing smart,
　　　Repentance melt, or Gratitude disarm ?

107 " Ah no.　Where Winter Scythia's waste enchains,
　　　And monstrous shapes roar to the ruthless storm,
　　Not Phœbus' smile can cheer the dreadful plains,
　　　Or soil accursed with balmy life inform.

108 " Then, Envy, then is thy triumphant hour,
　　　When mourns Benevolence his baffled scheme :
　　When Insult mocks the clemency of Power,
　　　And loud dissension's livid firebrands gleam :

109 " When squint-eyed Slander plies the unhallow'd tongue,
　　　From poison'd maw when Treason weaves his line,
　　And Muse apostate (infamy to song !)
　　　Grovels, low muttering, at Sedition's shrine.

110 " Let not my prince forego the peaceful shade,
　　　The whispering grove, the fountain and the plain :
　　Power, with the oppressive weight of pomp array'd,
　　.　Pants for simplicity and ease in vain.

111   " The yell of frantic Mirth may stun his ear,
      But frantic Mirth soon leaves the heart forlorn ;
And Pleasure flies that high tempestuous sphere :
      Far different scenes her lucid paths adorn.

112   " She loves to wander on the untrodden lawn,
      Or the green bosom of reclining hill,
Soothed by the careless warbler of the dawn,
      Or the lone plaint of ever-murmuring rill.

113   " Or from the mountain glade's aërial brow,
      While to her song a thousand echoes call,
Marks the wide woodland wave remote below,
      Where shepherds pipe unseen, and waters fall.

114   " Her influence oft the festive hamlet proves,
      Where the high carol cheers the exulting ring ;
And oft she roams the maze of wildering groves,
      Listening the unnumber'd melodies of Spring.

115   " Or to the long and lonely shore retires ;
      What time, loose-glimmering to the lunar beam,
Faint heaves the slumberous wave, and starry fires
      Gild the blue deep with many a lengthening gleam.

116   " Then to the balmy bower of Rapture borne,
      While strings self-warbling breathe Elysian rest,
Melts in delicious vision, till the morn
      Spangle with twinkling dew the flowery waste.

117   " The frolic Moments, purple-pinion'd. dance
      Around, and scatter roses as they play ;
And the blithe Graces, hand in hand, advance,
      Where, with her loved compeers, she deigns to stray

118 " Mild Solitude, in veil of rustic dye,
  Her sylvan spear with moss-grown ivy bound;
And Indolence, with sweetly languid eye,
  And zoneless robe that trails along the ground ;

119 " But chiefly Love—O thou, whose gentle mind
  Each soft indulgence Nature framed to share ;
Pomp, wealth, renown, dominion, all resign'd,
  Oh, haste to Pleasure's bower, for Love is there.

120 " Love, the desire of Gods ! the feast of heaven !
  Yet to Earth's favour'd offspring not denied !
Ah! let not thankless man the blessing given
  Enslave to Fame, or sacrifice to Pride.

121 " Nor I from Virtue's call decoy thine ear ;
  Friendly to Pleasure are her sacred laws :
Let Temperance' smile the cup of gladness cheer;
  That cup is death, if he withhold applause.

122 " Far from thy haunt be Envy's baneful sway,
  And Hate, that works the harass'd soul to storm ;
But woo Content to breathe her soothing lay,
  And charm from Fancy's view each angry form.

123 " No savage joy the harmonious hours profane !
  Whom Love refines, can barbarous tumults please ?
Shall rage of blood pollute the sylvan reign ?
  Shall Leisure wanton in the spoils of Peace ?

124 " Free let the feathery race indulge the song,
  Inhale the liberal beam, and melt in love :
Free let the fleet hind bound her hills along,
  And in pure streams the watery nations rove.

125 " To joy in Nature's universal smile
        Well suits, O man, thy pleasurable sphere ;
    But why should Virtue doom thy years to toil ?
        Ah! why should Virtue's laws be deem'd severe ?

126 " What meed, Beneficence, thy care repays ?
        What, Sympathy, thy still returning pang ?
    And why his generous arm should Justice raise,
        To dare the vengeance of a tyrant's fang ?

127 " From thankless spite no bounty can secure ;
        Or froward wish of discontent fulfil,
    That knows not to regret thy bounded power,
        But blames with keen reproach thy partial will.

128 " To check the impetuous all-involving tide
        Of human woes, how impotent thy strife !
    High o'er thy mounds devouring surges ride,
        Nor reck thy baffled toils, or lavish'd life.

129 " The bower of bliss, the smile of love be thine,
        Unlabour'd ease, and leisure's careless dream.
    Such be their joys who bend at Venus' shrine,
        And own her charms beyond compare supreme."

130 Warm'd as she spoke, all panting with delight,
        Her kindling beauties breathed triumphant bloom ;
    And Cupids flutter'd round in circlets bright,
        And Flora pour'd from all her stores perfume.

131 " Thine be the prize," exclaim'd the enraptured youth,
        " Queen of unrivall'd charms, and matchless joy."—
    O blind to fate, felicity, and truth !
        But such are they whom Pleasure's snares decoy.

132 The Sun was sunk ; the vision was no more ;
    Night downward rush'd tempestuous, at the frown
Of Jove's awaken'd wrath : deep thunders roar,
    And forests howl afar, and mountains groan,

133 And sanguine meteors glare athwart the plain ;
    With horror's scream the Ilian towers resound,
Raves the hoarse storm along the bellowing main,
    And the strong earthquake rends the shuddering
      ground.

THE TRIUMPH OF MELANCHOLY.

1 MEMORY, be still! why throng upon the thought
    These scenes deep-stain'd with Sorrow's sable dye ?
Hast thou in store no joy-illumined draught,
    To cheer bewilder'd Fancy's tearful eye ?

2 Yes—from afar a landscape seems to rise,
    Deck'd gorgeous by the lavish hand of Spring :
Thin gilded clouds float light along the skies,
    And laughing Loves disport on fluttering wing.

3 How blest the youth in yonder valley laid!
    Soft smiles in every conscious feature play,
While to the gale low murmuring through the glade,
    He tempers sweet his sprightly-warbling lay.

4 Hail, Innocence ! whose bosom, all serene,
    Feels not fierce Passion's raving tempest roll !
Oh, ne'er may Care distract that placid mien !
    Oh, ne'er may Doubt's dark shades o'erwhelm thy soul!

5 Vain wish ! for, lo ! in gay attire conceal'd,
　　Yonder she comes, the heart-inflaming fiend !
(Will no kind power the helpless stripling shield ?)
　　Swift to her destined prey see Passion bend !

6 O smile accursed, to hide the worst designs !
　　Now with blithe eye she woo's him to be blest,
While round her arm unseen a serpent twines—
　　And, lo ! she hurls it hissing at his breast.

7 And, instant, lo ! his dizzy eyeball swims
　　Ghastly, and reddening darts a threatful glare ;
Pain with strong grasp distorts his writhing limbs,
　　And Fear's cold hand erects his bristling hair !

8 Is this, O life, is this thy boasted prime ?
　　And does thy spring no happier prospect yield ?
Why gilds the vernal sun thy gaudy clime,
　　When nipping mildews waste the flowery field ?

9 How Memory pains !　Let some gay theme beguile
　　The musing mind, and soothe to soft delight.
Ye images of woe, no more recoil ;
　　Be life's past scenes wrapt in oblivious night.

10 Now when fierce Winter, arm'd with wasteful power,
　　Heaves the wild deep that thunders from afar,
How sweet to sit in this sequester'd bower,
　　To hear, and but to hear, the mingling war !

11 Ambition here displays no gilded toy
　　That tempts on desperate wing the soul to rise,
Nor Pleasure's flower-embroider'd paths decoy,
　　Nor Anguish lurks in Grandeur's gay disguise.

12 Oft has Contentment cheer'd this lone abode
    With the mild languish of her smiling eye;
Here Health has oft in blushing beauty glow'd,
    While loose-robed Quiet stood enamour'd by.

13 Even the storm lulls to more profound repose :
    The storm these humble walls assails in vain :
Screen'd is the lily when the whirlwind blows,
    While the oak's stately ruin strews the plain.

14 Blow on, ye winds ! Thine, Winter, be the skies ;
    Roll the old ocean, and the vales lay waste :
Nature thy momentary rage defies;
    To her relief the gentler seasons haste.

15 Throned in her emerald car, see Spring appear !
    (As Fancy wills, the landscape starts to view)
Her emerald car the youthful Zephyrs bear,
    Fanning her bosom with their pinions blue.

16 Around the jocund Hours are fluttering seen;
    And, lo ! her rod the rose-lipp'd power extends.
And, lo ! the lawns are deck'd in living green,
    And Beauty's bright-eyed train from heaven descends.

17 Haste, happy days, and make all nature glad—
    But will all nature joy at your return ?
Say, can ye cheer pale Sickness' gloomy bed,
    Or dry the tears that bathe the untimely urn ?

18 Will ye one transient ray of gladness dart
    'Cross the dark cell where hopeless slavery lies ?
To ease tired Disappointment's bleeding heart,
    Will all your stores of softening balm suffice ?

19 When fell Oppression in his harpy fangs
      From Want's weak grasp the last sad morsel bears,
  Can ye allay the heart-wrung parent's pangs,
      Whose famish'd child craves help with fruitless tears?

20 For ah! thy reign, Oppression, is not past,
      Who from the shivering limbs the vestment rends,
  Who lays the once rejoicing village waste,
      Bursting the ties of lovers and of friends.

21 O ye, to Pleasure who resign the day,
      As loose in Luxury's clasping arms you lie,
  O yet let pity in your breast bear sway,
      And learn to melt at Misery's moving cry.

22 But hop'st thou, Muse, vain-glorious as thou art,
      With the weak impulse of thy humble strain,
  Hop'st thou to soften Pride's obdurate heart,
      When Errol's bright example shines in vain?

23 Then cease the theme.   Turn, Fancy, turn thine eye,
      Thy weeping eye, nor further urge thy flight;
  Thy haunts, alas! no gleams of joy supply,
      Or transient gleams, that flash and sink in night.

24 Yet fain the mind its anguish would forego—
      Spread then, historic Muse, thy pictured scroll;
  Bid thy great scenes in all their splendour glow,
      And swell to thought sublime the exalted soul.

25 What mingling pomps rush boundless on the gaze!
      What gallant navies ride the heaving deep!
  What glittering towns their cloud-wrapt turrets raise!
      What bulwarks frown horrific o'er the steep!

26 Bristling with spears, and bright with burnish'd shields,
    The embattled legions stretch their long array;
Discord's red torch, as fierce she scours the fields,
    With bloody tincture stains the face of day.

27 And now the hosts in silence wait the sign.
    How keen their looks whom Liberty inspires!
Quick as the Goddess darts along the line,
    Each breast impatient burns with noble fires.

28 Her form how graceful!　In her lofty mien
    The smiles of Love stern Wisdom's frown control;
Her fearless eye, determined though serene,
    Speaks the great purpose, and the unconquer'd soul.

29 Mark, where Ambition leads the adverse band,
    Each feature fierce and haggard, as with pain!
With menace loud he cries, while from his hand
    He vainly strives to wipe the crimson stain.

30 Lo! at his call, impetuous as the storms,
    Headlong to deeds of death the hosts are driven:
Hatred to madness wrought, each face deforms,
    Mounts the black whirlwind, and involves the heaven.

31 Now, Virtue, now thy powerful succour lend,
    Shield them for Liberty who dare to die—
Ah, Liberty! will none thy cause befriend?
    Are these thy sons, thy generous sons, that fly?

32 Not Virtue's self, when Heaven its aid denies,
    Can brace the loosen'd nerves or warm the heart!
Not Virtue's self can still the burst of sighs,
    When festers in the soul Misfortune's dart.

33 See where, by heaven-bred terror all dismay'd
    The scattering legions pour along the plain ;
Ambition's car, with bloody spoils array'd,
    Hews its broad way, as Vengeance guides the rein.

34 But who is he that, by yon lonely brook,
    With woods o'erhung and precipices rude, [1]
Abandon'd lies, and with undaunted look
    Sees streaming from his breast the purple flood ?

35 Ah, Brutus ! ever thine be Virtue's tear !
    Lo ! his dim eyes to Liberty he turns,
As scarce supported on her broken spear
    O'er her expiring son the goddess mourns.

36 Loose to the wind her azure mantle flies,
    From her dishevell'd locks she rends the plume ;
No lustre lightens in her weeping eyes,
    And on her tear-stain'd cheek no roses bloom.

37 Meanwhile the world, Ambition, owns thy sway,
    Fame's loudest trumpet labours in thy praise,
For thee the Muse awakes her sweetest lay,
    And Flattery bids for thee her altars blaze.

38 Nor in life's lofty bustling sphere alone,
    The sphere where monarchs and where heroes toil,
Sink Virtue's sons beneath Misfortune's frown,
    While Guilt's thrill'd bosom leaps at Pleasure's smile

39 Full oft, where Solitude and Silence dwell,
    Far, far remote, amid the lowly plain,
Resounds the voice of Woe from Virtue's cell:
    Such is man's doom, and Pity weeps in vain.

[1] Such, according to the description given by Plutarch, was the scene of Brutus's death.

40 Still grief recoils—How vainly have I strove
  Thy power, O Melancholy, to withstand !
Tired I submit ; but yet, O yet remove
  Or ease the pressure of thy heavy hand.

41 Yet for a while let the bewilder'd soul
  Find in society relief from woe ;
O yield a while to Friendship's soft control ;
  Some respite, Friendship, wilt thou not bestow ?

42 Come, then, Philander ! for thy lofty, mind
  Looks down from far on all that charms the great ;
For thou canst bear, unshaken and resign'd,
  The brightest smiles, the blackest frowns of Fate :

43 Come thou, whose love unlimited, sincere,
  Nor faction cools, nor injury destroys ;
Who lend'st to misery's moans a pitying ear,
  And feel'st with ecstasy another's joys :

44 Who know'st man's frailty : with a favouring eye,
  And melting heart, behold'st a brother's fall ;
Who, unenslaved by custom's narrow tie,
  With manly freedom follow'st reason's call.

45 And bring thy Delia, softly-smiling fair,
  Whose spotless soul no sordid thoughts deform :
Her accents mild would still each throbbing care,
  And harmonize the thunder of the storm.

46 Though blest with wisdom, and with wit refined,
  She courts not homage, nor desires to shine :
In her each sentiment sublime is join'd
  To female sweetness, and a form divine.

47 Come, and dispel the deep surrounding shade:
        Let chasten'd mirth the social hours employ;
    O catch the swift-wing'd hour before 'tis fled,
        On swiftest pinion flies the hour of joy.

48 Even while the careless disencumber'd soul
        Dissolving sinks to joy's oblivious dream,
    Even then to time's tremendous verge we roll
        With haste impetuous down life's surgy stream.

49 Can Gaiety the vanish'd years restore,
        Or on the withering limbs fresh beauty shed,
    Or soothe the sad inevitable hour,
        Or cheer the dark, dark mansions of the dead?

50 Still sounds the solemn knell in Fancy's ear,
        That call'd Cleora to the silent tomb;
    To her how jocund roll'd the sprightly year!
        How shone the nymph in beauty's brightest bloom!

51 Ah! beauty's bloom avails not in the grave,
        Youth's lofty mien, nor age's awful grace:
    Moulder unknown the monarch and the slave,
        Whelm'd in the enormous wreck of human race.

52 The thought-fix'd portraiture, the breathing bust,
        The arch with proud memorials array'd,
    The long-lived pyramid shall sink in dust
        To dumb oblivion's ever-desert shade.

53 Fancy from comfort wanders still astray.
        Ah, Melancholy! how I feel thy power!
    Long have I labour'd to elude thy sway!
        But 'tis enough, for I resist no more.

54 The traveller thus, that o'er the midnight waste
    Through many a lonesome path is doom'd to roam,
Wilder'd and weary sits him down at last ;
    For long the night, and distant far his home.

ELEGY.

1 TIRED with the busy crowds, that all the day
    Impatient throng where Folly's altars flame,
My languid powers dissolve with quick decay,
    Till genial Sleep repair the sinking frame.

2 Hail, kind reviver ! that canst lull the cares,
    And every weary sense compose to rest,
Lighten the oppressive load which anguish bears,
    And warm with hope the cold desponding breast.

3 Touch'd by thy rod, from Power's majestic brow
    Drops the gay plume ; he pines a lowly clown ;
And on the cold earth stretch'd, the son of Woe
    Quaffs Pleasure's draught, and wears a fancied crown.

4 When roused by thee, on boundless pinions borne,
    Fancy to fairy scenes exults to rove,
Now scales the cliff gay-gleaming on the morn,
    Now sad and silent treads the deepening grove ;

5 Or skims the main, and listens to the storms,
    Marks the long waves roll far remote away ;
Or, mingling with ten thousand glittering forms,
    Floats on the gale, and basks in purest day.

6   Haply, ere long, pierced by the howling blast,
     Through dark and pathless deserts I shall roam,
  Plunge down the unfathom'd deep, or shrink aghast
     Where bursts the shrieking spectre from the tomb:

7   Perhaps loose Luxury's enchanting smile
     Shall lure my steps to some romantic dale,
  Where Mirth's light freaks the unheeded hours beguile,
     And airs of rapture warble in the gale.

8   Instructive emblem of this mortal state!
     Where scenes as various every hour arise
  In swift succession, which the hand of Fate
     Presents, then snatches from our wondering eyes.

9   Be taught, vain man, how fleeting all thy joys,
     Thy boasted grandeur and thy glittering store:
  Death comes, and all thy fancied bliss destroys;
     Quick as a dream it fades, and is no more.

10   And, sons of Sorrow! though the threatening storm
     Of angry Fortune overhang awhile,
  Let not her frowns your inward peace deform;
     Soon happier days in happier climes shall smile.

11   Through Earth's throng'd visions while we toss forlorn,
     'Tis tumult all, and rage, and restless strife;
  But these shall vanish like the dreams of morn,
     When Death awakes us to immortal life.

ELEGY.

WRITTEN IN THE YEAR 1758.

STILL shall unthinking man substantial deem
The forms that fleet through life's deceitful dream ?
Till at some stroke of Fate the vision flies,
And sad realities in prospect rise ;
And, from Elysian slumbers rudely torn,
The startled soul awakes, to think, and mourn.
   O ye, whose hours in jocund train advance,
Whose spirits to the song of gladness dance,
Who flowery plains in endless pomp survey,
Glittering in beams of visionary day ;   1
O yet, while Fate delays the impending woe,
Be roused to thought, anticipate the blow ;
Lest, like the lightning's glance, the sudden ill
Flash to confound, and penetrate to kill ;
Lest, thus encompass'd with funereal gloom,
Like me, ye bend o'er some untimely tomb,
Pour your wild ravings in Night's frighted ear,
And half pronounce Heaven's sacred doom severe.
   Wise, beauteous, good ! O every grace combined,
That charms the eye, or captivates the mind !   2(
Fresh, as the floweret opening on the morn,
Whose leaves bright drops of liquid pearl adorn !
Sweet, as the downy pinion'd gale, that roves
To gather fragrance in Arabian groves !
Mild, as the melodies at close of day,
That, heard remote, along the vale decay !
Yet, why with these compared ?   What tints so fine,
What sweetness, mildness, can be match'd with thine ?

Why roam abroad, since recollection true   29
Restores the lovely form to fancy's view?
Still let me gaze, and every care beguile,
Gaze on that cheek, where all the graces smile;
That soul-expressing eye, benignly bright,
Where Meekness beams ineffable delight;
That brow, where Wisdom sits enthroned serene,
Each feature forms, and dignifies the mean:
Still let me listen, while her words impart
The sweet effusions of the blameless heart;
Till all my soul, each tumult charm'd away,
Yields, gently led, to Virtue's easy sway.   40
    By thee inspired, O Virtue, age is young,
And music warbles from the faltering tongue:
Thy ray creative cheers the clouded brow,
And decks the faded cheek with rosy glow,
Brightens the joyless aspect, and supplies
Pure heavenly lustre to the languid eyes:
But when youth's living bloom reflects thy beams,
Resistless on the view the glory streams:
Love, wonder, joy, alternately alarm,
And beauty dazzles with angelic charm.   50
    Ah, whither fled?   ye dear illusions, stay!
Lo! pale and silent lies the lovely clay.
How are the roses on that cheek decay'd,
Which late the purple light of youth display'd!
Health on her form each sprightly grace bestow'd:
With life and thought each speaking feature glow'd.
Fair was the blossom, soft the vernal sky;
Elate with hope, we deem'd no tempest nigh:
When, lo! a whirlwind's instantaneous gust
Left all its beauties withering in the dust.   60
    Cold the soft hand that soothed Woe's weary head!
And quench'd the eye, the pitying tear that shed!

And mute the voice, whose pleasing accents stole,　　6
Infusing balm into the rankled soul !
O Death, why arm with cruelty thy power,
And spare the idle weed, yet lop the flower ?
Why fly thy shafts in lawless error driven ?
Is Virtue then no more the care of Heaven ?
But, peace, bold thought ! be still, my bursting heart !
We, not Eliza, felt the fatal dart.　　7

　　Escaped the dungeon, does the slave complain,
Nor bless the friendly hand that broke the chain ?
Say, pines not Virtue for the lingering morn,
On this dark wild condemn'd to roam forlorn ;
Where Reason's meteor rays, with sickly glow,
O'er the dun gloom a dreadful glimmering throw ;
Disclosing, dubious, to the affrighted eye
O'erwhelming mountains tottering from on high,
Black billowy deeps in storms perpetual tost,
And weary ways in wildering labyrinths lost ?　　8
O happy stroke, that bursts the bonds of clay,
Darts through the rending gloom the blaze of day,
And wings the soul with boundless flight to soar,
Where dangers threat, and fears alarm no more.

　　Transporting thought ! here let me wipe away
The tear of Grief, and wake a bolder lay.
But ah ! the swimming eye o'erflows anew ;
Nor check the sacred drops to pity due :
Lo ! where in speechless, hopeless anguish bend
O'er her loved dust, the parent, brother, friend !　　9
How vain the hope of man ! but cease thy strain,
Nor sorrow's dread solemnity profane ;
Mix'd with yon drooping mourners, on her bier
In silence shed the sympathetic tear.

RETIREMENT.   1758.

1 WHEN in the crimson cloud of even
    The lingering light decays,
And Hesper on the front of heaven
    His glittering gem displays;
Deep in the silent vale, unseen,
    Beside a lulling stream,
A pensive Youth, of placid mien,
    Indulged this tender theme :

2 " Ye cliffs, in hoary grandeur piled
    High o'er the glimmering dale;
Ye woods, along whose windings wild
    Murmurs the solemn gale :
Where Melancholy strays forlorn,
    And Woe retires to weep,
What time the wan Moon's yellow horn
    Gleams on the western deep !

3 " To you, ye wastes, whose artless charms
    Ne'er drew ambition's eye,
'Scaped a tumultuous world's alarms,
    To your retreats I fly.
Deep in your most sequester'd bower
    Let me at last recline,
Where Solitude, mild, modest power,
    Leans on her ivied shrine.

4 " How shall I woo thee, matchless fair ?
    Thy heavenly smile how win ?
Thy smile that smooths the brow of Care,
    And stills the storm within.

O wilt thou to thy favourite grove
  Thine ardent votary bring,
And bless his hours, and bid them move
  Serene on silent wing ?

5 " Oft let Remembrance soothe his mind
    With dreams of former days,
When in the lap of Peace reclined
  He framed his infant lays ;
When Fancy roved at large, nor Care
  Nor cold distrust alarm'd,
Nor Envy, with malignant glare,
  His simple youth had harm'd.

6 " 'Twas then, O Solitude, to thee
  His early vows were paid,
From heart sincere, and warm, and free,
  Devoted to the shade.
Ah ! why did Fate his steps decoy
  In stormy paths to roam,
Remote from all congenial joy ?——
  O take the wanderer home !

7 " Thy shades, thy silence now be mine,
  Thy charms my only theme ;
My haunt the hollow cliff, whose pine
  Waves o'er the gloomy stream.
Whence the scared owl on pinions gray
  Breaks from the rustling boughs,
And down the lone vale sails away
  To more profound repose.

8 " Oh, while to thee the woodland pours
  Its wildly-warbling song,

And balmy from the bank of flowers
 The Zephyr breathes along;
Let no rude sound invade from far,
 No vagrant foot be nigh,
No ray from Grandeur's gilded car
 Flash on the startled eye.

9 " But if some pilgrim through the glade
  Thy hallow'd bowers explore,
 O guard from harm his hoary head,
  And listen to his lore;
 For he of joys divine shall tell,
  That wean from earthly woe,
 And triumph o'er the mighty spell
  That chains his heart below.

10 " For me no more the path invites
  Ambition loves to tread;
 No more I climb those toilsome heights
  By guileful hope misled;
 Leaps my fond fluttering heart no more
  To Mirth's enlivening strain;
 For present pleasure soon is o'er,
  And all the past is vain."

THE HERMIT.

1 AT the close of the day, when the hamlet is still,
 And mortals the sweets of forgetfulness prove,
 When nought but the torrent is heard on the hill,
 And nought but the nightingale's song in the grove

'Twas thus, by the cave of the mountain afar,
While his harp rung symphonious, a hermit began :
No more with himself or with nature at war,
He thought as a sage, though he felt as a man.

2 " Ah ! why, all abandon'd to darkness and woe,
Why, lone Philomela, that languishing fall ?
For Spring shall return, and a lover bestow,
And sorrow no longer thy bosom enthrall.
But if pity inspire thee, renew the sad lay,
Mourn, sweetest complainer, man calls thee to mourn :
O, soothe him whose pleasures like thine pass away :
Full quickly they pass—but they never return.

3 " Now gliding remote on the verge of the sky,
The Moon, half extinguish'd, her crescent displays :
But lately I mark'd when majestic on high
She shone, and the planets were lost in her blaze.
Roll on, thou fair orb, and with gladness pursue
The path that conducts thee to splendour again.
But man's faded glory what change shall renew ?
Ah, fool ! to exult in a glory so vain !

4 " 'Tis night, and the landscape is lovely no more ;
I mourn, but, ye woodlands, I mourn not for you ;
For morn is approaching, your charms to restore,
Perfumed with fresh fragrance, and glittering with dew
Nor yet for the ravage of winter I mourn ;
Kind Nature the embryo blossom will save.
But when shall spring visit the mouldering urn ?
O when shall it dawn on the night of the grave ?

5 " 'Twas thus, by the glare of false Science betray'd,
That leads to bewilder, and dazzles to blind ;

My thoughts wont to roam, from shade onward to shade,
Destruction before me, and sorrow behind.
'O pity, great Father of light,' then I cried,
'Thy creature, who fain would not wander from thee :
Lo, humbled in dust, I relinquish my pride :
From doubt and from darkness thou only canst free.'

6 "And darkness and doubt are now flying away;
No longer I roam in conjecture forlorn :
So breaks on the traveller, faint, and astray,
The bright and the balmy effulgence of morn.
See Truth, Love, and Mercy in triumph descending,
And nature all glowing in Eden's first bloom !
On the cold cheek of Death smiles and roses are blending,
And Beauty immortal awakes from the tomb."

ON

THE REPORT OF A MONUMENT TO BE ERECTED IN WESTMINSTER ABBEY, TO THE MEMORY OF A LATE AUTHOR (CHURCHILL).

(WRITTEN IN 1765.)

[PART OF A LETTER TO A PERSON OF QUALITY.]

Lest your Lordship, who are so well acquainted with everything that relates to true honour, should think hardly of me for attacking the memory of the dead, I beg leave to offer a few words in my own vindication.

If I had composed the following verses, with a view to gratify private resentment, to promote the interest of any faction, or to recommend myself to the patronage of any person whatsoever, I should have been altogether inexcusable. To attack the memory of the dead from selfish considerations, or from mere wantonness of malice, is an enormity which none can hold in greater detestation than I. But I composed them from very different motives ; as every intelligent reader, who peruses them with attention, and who is willing to believe me upon my own testimony, will undoubtedly perceive. My motives proceeded from a sincere desire to do some small service to my country, and to the cause of truth and virtue. The promoters of faction I ever did, and ever will, consider as the enemies of mankind : to the memory of such I owe no veneration: to the writings of such I owe no indulgence.

Your Lordship knows that (Churchill) owed the greatest share of his renown to the most incompetent of all judges, the mob: actuated by the most unworthy of all principles, a spirit of insolence, and inflamed by the vilest of all human passions, hatred to their fellow-citizens. Those who joined the cry in his favour seemed to me to be swayed rather by fashion than by real sentiment : he therefore might have lived and died unmolested by me, confident as I am, that posterity, when the present unhappy dissensions are forgotten, will do ample justice to his real character. But when I saw the extravagant honours that were paid to his memory, and heard that a monument in Westminster Abbey was intended for one whom even his admirers acknowledge to have been an incendiary and a debauchee ; I could not help wishing that my countrymen would reflect a little on what they were doing, before they consecrated, by what posterity would think the public voice, a character, which no friend to virtue or true taste can approve. 'It was this sentiment, enforced by the earnest request of a friend, which produced the following little poem ; in which I have said nothing of (Churchill's) manners that is not warranted by the best authority : nor of his writings, that is not perfectly agreeable to the opinion of many of the most competent judges in Britain.

ABERDEEN, *January* 1765.

BUFO, begone ! with thee may Faction's fire,
That hatch'd thy salamander-fame, expire.
Fame, dirty idol of the brainless crowd,
What half-made moon-calf can mistake for good !
Since shared by knaves of high and low degree ;
Cromwell and Cataline : Guido Faux, and thee.
  By nature uninspired, untaught by art ;
With not one thought that breathes the feeling heart,
With not one offering vow'd to Virtue's shrine,
With not one pure unprostituted line ;   10
Alike debauch'd in body, soul, and lays ;—
For pension'd censure, and for pension'd praise,
For ribaldry, for libels, lewdness, lies,
For blasphemy of all the good and wise :

Coarse violence in coarser doggrel writ,   15
Which bawling blackguards spell'd, and took for wit :
For conscience, honour, slighted, spurn'd, o'erthrown:——
Lo ! Bufo shines the minion of renown.
    Is this the land that boasts a Milton's fire,
And magic Spenser's wildly warbling lyre ?   20
The land that owns the omnipotence of song,
When Shakspeare whirls the throbbing heart along ?
The land, where Pope, with energy divine,
In one strong blaze bade wit and fancy shine :
Whose verse, by truth in virtue's triumph born,
Gave knaves to infamy, and fools to scorn ;
Yet pure in manners, and in thought refined,
Whose life and lays adorn'd and bless'd mankind ?
Is this the land, where Gray's unlabour'd art
Soothes, melts, alarms, and ravishes the heart :   30
While the lone wanderer's sweet complainings flow
In simple majesty of manly woe :
Or while, sublime, on eagle pinion driven,
He soars Pindaric heights, and sails the waste of Heaven ?
Is this the land, o'er Shenstone's recent urn,
Where all the Loves and gentler Graces mourn ?
And where, to crown the hoary bard of night,[1]
The Muses and the Virtues all unite ?
Is this the land where Akenside displays
The bold yet temperate flame of ancient days ?   40
Like the rapt sage,[2] in genius as in theme,
Whose hallow'd strain renown'd Illyssus' stream :
Or him, the indignant bard,[3] whose patriot ire,
Sublime in vengeance, smote the dreadful lyre :
For truth, for liberty, for virtue warm,
Whose mighty song unnerved a tyrant's arm,

  [1] 'Hoary bard of night:' Dr Young. — [2] 'Rapt sage:' Plato. — [3] 'Indignant bard:' Alceus ; see Akenside's 'Ode on Lyric Poetry.'

———

Hush'd the rude roar of discord, rage, and lust,   4
And spurn'd licentious demagogues to dust.
  Is this the queen of realms? the glorious isle,
Britannia, blest in Heaven's indulgent smile?
Guardian of truth, and patroness of art,
Nurse of the undaunted soul, and generous heart!
Where, from a base unthankful world exiled,
Freedom exults to roam the careless wild :
Where taste to science every charm supplies,
And genius soars unbounded to the skies?
  And shall a Bufo's most polluted name
Stain her bright tablet of untainted fame?
Shall his disgraceful name with theirs be join'd,
Who wish'd and wrought the welfare of their kind?   6
His name, accurst, who, leagued with ———[1] and Hell,
Labour'd to rouse, with rude and murderous yell,
Discord the fiend, to toss rebellion's brand,
To whelm in rage and woe a guiltless land :
To frustrate wisdom's, virtue's noblest plan,
And triumph in the miseries of man.
  Drivelling and dull, when crawls the reptile Muse,
Swoln from the sty, and rankling from the stews,
With envy, spleen, and pestilence replete,
And gorged with dust she lick'd from Treason's feet: 7
Who once, like Satan, raised to Heaven her sight,
But turn'd abhorrent from the hated light :——
O'er such a Muse shall wreaths of glory bloom?
No—shame and execration be her doom.
  Hard-fated Bufo, could not dulness save
Thy soul from sin, from infamy thy grave?
Blackmore and Quarles, those blockheads of renown,
Lavish'd their ink, but never harm'd the town.
Though this, thy brother in discordant song,
Harass'd the ear, and cramp'd the labouring tongue :   8

[1] Wilkes.

And that, like thee, taught staggering prose to stand, 8
And limp on stilts of rhyme around the land.
Harmless they dozed a scribbling life away,
And yawning nations own'd the innoxious lay,
But from thy graceless, rude, and beastly brain,
What fury breathed the incendiary strain ?
    Did hate to vice exasperate thy style?
No——Bufo match'd the vilest of the vile.
Yet blazon'd was his verse with Virtue's name——
Thus prudes look down to hide their want of shame : 9
Thus hypocrites to truth, and fools to sense,
And fops to taste, have sometimes made pretence :
Thus thieves and gamesters swear by honour's laws :
Thus pension-hunters bawl " their country's cause :"
Thus furious Teague for moderation raved,
And own'd his soul to liberty enslaved.
    Nor yet, though thousand cits admire thy rage,
Though less of fool than felon marks thy page :
Nor yet, though here and there one lonely spark
Of wit half brightens through the involving dark,
To show the gloom more hideous for the foil,
But not repay the drudging reader's toil ;
(For who for one poor pearl of clouded ray
Through Alpine dunghills delves his desperate way?
Did genius to thy verse such bane impart ?
No.   'Twas the demon of thy venom'd heart,
(Thy heart with rancour's quintessence endued),
And the blind zeal of a misjudging crowd.
    Thus from rank soil a poison'd mushroom sprung,
Nursling obscene of mildew and of dung :   11
By Heaven design'd on its own native spot
Harmless to enlarge its bloated bulk, and rot.
But gluttony the abortive nuisance saw ;
It roused his ravenous, undiscerning maw :

Gulp'd down the tasteless throat, the mess abhorr'd   115
Shot fiery influence round the maddening board.
   O had thy verse been impotent as dull,
Nor spoke the rancorous heart, but lumpish scull ;
Had mobs distinguish'd, they who howl'd thy fame.
The icicle from the pure diamond's flame,   120
From fancy's soul thy gross imbruted sense,
From dauntless truth thy shameless insolence,
From elegance confusion's monstrous mass,
And from the lion's spoils the skulking ass,
From rapture's strain the drawling doggrel line,
From warbling seraphim the grunting swine ;
With gluttons, dunces, rakes, thy name had slept,
Nor o'er her sullied fame Britannia wept :
Nor had the Muse, with honest zeal possess'd,
To avenge her country, by thy name disgraced,   130
Raised this bold strain for virtue, truth, mankind,
And thy fell shade to infamy resign'd.
   When frailty leads astray the soul sincere,
Let mercy shed the soft and manly tear.
When to the grave descends the sensual sot,
Unnamed, unnoticed, let his carrion rot.
When paltry rogues, by stealth, deceit, or force,
Hazard their necks, ambitious of your purse :
For such the hangman wreaths his trusty gin,
And let the gallows expiate their sin.   140
But when a ruffian, whose portentous crimes,
Like plagues and earthquakes terrify the times,
Triumphs through life, from legal judgment free,
For Hell may hatch what law could ne'er foresee :
Sacred from vengeance shall his memory rest ?—
Judas, though dead, though damn'd, we still detest.

THE BATTLE OF THE PIGMIES AND CRANES.

(FROM THE " PYGMÆO-GERANO-MACHIA " OF ADDISON.)

1762.

THE Pigmy people, and the feather'd train,
Mingling in mortal combat on the plain,
I sing.   Ye Muses, favour my designs,
Lead on my squadrons and arrange the lines ;
The flashing swords and fluttering wings display,
And long bills nibbling in the bloody fray ;
Cranes darting with disdain on tiny foes,
Conflicting birds and men, and war's unnumber'd woes !
   The wars and woes of heroes six feet long
Have oft resounded in Pierian song.   10
Who has not heard of Colchos' golden fleece,
And Argo mann'd with all the flower of Greece ?
Of Thebes' fell brethren ; Theseus stern of face ;
And Peleus' son, unrivall'd in the race ;
Eneas, founder of the Roman line,
And William, glorious on the banks of Boyne ?
Who has not learn'd to weep at Pompey's woes,
And over Blackmore's epic page to doze ?
'Tis I, who dare attempt unusual strains,
Of hosts unsung, and unfrequented plains ;   20
The small shrill trump, and chiefs of little size,
And armies rushing down the darken'd skies.
   Where India reddens to the early dawn,
Winds a deep vale from vulgar eye withdrawn :
Bosom'd in groves the lowly region lies,
And rocky mountains round the border rise.

Here, till the doom of fate its fall decreed,   27
The empire flourish'd of the pigmy breed ;
Here Industry perform'd, and Genius plann'd,
And busy multitudes o'erspread the land.
But now to these lone bounds if pilgrim stray,
Tempting through craggy cliffs the desperate way,
He finds the puny mansion fallen to earth,
Its godlings mouldering on the abandon'd hearth ;
And starts where small white bones are spread around,
" Or little[1] footsteps lightly print the ground ;"
While the proud crane her nest securely builds,
Chattering amid the desolated fields.
   But different fates befell her hostile rage,
While reign'd invincible through many an age   40
The dreaded pigmy : roused by war's alarms,
Forth rush'd the madding manikin to arms.
Fierce to the field of death the hero flies ;
The faint crane fluttering flaps the ground and dies ;
And by the victor borne (o'erwhelming load!)
With bloody bill loose-dangling marks the road.
And oft the wily dwarf in ambush lay,
And often made the callow young his prey ;
With slaughter'd victims heap'd his board, and smiled,
To avenge the parent's trespass on the child.   50
Oft, where his feather'd foe had rear'd her nest,
And laid her eggs and household gods to rest,
Burning for blood in terrible array,
The eighteen-inch militia burst their way :
All went to wreck ; the infant foeman fell,
Whence scarce his chirping bill had broke the shell.
   Loud uproar hence and rage of arms arose,
And the fell rancour of encountering foes ;
Hence dwarfs and cranes one general havoc whelms,
And Death's grim visage scares the pigmy realms.   60

[1] ' Or little,' &c. : from Gray's Elegy.

Not half so furious blazed the warlike fire   6
Of mice, high theme of the Mæonian lyre ;
When bold to battle march'd the accoutred frogs,
And the deep tumult thunder'd through the bogs.
Pierced by the javelin bulrush on the shore
Here agonizing roll'd the mouse in gore ;
And there the frog (a scene full sad to see !)
Shorn of one leg, slow sprawl'd along on three ;
He vaults no more with vigorous hops on high,
But mourns in hoarsest croaks his destiny.
    And now the day of woe drew on apace,
A day of woe to all the pigmy race,
When dwarfs were doom'd (but penitence was vain)
To rue each broken egg, and chicken slain.
For, roused to vengeance by repeated wrong,
From distant climes the long-bill'd legions throng :
From Strymon's lake, Cäyster's plashy meads,
And fens of Scythia, green with rustling reeds ;
From where the Danube winds through many a land,
And Mareotis leaves the Egyptian strand ;   8
To rendezvous they waft on eager wing,
And wait, assembled, the returning spring.
Meanwhile they trim their plumes for length of flight,
Whet their keen beaks and twisting claws for fight :
Each crane the pigmy power in thought o'erturns,
And every bosom for the battle burns.
    When genial gales the frozen air unbind,
The screaming legions wheel, and mount the wind ;
Far in the sky they form their long array,
And land and ocean stretch'd immense survey
Deep, deep beneath ; and, triumphing in pride
With clouds and winds commix'd, innumerous ride.
'Tis wild obstreperous clangour all, and heaven
Whirls, in tempestuous undulation driven.

Nor less the alarm that shook the world below, 95
Where march'd in pomp of war the embattled foe:
Where manikins with haughty step advance,
And grasp the shield, and couch the quivering lance:
To right and left the lengthening lines they form,
And rank'd in deep array await the storm. 1(
High in the midst the chieftain-dwarf was seen,
Of giant stature and imperial mien :
Full twenty inches tall, he strode along,
And view'd with lofty eye the wondering throng ;
And while with many a scar his visage frown'd,
Bared his broad bosom, rough with many a wound
Of beaks and claws, disclosing to their sight
The glorious meed of high heroic might.
For with insatiate vengeance he pursued,
And never-ending hate, the feathery brood. 110
Unhappy they, confiding in the length
Of horny beak, or talon's crooked strength,
Who durst abide his rage ; the blade descends,
And from the panting trunk the pinion rends:
Laid low in dust the pinion waves no more,
The trunk disfigured stiffens in its gore.
What hosts of heroes fell beneath his force!
What heaps of chicken carnage mark'd his course!
How oft, O Strymon, thy lone banks along,
Did wailing Echo waft the funeral song! 120
And now from far the mingling clamours rise,
Loud and more loud rebounding through the skies.
From skirt to skirt of Heaven, with stormy sway,
A cloud rolls on, and darkens all the day.
Near and more near descends the dreadful shade,
And now in battailous array display'd,
On sounding wings, and screaming in their ire,
The cranes rush onward, and the fight require.

G

The pigmy warriors eye with fearless glare   129
The host thick swarming o'er the burden'd air ;
Thick swarming now, but to their native land
Doom'd to return a scanty straggling band.——
When sudden, darting down the depth of heaven,
Fierce on the expecting foe the cranes are driven,
The kindling frenzy every bosom warms,
The region echoes to the crash of arms ;
Loose feathers from the encountering armies fly,
And in careering whirlwinds mount the sky.
To breathe from toil upsprings the panting crane,
Then with fresh vigour downwards darts again.   140
Success in equal balance hovering hangs.
Here, on the sharp spear, mad with mortal pangs,
The bird transfix'd in bloody vortex whirls,
Yet fierce in death the threatening talon curls ;
There, while the life-blood bubbles from his wound,
With little feet the pigmy beats the ground :
Deep from his breast the short, short sob he draws,
And, dying, curses the keen-pointed claws.
Trembles the thundering field, thick cover'd o'er
With falchions, mangled wings, and streaming gore ; 150
And pigmy arms, and beaks of ample size,
And here a claw, and there a finger, lies.
    Encompass'd round with heaps of slaughter'd foes,
All grim in blood the pigmy champion glows ;
And on the assailing host impetuous springs,
Careless of nibbling bills and flapping wings ;
And 'midst the tumult wheresoe'er he turns,
The battle with redoubled fury burns ;
From every side the avenging cranes amain
Throng, to o'erwhelm this terror of the plain.   160
When suddenly (for such the will of Jove)
A fowl enormous, sousing from above,

The gallant chieftain clutch'd, and, soaring high,   163
(Sad chance of battle!) bore him up the sky.
The cranes pursue, and, clustering in a ring,
Chatter triumphant round the captive king.
But, ah! what pangs each pigmy bosom wrung,
When, now to cranes a prey, on talons hung,
High in the clouds they saw their helpless lord,
His wriggling form still lessening as he soar'd.   170
   Lo! yet again with unabated rage,
In mortal strife the mingling hosts engage.
The crane with darted bill assaults the foe,
Hovering; then wheels aloft to 'scape the blow:
The dwarf in anguish aims the vengeful wound;
But whirls in empty air the falchion round.
   Such was the scene, when 'midst the loud alarms
Sublime the eternal Thunderer rose in arms,
When Briareus, by mad ambition driven,
Heaved Pelion huge, and hurl'd it high at heaven.   180
Jove roll'd redoubling thunders from on high,
Mountains and bolts encounter'd in the sky;
Till one stupendous ruin whelm'd the crew,
Their vast limbs weltering wide in brimstone blue.
   But now at length the pigmy legions yield,
And, wing'd with terror, fly the fatal field.
They raise a weak and melancholy wail,
All in distraction scattering o'er the vale.
Prone on their routed rear the cranes descend;
Their bills bite furious, and their talons rend;   190
With unrelenting ire they urge the chase,
Sworn to exterminate the hated race.
   'Twas thus the pigmy name, once great in war,
For spoils of conquer'd cranes renown'd afar,
Perish'd. For, by the dread decree of Heaven,
Short is the date to earthly grandeur given,

And vain are all attempts to roam beyond   197
Where fate has fix'd the everlasting bound.
Fallen are the trophies of Assyrian power,
And Persia's proud dominion is no more:
Yea, though to both superior far in fame,
Thine empire, Latium, is an empty name !
　And now, with lofty chiefs of ancient time,
The pigmy heroes roam the Elysian clime.
Or, if belief to matron-tales be due,
Full oft, in the belated shepherd's view,
Their frisking forms, in gentle green array'd,
Gambol secure amid the moonlight glade:
Secure, for no alarming cranes molest,
And all their woes in long oblivion rest: 210
Down the deep vale and narrow winding way
They foot it featly, ranged in ringlets gay:
'Tis joy and frolic all, where'er they rove,
And Fairy-people is the name they love.

THE HARES.

A FABLE.

Yes, yes, I grant the sons of Earth
Are doom'd to trouble from their birth.
We all of sorrow have our share;
But say, is yours without compare ?
Look round the world ; perhaps you 'll find
Each individual of our kind
Press'd with an equal load of ill,
Equal at least: look further still,

And own your lamentable case
Is little short of happiness.
In yonder hut that stands alone
Attend to Famine's feeble moan ;
Or view the couch where Sickness lies,
Mark his pale cheek, and languid eyes;
His frame by strong convulsion torn,
His struggling sighs, and looks forlorn.
Or see, transfixt with keener pangs,
Where o'er his hoard the miser hangs;
Whistles the wind ; he starts, he stares,
Nor Slumber's balmy blessing shares ;   20
Despair, Remorse, and Terror roll
Their tempests on his harass'd soul.
    But here perhaps it may avail
To enforce our reasoning with a tale.
    Mild was the morn, the sky serene,
The jolly hunting band convene,
The beagle's breast with ardour burns,
The bounding steed the champaign spurns,
And Fancy oft the game descries
Through the hound's nose and huntsman's eyes.   30
    Just then a council of the hares
Had met on national affairs.
The chiefs were set ; while o'er their head
The furze its frizzled covering spread.
Long lists of grievances were heard,
And general discontent appear'd.
" Our harmless race shall every savage
Both quadruped and biped ravage ?
Shall horses, hounds, and hunters still
Unite their wits to work us ill ?   40
The youth, his parent's sole delight,
Whose tooth the dewy lawns invite,

Whose pulse in every vein beats strong,   43
Whose limbs leap light the vales along,
May yet ere noontide meet his death,
And lie dismember'd on the heath.
For youth, alas! nor cautious age,
Nor strength, nor speed eludes their rage.
In every field we meet the foe,
Each gale comes fraught with sounds of woe ;   50
The morning but awakes our fears,
The evening sees us bathed in tears.
But must we ever idly grieve,
Nor strive our fortunes to relieve ?
Small is each individual's force ;
To stratagem be our recourse ;
And then, from all our tribes combined,
The murderer to his cost may find
No foes are weak whom Justice arms,
Whom Concord leads, and Hatred warms.   60
Be roused ; or liberty acquire,
Or in the great attempt expire."
　　He said no more, for in his breast
Conflicting thoughts the voice suppress'd :
The fire of vengeance seem'd to stream
From his swoln eyeball's yellow gleam.
　　And now the tumults of the war,
Mingling confusedly from afar,
Swell in the wind.　Now louder cries
Distinct of hounds and men arise.   70
Forth from the brake, with beating heart,
The assembled hares tumultuous start,
And, every straining nerve on wing,
Away precipitately spring.
The hunting band, a signal given,
Thick thundering o'er the plain are driven ;

O'er cliff abrupt, and shrubby mound,   77
And river broad, impetuous bound ;
Now plunge amid the forest shades,
Glance through the openings of the glades ;
Now o'er the level valley sweep,
Now with short step strain up the steep ;
While backward from the hunter's eyes
The landscape like a torrent flies.
At last an ancient wood they gain'd,
By pruner's axe yet unprofaned.
High o'er the rest, by nature rear'd,
The oak's majestic boughs appear'd ;
Beneath, a copse of various hue
In barbarous luxuriance grew.   90
No knife had curb'd the rambling sprays,
No hand had wove the implicit maze.
The flowering thorn, self-taught to wind,
The hazel's stubborn stem entwined,
And bramble twigs were wreathed around,
And rough furze crept along the ground.
Here sheltering from the sons of murther,
The hares their tired limbs drag no further.
   But, lo ! the western wind ere long
Was loud, and roar'd the woods among ;   100
From rustling leaves and crashing boughs
The sound of woe and war arose.
The hares distracted scour the grove,
As terror and amazement drove ;
But danger, wheresoe'er they fled,
Still seem'd impending o'er their head.
Now crowded in a grotto's gloom,
All hope extinct, they wait their doom.
Dire was the silence, till, at length,
Even from despair deriving strength,   110

With bloody eye and furious look,   111
A daring youth arose and spoke :
  " O wretched race, the scorn of Fate,
Whom ills of every sort await !
O cursed with keenest sense to feel
The sharpest sting of every ill !
Say ye, who, fraught with mighty scheme,
Of liberty and vengeance dream,
What now remains ? To what recess
Shall we our weary steps address,   120
Since Fate is evermore pursuing
All ways, and means to work our ruin ?
Are we alone, of all beneath,
Condemn'd to misery worse than death ?
Must we, with fruitless labour, strive
In misery worse than death to live ?
No. Be the smaller ill our choice ;
So dictates Nature's powerful voice.
Death's pang will in a moment cease ;
And then, all hail, eternal peace !"   130
Thus while he spoke, his words impart
The dire resolve to every heart.
  A distant lake in prospect lay,
That, glittering in the solar ray,
Gleam'd through the dusky trees, and shot
A trembling light along the grot.
Thither with one consent they bend,
Their sorrows with their lives to end ;
While each, in thought, already hears
The water hissing in his ears.   140
  Fast by the margin of the lake,
Conceal'd within a thorny brake,
A linnet sat, whose careless lay
Amused the solitary day.

Careless he sung, for on his breast 145
Sorrow no lasting trace impress'd;
When suddenly he heard a sound
Of swift feet traversing the ground.
Quick to the neighbouring tree he flies,
Thence trembling casts around his eyes; 150
No foe appear'd, his fears were vain;
Pleased he renews the sprightly strain.
 The hares whose noise had caused his fright,
Saw with surprise the linnet's flight.
" Is there on earth a wretch," they said,
" Whom our approach can strike with dread ? "
An instantaneous change of thought
To tumult every bosom wrought.
 So fares the system-building sage,
Who, plodding on from youth to age, . 160
At last on some foundation dream
Has rear'd aloft his goodly scheme,
And proved his predecessors fools,
And bound all nature by his rules;
So fares he in that dreadful hour,
When injured Truth exerts her power,
Some new phenomenon to raise,
Which, bursting on his frighted gaze,
From its proud summit to the ground
Proves the whole edifice unsound. 170
 " Children," thus spoke a hare sedate,
Who oft had known the extremes of fate,
" In slight events the docile mind
May hints of good instruction find,
That our condition is the worst,
And we with such misfortunes curst,
As all comparison defy,
Was late the universal cry;

When, lo ! an accident so slight   172
As yonder little linnet's flight,
Has made your stubborn hearts confess
(So your amazement bids me guess)
That all our load of woes and fears
Is but a part of what he bears.
Where can he rest secure from harms,
Whom even a helpless hare alarms ?
Yet he repines not at his lot ;
When past, the danger is forgot :
On yonder bough he trims his wings,
And with unusual rapture sings :   190
While we, less wretched, sink beneath
Our lighter ills, and rush to death.
No more of this unmeaning rage,
But hear, my friends, the words of age :
  " When, by the winds of autumn driven,
The scatter'd clouds fly 'cross the heaven,
Oft have we, from some mountain's head,
Beheld the alternate light and shade
Sweep the long vale.   Here, hovering, lowers
The shadowy cloud ; there downward pours,   200
Streaming direct, a flood of day,
Which from the view flies swift away ;
It flies, while other shades advance,
And other streaks of sunshine glance.
Thus chequer'd is the life below
With gleams of joy and clouds of woe.
Then hope not, while we journey on,
Still to be basking in the sun ;
Nor fear, though now in shades ye mourn,
That sunshine will no more return.   210
If, by your terrors overcome,
Ye fly before the approaching gloom,

The rapid clouds your flight pursue, 213
And darkness still o'ercasts your view.
Who longs to reach the radiant plain
Must onward urge his course amain:
For doubly swift the shadow flies,
When 'gainst the gale the pilgrim plies.
At least be firm, and undismay'd
Maintain your ground! the fleeting shade 220
Ere long spontaneous glides away,
And gives you back the enlivening ray.
Lo, while I speak, our danger past!
No more the shrill horn's angry blast
Howls in our ear: the savage roar
Of war and murder is no more.
Then snatch the moment fate allows,
Nor think of past or future woes."
   He spoke; and hope revives; the lake
That instant one and all forsake, 230
In sweet amusement to employ
The present sprightly hour of joy.
   Now from the western mountain's brow,
Compass'd with clouds of various glow,
The sun a broader orb displays,
And shoots aslope his ruddy rays.
The lawn assumes a fresher green,
And dew-drops spangle all the scene.
The balmy zephyr breathes along,
The shepherd sings his tender song, 240
With all their lays the groves resound,
And falling waters murmur round:
Discord and care were put to flight,
And all was peace and calm delight.

THE WOLF AND SHEPHERDS.

A FABLE.

(WRITTEN IN 1757, AND FIRST PUBLISHED IN 1766.)

LAWS, as we read in ancient sages,
Have been like cobwebs in all ages :
Cobwebs for little flies are spread,
And laws for little folks are made ;
But if an insect of renown,
Hornet or beetle, wasp or drone,
Be caught in quest of sport or plunder,
The flimsy fetter flies in sunder.
　　Your simile perhaps may please one
With whom wit holds the place of reason :　　10
But can you prove that this in fact is
Agreeable to life and practice ?
　　Then hear, what in his simple way
Old Æsop told me t' other day.
In days of yore, but (which is very odd)
Our author mentions not the period,
We mortal men, less given to speeches,
Allow'd the beasts sometimes to teach us.
But now we all are prattlers grown,
And suffer no voice but our own ;　　20
With us no beast has leave to speak,
Although his honest heart should break.
'Tis true, your asses and your apes,
And other brutes in human shapes,
And that thing made of sound and show,
Which mortals have misnamed a beau,

(But in the language of the sky   27
Is call'd a two-legg'd butterfly),
Will make your very heartstrings ache
With loud and everlasting clack,   .
And beat your auditory drum,
Till you grow deaf, or they grow dumb.
      But to our story we return :
'Twas early on a Summer morn,
A Wolf forsook the mountain den,
And issued hungry on the plain.
Full many a stream and lawn he past
And reach'd a winding vale at last;
Where from a hollow rock he spied
The shepherds drest in flowery pride.   40
Garlands were strew'd, and all was gay,
To celebrate a holiday.
The merry tabor's gamesome sound
Provoked the sprightly dance around.
Hard by a rural board was rear'd,
On which in fair array appear'd
The peach, the apple, and the raisin,
And all the fruitage of the season.
But, more distinguish'd than the rest,
Was seen a wether ready drest,   50
That smoking, recent from the flame,
Diffused a stomach-rousing steam.
Our Wolf could not endure the sight,
Courageous grew his appetite :
His entrails groan'd with tenfold pain,
He lick'd his lips, and lick'd again :
At last, with lightning in his eyes,
He bounces forth, and fiercely cries :
" Shepherds, I am not given to scolding,
But now my spleen I cannot hold in.   60

By Jove, such scandalous oppression
Would put an elephant in passion.
You, who your flocks (as you pretend)
By wholesome laws from harm defend,
Which make it death for any beast,
How much soe'er by hunger press'd,
To seize a sheep by force or stealth,
For sheep have right to life and health;
Can you commit, uncheck'd by shame,
What in a beast so much you blame?
What is a law, if those who make it
Become the forwardest to break it?
The case is plain: you would reserve
All to yourselves, while others starve.
Such laws from base self-interest spring,
Not from the reason of the thing—"
. He was proceeding, when a swain
Burst out,—" And dares a wolf arraign
His betters, and condemn their measures,
And contradict their wills and pleasures?
We have establish'd laws, 'tis true,
But laws are made for such as you.
Know, sirrah, in its very nature
A law can't reach the legislature.
For laws, without a sanction join'd,
As all men know, can never bind;
But sanctions reach not us the makers,
For who dares punish us, though breakers?
'Tis therefore plain, beyond denial,
That laws were ne'er design'd to tie all;
But those, whom sanctions reach alone:
We stand accountable to none.
Besides, 'tis evident, that, seeing
Laws from the great derive their being,

They as in duty bound should love   9
The great, in whom they live and move,
And humbly yield to their desires :
'Tis just what gratitude requires.
What suckling, dandled on the lap,
Would tear away its mother's pap ?   10
But hold——Why deign I to dispute
With such a scoundrel of a brute ?
Logic is lost upon a knave,
Let action prove the law our slave."
   An angry nod his will declared
To his gruff yeoman of the guard ;
The full-fed mongrels, train'd to ravage,
Fly to devour the shaggy savage.
   The beast had now no time to lose
In chopping logic with his foes ;   11(
" This argument," quoth he, " has force,
And swiftness is my sole resource."
   He said, and left the swains their prey,
And to the mountains scour'd away.

SONG ;

IN IMITATION OF SHAKSPEARE'S " BLOW, BLOW, THOU WINTER WIND."

1 BLOW, blow, thou vernal gale !
   Thy balm will not avail
     To ease my aching breast ;
   Though thou the billows smooth,
   Thy murmurs cannot soothe
     My weary soul to rest.

2 Flow, flow, thou tuneful stream !
  Infuse the easy dream
    Into the peaceful soul;
  But thou canst not compose
  The tumult of my woes,
    Though soft thy waters roll.

3 Blush, blush, ye fairest flowers!
  Beauties surpassing yours
    My Rosalind adorn ;
  Nor is the Winter's blast,
  That lays your glories waste,
    So killing as her scorn.

4 Breathe, breathe, ye tender lays,
  That linger down the maze
    Of yonder winding grove ;
  O let your soft control
  Bend her relenting soul
    To pity and to love.

5 Fade, fade, ye flowerets fair !
  Gales, fan no more the air !
    Ye streams, forget to glide ;
  Be hush'd each vernal strain ;
  Since nought can soothe my pain,
    Nor mitigate her pride.

TO LADY CHARLOTTE GORDON,

DRESSED IN A TARTAN SCOTCH BONNET, WITH PLUMES, ETC.

1 WHY, lady, wilt thou bind thy lovely brow
   With the dread semblance of that warlike helm;
That nodding plume, and wreath of various glow,
   That graced the chiefs of Scotia's ancient realm ?

2 Thou know'st that Virtue is of power the source,
   And all her magic to thy eyes is given ;
We own their empire, while we feel their force,
   Beaming with the benignity of heaven.

3 The plumy helmet and the martial mien
   Might dignify Minerva's awful charms ;
But more resistless far the Idalian queen—
   Smiles, graces, gentleness, her only arms.

EPITAPH :

BEING PART OF AN INSCRIPTION DESIGNED FOR A MONU-MENT ERECTED BY A GENTLEMAN TO THE MEMORY OF HIS LADY.

FAREWELL, my best beloved ! whose heavenly mind
Genius with virtue, strength with softness join'd ;
Devotion, undebased by pride or art,
With meek simplicity, and joy of heart:

H

Though sprightly, gentle; though polite, sincere;
And only of thyself a judge severe:
Unblamed, unequall'd in each sphere of life,
The tenderest daughter, sister, parent, wife.
In thee, their patroness the afflicted lost;
Thy friends their pattern, ornament, and boast;
And I—but ah, can words my loss declare,
Or paint the extremes of transport and despair!
O thou, beyond what verse or speech can tell—
My guide, my friend, my best beloved, farewell!

EPITAPH

ON TWO YOUNG MEN OF THE NAME OF LEITCH, WHO WERE
DROWNED IN CROSSING THE RIVER SOUTHESK. 1757.

O THOU! whose steps in sacred reverence tread
These lone dominions of the silent dead;
On this sad stone a pious look bestow,
Nor uninstructed read this tale of woe;
And while the sigh of sorrow heaves thy breast,
Let each rebellious murmur be suppress'd;
Heaven's hidden ways to trace, for us how vain!
Heaven's wise decrees, how impious to arraign!
Pure from the stains of a polluted age,
In early bloom of life they left the stage:
Not doom'd in lingering woe to waste their breath,
One moment snatch'd them from the power of Death:
They lived united, and united died;
Happy the friends whom Death cannot divide!

EPITAPH, INTENDED FOR HIMSELF.

1 ESCAPED the gloom of mortal life, a soul
   Here leaves its mouldering tenement of clay,
Safe where no cares their whelming billows roll,
   No doubts bewilder, and no hopes betray.

2 Like thee, I once have stemm'd the sea of life;
   Like thee, have languish'd after empty joys;
Like thee, have labour'd in the stormy strife;
   Been grieved for trifles, and amused with toys.

3 Yet, for a while, 'gainst Passion's threatful blast
   Let steady Reason urge the struggling oar;
Shot through the dreary gloom, the morn at last
   Gives to thy longing eye the blissful shore.

4 Forget my frailties, thou art also frail;
   Forgive my lapses, for thyself mayst fall;
Nor read, unmoved, my artless tender tale,
   I was a friend, O man! to thee, to all.

END OF BEATTIE'S POEMS.

POETICAL WORKS

OF

ROBERT BLAIR.

THE LIFE OF ROBERT BLAIR.

THE paradox of Dr Johnson, in reference to sacred poetry, has long ago fallen into disrepute. It seems singular indeed, how it ever obtained credence, even although supported by one of the most powerful pens that ever wrote in Britain, when we remember that, previous to that author's day, the best poetry in the world *had* been sacred. The Holy Scriptures then existed, with that poetry which bursts out at their every pore, besides being collected here and there into masses of rich song, "pressed down, shaken together, and running over." Dante, too, had written his great work, which, as if to mark it out for ever from things unclean and common, he had called the "*Divina* Commedia," and which was worthy of the name. Tasso's "Gerusalemme Liberata" had a religious moral, as well as a title suggestive of religious ideas. Spenser's "Faery Queen" was sacred, if not in all the parts, yet at least in the pervading spirit of its poetry. Cowley's "Davideis," Herbert's "Temple," Milton's "Paradise Lost" and "Paradise Regained," and Young's "Night Thoughts," existed then, were all admitted to be more or less masterpieces, and were all sacred in their subjects and aims. Blair's "Grave" too, had, ere Johnson's day, appeared, and furnished a good example of a solemn and religious theme, treated with genuine poetic power.

We need not say what a flood of sacred song has arisen since, and drowned the dictum of the lexicographer in the waves. Nay, an opinion is gaining ground, that all lofty poetry tends toward the sacred, and lies under the shadow of the divine. Poetry is like fire, which, even when employed in culinary or destructive purposes, points its column upwards, and seems to transmit the flower and essence of its conquests to heaven. All poetry that does not thus ascend is either morbid in spirit, or secondary in merit.

We come now to the life of one of our best religious poets, —ROBERT BLAIR,—whose short poem, " the Grave," is so admirable as to excite keen regret that it is almost the only specimen extant of his gifted and original mind.

The facts of his life are more than usually scanty, and our biography, therefore, must be brief and meagre. Robert Blair was born in Edinburgh, in 1699. It is curious, by the way, how few poets the Modern Athens has produced. It has bred lawyers, statists, critics, savans, in plenty, but reared but few men of transcendant genius, and, so far as we remember, only five good poets,—Scott, Ferguson, Ramsay, Falconer, and Blair,—whom the manufacturing town of Paisley nearly matches with its Tannahill, Motherwell, Alexander and John Wilson. Blair was the eldest son of the Rev. David Blair, who was a minister of the Old Church of Edinburgh, and one of the chaplains to the King. His mother was Euphemia Nisbet, daughter of Alexander Nisbet, Esq., of Carfin. His grandfather, Robert Blair, of Irvine,—descended from the ancient family of Blair *of that ilk* (*i. e.*, of Blair), in Ayrshire,—distinguished himself, in the troublous times of the Solemn League and Covenant, as a powerful preacher, an able negociator, and a brave, determined man. The celebrated Hugh Blair, —whose writings, once so popular, seem now nearly forgotten, —was our poet's cousin, although younger by nineteen years. Robert lost his father while yet a boy, but enjoyed the anxious care and admirable training of an excellent mother. He studied first at the University of Edinburgh, and afterwards in Holland. Of the particulars of either part of his curriculum nothing is known. On his return from abroad, he seems to have received license to preach, and to have hung about Edinburgh for a few years, an unemployed probationer. This was of less consequence, as he had some hereditary property. It gave him, too, abundant leisure for study, and he employed it well—cultivating natural history and the cognate sciences—publishing a few fugitive verses, which made very little impression on the public—and drawing out the first rude draught of the poem which was destined to make him immortal,—" The Grave." In 1731, when he was in his thirty-second year, he was appointed to the living of Athelstaneford, a parish in East Lothian, where he continued to reside all the rest of his life. Dissenter though the author of this biography be, he is free to confess, that there is very much that is enviable in the position of a parish minister, particularly in the country. Possessed of an easy competence, and a manageable field of labour, surrounded by the simplicities of rural manners, and the picturesque features of rural scenery,—lord of his sphere of duty, and master of his time,—his life can be, and often is, one of the most useful and happy, honourable in its toils, and graceful in its relaxations, to be found on earth. Where could we expect elegant studies to be prosecuted with more success, or whence could we expect more works of sanctified learning and genius to issue, than in and from the " manses " of Scotland, always so beautifully situated, now on the brink of the mountain stream, singing its wild way through the woods,—now in the centre of rich orchards and fertile fields,—now on sunny braes, overlooking the whole parish, prostrate in its loveliness at their feet,—and now surrounded and shadowed by broad old oaks and tall black pine-trees? And so, accordingly, it has been, although not perhaps to the extent we might have wished or expected. Philosophy of the deepest order has been studied—inquiries the most profound and extensive into natural science and history have been prosecuted ; and painting, music, and poetry, have found enthusiastic and gifted votaries, who, at the same time, have not neglected their higher vocation,—in the quiet manses of our country ; and we rejoice to know that this state of things continues, and is not confined to the Established Church, but may be asserted with equal or greater force to exist in others.

At Athelstaneford, Blair seems to have realised this ideal of a country minister. He was attentive to his pastoral duties, and the correspondent of Doddridge and the author of " The

Grave," could not fail to be an evangelical, a practical, and a powerful preacher. He at the same time diligently prosecuted his favourite studies, which were botany, natural history, and poetry. Possessing a considerable fortune, he lived on a footing of equality and friendship with the gentry of the neighbourhood, and others of similar rank in distant parts of Scotland. Sir Francis Kinloch of Gilmerton and John Callander of Craigforth are mentioned as two of his intimates. We are tempted to figure the author of " The Grave " as a morose and melancholy *solitaire* — musing amid midnight churchyards—stumbling over bones—and returning home to light his lamp, inserted in a gaping skull, and to write out his gloomy cogitations. This is very far from being his real character. He was more frequently seen wandering amidst the flowery nooks of summer, with a microscope in his hand ; or, on his way home from his pastoral visitations, stopping to analyse the fungi and the mosses which met him on his path ; or musing above the long liquid lapse of some wayside stream, down which were floating the red leaves of autumn ; or turning a telescope of his own construction aloft to the gleaming host of heaven. In his mode of spending his time, as well as in some of the stern features of his genius, he resembled Crabbe, who, believing that every weed was a flower, spent much of his time amidst the fields and on the sea-shores ; who extracted delight out of the meanest fungus, even as he extracted poetry out of the humblest characters ; and whose life, like Blair's, was a harmless dream.

After spending seven years of studious solitude, he, in 1738, married his relation, Isabella Law, daughter of Mr Law of Elvingston, who had been professor of moral philosophy in the University of Edinburgh, and whose death, which had happened ten years before, he had mourned in some rather lame verses, which our readers will find in this edition. Her brother was the sheriff-depute of East Lothian. She is described as a lady of great beauty and amiable manners, and succeeded in making the poet very happy. She bore him five sons and one daughter. Of these, Robert arose, through various gradations of honour at the Scottish bar, to be President of the Court of

Session, and died in 1811. He was a man of massive and powerful intellect. It is, we think, in *Peter's Letters* that Lockhart gives a glowing portraiture of President Blair's remarkable powers. He had not the genius or " hairbrained sentimental trace " of his father, but had inherited that clear, stern understanding, and that profound insight into men and manners, which are met with in every page of " The Grave."

Of this poem the author had, we said, drawn a first outline when a youth in Edinburgh. This he completed after his settlement at Athelstaneford ; and, about the year 1742, he began to make arrangements for its publication. He had, probably through his neighbour, the celebrated Colonel Gardiner, who fell at the battle of Prestonpans, become acquainted with Isaac Watts, who paid him, he says in one of his letters, " many civilities." To him he forwarded the MS. of his poem. Dr Watts, with characteristic candour and good taste, admired it, and offered it to two different London booksellers, both of whom, however, declined to publish it, expressing a doubt whether any person living three hundred miles from town could write so as to be acceptable to the fashionable and the polite ! No poetry at that time went down except imitations of Pope. Blair got back his MS., and, nothing daunted, sent it to Philip Doddridge, who was also an intimate of Colonel Gardiner's, requesting his opinion, which appears to have been as favourable as that of Dr Watts. At length it was published in London in the year 1743, and reprinted at Edinburgh in 1747, a year after its author's death.

Between that event and the appearance of his poem, nothing remarkable occurred. The success of his work must have shed additional sweetness into a cup which was rich before. " His tastes," says one of his biographers, " were elegant and domestic. Books and flowers seem to have been the only rivals in his thoughts. His rambles were from his fireside to his garden ; and, although the only record of his genius is of a gloomy character, it is evident that his habits and life contributed to render him cheerful and happy." At last that awful chasm, the terrors, grandeurs, and moral lessons of which he had so powerfully sung, opened its jaws to receive him, and the Grave crowned its laureate with its cold and earthy crown. He was seized with fever, caught probably in the exercise of his pastoral functions, and expired on the 4th of February 1746, at the early age of forty-seven, when his body and mind were both in full vigour, and when, speaking after the manner of men, yet greater works than "The Grave" were before him. He left his wife, who lived till 1774, and five children behind him. His body reposes in the church-yard of Athelstaneford, without a monument, and with no-thing but the initials R. B. to mark the spot.

The fact that he died comparatively so young, sufficiently accounts for the paucity of his poems. He had found a vein of rich and virgin gold; he had thrown out one mass of ore, and was, as it were, resting on his pickaxe ere recommencing his labour, when he was smitten down by a workman who never rests nor slumbers. Still let us thankfully accept what he has produced; the more as it is so distinctively original, so free from any serious alloy, and so impressively religious in its spirit and tone.

This masterpiece of Blair's genius is not a great poem so much as it is a magnificent portion, fragment, or book of a great poem. The most, alike of its merits and its faults, spring from the fact, that it keeps close to its subject——it daguerreotypes its dreadful theme. Many have objected to its conclusion as lame and impotent, and would have wished a loftier swell of hopeful anticipation of the Resurrection at the close; but this, in fact, would have started the subject of another poem. Blair was writing of the power and triumphs of the tomb. He left it to others, or possibly to another poem by himself, to celebrate the victory over it, to be gained at the resurrection. Enough for his purpose to allude to it at the close, in such a way as to intimate his own belief in its reality. Surely he expects too much who requires the painter of "Night" to introduce "Morning" into the same picture.

The shortness of the poem has been objected to it. But this, we think, shows the poet's good sense. The subject is too uniform and too gloomy for a long poem. "The Grave, in twelve books" would have been totally unreadable. It was far better to give, as Blair has given, a strong, stern, rapid, and concentrated sketch of the grisly gulf. The grave, in one respect, has no unity, and no story. It stands by itself, hollow, solitary, with its momentary ghastly yawnings, its general repose, and the dark mysteries which, whether open or shut, it conceals in its silent bosom. Reverence, as well as good taste, requires the poet who would venture on such a theme, to approach it trembling, and to withdraw from it in haste.

Yet Blair has been accused of a want of reverence in his treatment of this awful subject, nor is this objection altogether unfounded; the poet does treat " the Grave " in a somewhat abrupt and cavalier fashion, and does not seem sufficiently afraid of it. He was young when he wrote the greater part of the poem, and of young poets we may ask as Wordsworth asks about little children, " What can they know of death ? " It had never knocked at his door or glared in at his window. He was, besides, of a bold and daring genius. He consulted rather strong effect than minute finish. The tone and style of his poem, consequently, are somewhat hirsute and un-polished. Campbell says of him, judiciously, " Blair may be a homely and even a gloomy poet in the eye of fastidious criticism; but there is a masculine and pronounced character even in his gloom and homeliness that keeps it most distinctly apart from either dulness or vulgarity. His style pleases us like the powerful expression of a countenance without regular beauty." He excels most in describing the darkest and most terrible ideas suggested by the subject, and seems almost to exult, while depicting the triumphs of the grave over the rich, the strong, the lofty, and the powerful. Death himself he assails in language approaching virulence, as when he says

> O great maneater,
> Unheard-of epicure, without a fellow,
> Thou must render up thy dead,
> And with high interest too.

This exulting spirit, however, springs in him, less from ferocious feeling than from conscious rejoicing power. He is not a savage, brandishing his bloody tomahawk, so much as a Michael Angelo, hewing, with heat and haste, at one of his terrible pieces of statuary. He characterizes the miser severely; he lashes the proud wicked man whom he sees pompously hearsed into Hell; with stern irony he pursues the beauty from her looking-glass to the clods where

> "The high-fed worm, in lazy volumes roll'd,
> Feeds on her damask cheek;"

he derides the baffled son of Esculapius, who is deserted and deceived by his own drugs; and he exerts all the fearful force of his genius to show us the suicide in that "Other Place," where

> "The common damn'd shun his society,
> And look upon themselves as fiends less foul."

But the fine imagery and the rapid touch serve alike to show that though he is angry, it is with the wrath of a man—not with the malignity of a demon. We have sometimes been induced to fancy that Pollok, in the "Course of Time," loves to linger amid the ruins of fallen and lost natures; and finds a savage luxury in the contemplation of the agonies of those whom he represents as damned. He tells us that he loved no scenery so well as that of solitary wastes, where nature was utterly barren and seemed willing to decay—where the dark wings of monotonous gloom and eternal silence met and sullenly embraced over the dreary region; and he seems to have had the same passion for moral as for physical desolations. Blair, on the other hand, never tarries long in such scenes; he does not dwell amidst, and brood over them like an owl, but crosses them with the swift brushing wing of a bird returning to her evening nest. He never goes out of his way to search for them—he sees and shows them merely because they meet him on his path. There is nothing morbid nor much that is melancholy in this poem. He takes the hard fact as it is, and paints it with all his force, but he does not seek to exaggerate or discolour it. He shows "the Grave" in various lights, at morning, night, and noon—not under the uniform weight of a leaden midnight sky, or only by the ghastly illumination of a waning moon.

Southey, in his " Life of Cowper," has fallen into the mistake of supposing Blair one of the imitators of Young. Now, in fact, Blair's poem was *written* before the " Last Day " of Young, or the " Night Thoughts " had appeared. Its originality is indeed one of its greatest merits and charms. The author has copied no style, imitated no manner, and scorned to permit any living man or poet to stand between him and the cold stern reality of death, which he was to reflect in song. He is worthy, thus, of the name so often misapplied, of Poet — *i. e.* Maker. You see an original genius both in the beauties and the faults of the work. Its language, so simply strong and daring in its homeliness, its free and energetic motion, its fresh fearless touch, its fidelity to nature and to life, the quick succession and sharp brief poignancy of its pictures, its absence of elaboration, and carelessness about minute lights and shades—all combine to prove that the author has an eye, an imagination, and a purpose quite peculiar to himself. He treats " the Grave " with as much originality as if he had been contemporary with the earliest sepulchre—as if he had plucked grass from Abel's tomb ; and yet, while it has not lost to his eye its first fearful gloss and glory, it has gathered around it the dear or dismal associations of six thousand years ; and Adam and the " new-made widow " seem to be leaning side by side over its dust. We could have conceived of him treating the subject more reconditely, imaginatively, and metaphysically, but not of handling it with more direct and masculine power.

That he has done so, is, undoubtedly, one great cause of the poem's popularity. Had he woven any gossamer of reverie or philosophic conjecture over " the Grave," or even shown much personal interest in it, he might have gained a more peculiar set of admirers, but would not have won his way to the world's heart. As it is, the popularity of " The Grave " has been unbounded. Partly from the subject, partly from the shortness, partly from the signal truth and force of the poem, it rose rapidly to fame. It became " everybody's Grave." The poem was copied into all school collections. It lay along with *Robinson Crusoe* and Bunyan's *Pilgrim's Progress*, in the windows of cottages, and on the tables of wayside inns—achieving thus what Coleridge predicated over that well-thumbed copy of *Thomson's Seasons*, in the Welsh ale-house—" true fame!" It pervaded America. It was translated into other languages, and in its own it now transmigrated into a tract, now filled the page of a periodical, and now became a small separate book, telling its solemn tale to those who, though at first reluctant, as was the wedding guest to hear the Anciente Marinere, were at last compelled .to listen, if not to learn. Light ballads and other amusing and clever trifles, had before and have since thus " put a girdle round about the globe in forty minutes; " but here was the phenomenon of a sad and serious strain, with little merit or charm but Christian truth and rugged poetry, passing, as if on telegraphic wires, through the whole world in a moment of time. Perhaps we should add a reason, although a very subordinate one, for the popularity of the poem. It was its author's *first* and *last*. He wrote himself at once and easily *up*—he never tried and succeeded in writing himself laboriously *down*.

The only books which should gain permanent reputation are those which supply materials for thought, and are studded with moveable gems of expression. We think we may divide the poems of the past and present into two classes, which we may discriminate into *buildings* and *quarries*. Many works to which you can hardly deny the character of works of genius may be likened to elegant and splendid edifices, the structure of which you cannot but admire, although the secret of their architecture you do not understand, and although from them you neither do nor can extract a single stone. They stand up before the view, dazzling and confounding,—

" Distinct but distant, clear, but ah! how cold."

Other books, less magnificent in aspect and rougher in style, are yet so full of suggestive and germinating thought, that we must liken them to quarries, surrounded it may be by thorns and briars, and precipices, but containing the richest of matter, and communicating with the very depths of the earth.   Not to enter on the vexed questions connected with more celebrated poets, we may name Darwin and Dr Thomas Brown as two specimens of the building, and Robert Blair as an admirable example of the quarry. .In household words and sententious truths, he yields (taking his space into consideration), not even to Young, or Pope, or Cowper, but to Shakspeare alone.   His poem is a tissue of texts; many of his expressions might pass and have passed for bits of Hamlet. Take a few :—

> " Friendship, mysterious cement of the soul,
>   Sweetener of life, and solder of society."

> " Son of the morning, whither art thou gone ?
>   Where hast thou hid thy many-spangled head,
> And the majestic menace of thine eyes
>   Felt from afar ? "

> " Sorry pre-eminence of high descent !
>   Above the vulgar, born to *rot in state*."

Hence, by the way, Byron's famous lines,—

> " It seem'd the mockery of hell to fold
>   The *rottenness* of eighty years in gold."

The exquisite description of beauty in the grave has been already quoted.   That of the strong man dying is quite Shakspearian, and equally so is the picture commencing, " Death's shafts fly quick," particularly the passage about the sexton.   How much he has compressed in the few words of the celebrated description!—

> " The wind is up ; hark ! how it howls ! methinks
>   Till now I never heard a sound so dreary ;
> Doors creak, and windows clap, and night's foul bird,
>   Rook'd in the spire, screams loud."

Who Blair's favourite authors were, we are not informed, but internal evidence proves him to have frequently and profitably read Shakspeare; and in terseness of description, comprehensiveness of vision, careless grandeur of execution,

I

and short felicitous strokes of genius, he bears to him a considerable resemblance.

Blair's originality is proved by the fact, that many poets since have been either indebted to or inspired by his manly, noble verse. A great original, although he seldom steals himself, is the innocent cause of much theft in others, and his writings tempt, like the unbolted gate of a bank, to plunder. Young, although a truly gifted man, has kindled his night-lamp again and again at the phosphoric flame of " The Grave." The author of the " Night Thoughts " has written more sustained and sounding passages than Blair; his style is more antithetic, and his general mode of thought more ingenious; his book is a much larger one; he exhibits at times gleams of deeper insight; has occasional bursts of more impassioned earnestness; and his work has a personal interest, like an interrupted story or imperfect plot running through it: but " The Grave " is superior in ease, in nature, in healthy tone, and in those happy touches which light upon even genius only in rare and favoured hours. In some of these points, as well as in a certain power of rough moral anatomy, and vivid hurrying sarcasm (like one in haste lifting, handling, and striking with a red-hot falchion), Blair reminds us rather of Cowper; but the poet of " The Task " teaches a sterner morality, wears around him a mantle of austerer gloom, abounds more in Scriptural reference and in purely theological matter, and exhibits a more thoroughly bardic and prophetic spirit. James Grahame, the author of " The Sabbath," resembles Blair somewhat in happy pictorial flashes, and in the frequent rudeness of his versification; but is, on the whole, a milder, a more refined, a tenderer, and a weaker writer. It is clear that Pollok found the germ of his noble poem, " The Course of Time," in " The Grave." They resemble each other in their want of a plot, a hinge, a " backbone," both being collections of loosely-strung moral sketches, with no unity but that of spirit, as also in the homely force and boldness of the writing; and if Pollok in aught differ from Blair, it is partly in the length of his poem and its elaboration, and partly in that feverish, hectic heat, and that morbid intensity and fury of temperament, which are the sources of much of Pollok's strength, and of more of his weakness.

No poem on any similar subject, in our time, can be named with Blair's, except perhaps Bryant's " Thanatopsis." The moral tendency, however, and religious tone of the two poems are entirely different. " Thanatopsis" looks at the Grave solely in its physical and poetical aspects. It never mentions either the Resurrection or the Future State. An Indian would have coloured his poem on the sepulchre with finer and fierier lines, like the stamp of autumn on the fallen leaf. The main idea in it (an idea probably suggested by a line in " The Grave "—

> " What is this world ?
> What but a spacious burial-place unwall'd ? ")

is that of the earth as a great sepulchre; and its lesson is to inculcate on the death-devoted dust, which we call man, the duty of dropping into its kindred dust as quietly and gracefully as possible. It is, as a poem, chiefly remarkable for its solemn music, which reminds you of a burial-march, but is far inferior to the Scottish poem in lofty moral, in theological truth, and in illustrative power. Blair, and not Bryant, remains the laureate of the Grave.

It is much to have one's name and fame connected with one of the great centrical truths of the universe, especially when that truth is related to a fact. Suppose a writer to have produced a great poem on Light and the Sun—or on Absolute Being and God—or on Immortal Life and Heaven—how sublime and how enviable were his reputation! It were for ever bound up, in the bundle of life, with these great Ideas and Facts. Now, Blair has sung, in notes as yet unequalled, one of the cardinal, although one of the gloomiest thoughts and actualities in existence, and his name ought to stand proportionally high. He has, in a solemn yet happy hour, turned aside from the highways, and the byeways too, of the world, and gone a-musing and meditating, like Isaac in the evening fields, and found among these a field of the dead, a place of skulls; and, returning home, has recorded that one brief meditation in verse, and made it and himself immortal. Such, precisely, is this Poem, and such the experience of this Poet. As long as " the mourners go about the streets," or assemble in their crowds, blackening the silent *braes* on their way to the country churchyard—as long as the grass of the grave murmurs out its moral in the western wind, and the sunshine seems to sadden as it shines upon the memorials and monuments of the dead—so long shall men read the " The Grave," and turn with pensive joy and tearful gratitude to the memory of its poet.

BLAIR'S POEMS.

THE GRAVE.

WHILE some affect the sun, and some the shade,
Some flee the city, some the hermitage;
Their aims as various, as the roads they take
In journeying through life;—the task be mine,
To paint the gloomy horrors of the tomb;
The appointed place of rendezvous, where all
These travellers meet.—Thy succours I implore,
Eternal king! whose potent arm sustains
The keys of Hell and Death.—The Grave, dread thing!
Men shiver when thou'rt named: Nature appall'd   10
Shakes off her wonted firmness.   Ah! how dark
Thy long-extended realms, and rueful wastes!
Where nought but silence reigns, and night, dark night,
Dark as was chaos, ere the infant Sun
Was roll'd together, or had tried his beams
Athwart the gloom profound.—The sickly taper,
By glimmering through thy low-brow'd misty vaults
(Furr'd round with mouldy damps, and ropy slime),
Lets fall a supernumerary horror,
And only serves to make thy night more irksome.   20

Well do I know thee by thy trusty yew,   21
Cheerless, unsocial plant! that loves to dwell
'Midst skulls and coffins, epitaphs and worms :
Where light-heel'd ghosts, and visionary shades,
Beneath the wan cold moon (as fame reports)
Embodied, thick, perform their mystic rounds :
No other merriment, dull tree! is thine.
     See yonder hallow'd fane—the pious work
Of names once famed, now dubious or forgot,
And buried 'midst the wreck of things which were;   30
There lie interr'd the more illustrious dead.
The wind is up : hark! how it howls! Methinks
Till now I never heard a sound so dreary :
Doors creak, and windows clap, and night's foul bird,
Rook'd in the spire, screams loud : the gloomy aisles
Black-plaster'd, and hung round with shreds of 'scutcheons,
And tatter'd coats of arms, send back the sound,
Laden with heavier airs, from the low vaults,
The mansions of the dead.——Roused from their slumbers,
In grim array the grisly spectres rise,   40
Grin horrible, and, obstinately sullen,
Pass and repass, hush'd as the foot of night.
Again the screech-owl shrieks : ungracious sound!
I 'll hear no more; it makes one's blood run chill.
     Quite round the pile, a row of reverend elms,
Coeval near with that, all ragged show,
Long lash'd by the rude winds : some rift half down
Their branchless trunks; others so thin at top,
That scarce two crows could lodge in the same tree.
Strange things, the neighbours say, have happen'd here :
Wild shrieks have issued from the hollow tombs;   51
Dead men have come again, and walk'd about;
And the great bell has toll'd, unrung, untouch'd!

(Such tales their cheer at wake or gossipping,   54
When it draws near to witching time of night.)
    Oft, in the lone church-yard at night I 've seen,
By glimpse of moonshine chequering through the trees,
The schoolboy with his satchel in his hand,
Whistling aloud to bear his courage up,
And lightly tripping o'er the long flat stones   60
(With nettles skirted, and with moss o'ergrown),
That tell in homely phrase who lie below.
Sudden he starts! and hears, or thinks he hears,
The sound of something purring at his heels;
Full fast he flies, and dares not look behind him,
Till out of breath he overtakes his fellows;
Who gather round, and wonder at the tale
Of horrid apparition, tall and ghastly,
That walks at dead of night, or takes his stand
O'er some new-open'd grave, and, strange to tell!   70
Evanishes at crowing of the cock.
    The new-made widow too, I've sometimes spied,
Sad sight! slow moving o'er the prostrate dead:
Listless, she crawls along in doleful black,
Whilst bursts of sorrow gush from either eye,
Fast falling down her now untasted cheek.
Prone on the lowly grave of the dear man
She drops; whilst busy meddling memory,
In barbarous succession, musters up
The past endearments of their softer hours,   80
Tenacious of its theme.   Still, still she thinks
She sees him, and, indulging the fond thought,
Clings yet more closely to the senseless turf,
Nor heeds the passenger who looks that way.
    Invidious grave!——how dost thou rend in sunder
Whom love has knit, and sympathy made one!
A tie more stubborn far than nature's band.

Friendship ! mysterious cement of the soul;   88
Sweetener of life, and solder of society !
I owe thee much : thou hast deserved from me,
Far, far beyond what I can ever pay.
Oft have I proved the labours of thy love,
And the warm efforts of the gentle heart,
Anxious to please.——Oh ! when my friend and I
In some thick wood have wander'd heedless on,
Hid from the vulgar eye, and sat us down
Upon the sloping cowslip-cover'd bank,
Where the pure limpid stream has slid along
In grateful errors through the underwood,
Sweet murmuring,——methought the shrill-tongued thrush
Mended his song of love ; the sooty blackbird   101
Mellow'd his pipe, and soften'd every note;
The eglantine smelt sweeter, and the rose
Assumed a dye more deep; whilst every flower
Vied with its fellow-plant in luxury
Of dress.——Oh ! then the longest summer's day
Seem'd too, too much in haste : still the full heart
Had not imparted half ! 'twas happiness
Too exquisite to last.   Of joys departed,
Not to return, how painful the remembrance !   110
     Dull Grave !——thou spoil'st the dance of youthful blood,
Strik'st out the dimple from the cheek of mirth,
And every smirking feature from the face ;
Branding our laughter with the name of madness.
Where are the jesters now ? the men of health ·
Complexionally pleasant ? Where the droll,
Whose every look and gesture was a joke
To clapping theatres and shouting crowds,
And made even thick-lipp'd musing melancholy
To gather up her face into a smile   120

Before she was aware ? Ah ! sullen now,   121
And dumb as the green turf that covers them.
   Where are the mighty thunderbolts of war ?
The Roman Cæsars, and the Grecian chiefs,
The boast of story ? Where the hotbrain'd youth,
Who the tiara at his pleasure tore
From kings of all the then discover'd globe,
And cried, forsooth, because his arm was hamper'd,
And had not room enough to do its work ?——
Alas ! how slim, dishonourably slim,   130
And cramm'd into a place we blush to name !
Proud Royalty ! how alter'd in thy looks !
How blank thy features, and how wan thy hue !
Son of the morning, whither art thou gone ?
Where hast thou hid thy many-spangled head,
And the majestic menace of thine eyes,
Felt from afar ? Pliant and powerless now,
Like new-born infant wound up in his swathes,
Or victim tumbled flat upon its back,
That throbs beneath the sacrificer's knife.   140
Mute must thou bear the strife of little tongues,
And coward insults of the base-born crowd,
That grudge a privilege thou never hadst,
But only hoped for in the peaceful grave,
Of being unmolested and alone.
Arabia's gums and odoriferous drugs,
And honours by the heralds duly paid
In mode and form even to a very scruple :
Oh, cruel irony ! these come too late ;
And only mock whom they were meant to honour.   150
Surely there 's not a dungeon slave that 's buried
In the highway, unshrouded and uncoffin'd,
But lies as soft, and sleeps as sound as he.

Sorry pre-eminence of high descent,   154
Above the vulgar born, to rot in state!
   But see! the well plumed hearse comes nodding on,
Stately and slow; and properly attended
By the whole sable tribe that painful watch
The sick man's door, and live upon the dead,
By letting out their persons by the hour,   160
To mimic sorrow when the heart's not sad.
How rich the trappings, now they're all unfurl'd
And glittering in the sun! Triumphant entries
Of conquerors, and coronation pomps,
In glory scarce exceed.   Great gluts of people
Retard the unwieldy show; whilst from the casements
And houses' tops, ranks behind ranks close wedged
Hang bellying o'er.   But tell us, why this waste?
Why this ado in earthing up a carcase
That's fallen into disgrace, and in the nostril   170
Smells horrible?——Ye undertakers, tell us,
'Midst all the gorgeous figures you exhibit,
Why is the principal conceal'd, for which
You make this mighty stir?——'Tis wisely done;
What would offend the eye in a good picture,
The painter casts discreetly into shade.
   Proud lineage! now how little thou appear'st!
Below the envy of the private man!
Honour, that meddlesome officious ill,
Pursues thee even to death, nor there stops short;   180
Strange persecution! when the grave itself
Is no protection from rude sufferance.
   Absurd to think to overreach the grave,
And from the wreck of names to rescue ours!
The best-concerted schemes men lay for fame
Die fast away: only themselves die faster.
The far-famed sculptor, and the laurell'd bard,

Those bold insurancers of deathless fame,   188
Supply their little feeble aids in vain.
The tapering pyramid, the Egyptian's pride,
And wonder of the world; whose spiky top
Has wounded the thick cloud, and long outlived
The angry shaking of the winter's storm;
Yet spent at last by the injuries of heaven,
Shatter'd with age and furrow'd o'er with years,
The mystic cone, with hieroglyphics crusted,
At once gives way. Oh, lamentable sight!
The labour of whole ages tumbles down,
A hideous and mis-shapen length of ruins.
Sepulchral columns wrestle, but in vain,   200
With all-subduing Time: his cankering hand
With calm deliberate malice wasteth them:
Worn on the edge of days, the brass consumes,
The busto moulders, and the deep-cut marble,
Unsteady to the steel, gives up its charge.
Ambition, half convicted of her folly,
Hangs down the head, and reddens at the tale.
    Here, all the mighty troublers of the earth,
Who swam to sovereign rule through seas of blood;
The oppressive, sturdy, man-destroying villains,   210
Who ravaged kingdoms, and laid empires waste,
And in a cruel wantonness of power
Thinn'd states of half their people, and gave up
To want the rest; now, like a storm that's spent,
Lie hush'd, and meanly sneak behind the covert.
Vain thought! to hide them from the general scorn
That haunts and dogs them like an injured ghost
Implacable. Here, too, the petty tyrant,
Whose scant domains geographer ne'er noticed,
And, well for neighbouring grounds, of arm as short; 220
Who fix'd his iron talons on the poor,

And gripp'd them like some lordly beast of prey;   222
Deaf to the forceful cries of gnawing hunger,
And piteous, plaintive voice of misery
(As if a slave was not a shred of nature,
Of the same common nature with his lord) ;
Now tame and humble, like a child that's whipp'd,
Shakes hands with dust, and calls the worm his kinsman
Nor pleads his rank and birthright : Under ground
Precedency's a jest ; vassal and lord,   230
Grossly familiar, side by side consume.
    When self-esteem, or others' adulation,
Would cunningly persuade us we are something
Above the common level of our kind,
The Grave gainsays the smooth-complexion'd flattery,
And with blunt truth acquaints us what we are.
    Beauty,——thou pretty plaything, dear deceit !
That steals so softly o'er the stripling's heart,
And gives it a new pulse, unknown before,
The Grave discredits thee: thy charms expunged,   240
Thy roses faded, and thy lilies soil'd,
What hast thou more to boast of ?   Will thy lovers
Flock round thee now, to gaze and do thee homage ?
Methinks I see thee with thy head low laid,
Whilst, surfeited upon thy damask cheek,
The high-fed worm, in lazy volumes roll'd,
Riots unscared.   For this, was all thy caution ?
For this, thy painful labours at thy glass ?
To improve those charms and keep them in repair,
For which the spoiler thanks thee not.   Foul feeder !250
Coarse fare and carrion please thee full as well,
And leave as keen a relish on the sense.
Look how the fair one weeps !——the conscious tears
Stand thick as dew-drops on the bells of flowers :

Honest effusion! the swoln heart in vain   .   255
Works hard to put a gloss on its distress.*
    Strength, too,——thou surly, and less gentle boast
Of those that laugh loud at the village ring!
A fit of common sickness pulls thee down
With greater ease than e'er thou didst the stripling   260
That rashly dared thee to the unequal fight.
What groan was that I heard?——deep groan indeed!
With anguish heavy laden; let me trace it:
From yonder bed it comes, where the strong man,
By stronger arm belabour'd, gasps for breath
Like a hard-hunted beast. How his great heart
Beats thick! his roomy chest by far too scant
To give the lungs full play. What now avail
The strong-built, sinewy limbs, and well spread shoulders '
See how he tugs for life, and lays about him,   270
Mad with his pains!——Eager he catches hold
Of what comes next to hand, and grasps it hard,
Just like a creature drowning;——hideous sight!
Oh! how his eyes stand out, and stare full ghastly!
While the distemper's rank and deadly venom
Shoots like a burning arrow 'cross his bowels,
And drinks his marrow up.——Heard you that groan?
It was his last.——See how the great Goliath,
Just like a child that brawl'd itself to rest,   279
Lies still.——What mean'st thou then, O mighty boaster!
To vaunt of nerves of thine? What means the bull,
Unconscious of his strength, to play the coward,
And flee before a feeble thing like man,
That, knowing well the slackness of his arm,
Trusts only in the well-invented knife?
    With study pale, and midnight vigils spent,
The star-surveying sage, close to his eye
Applies the sight-invigorating tube;

And, travelling through the boundless length of space,
Marks well the courses of the far-seen orbs,   290
That roll with regular confusion there,
In ecstasy of thought.   But, ah, proud man!
Great heights are hazardous to the weak head;
Soon, very soon, thy firmest footing fails;
And down thou dropp'st into that darksome place,
Where nor device nor knowledge ever came.
  Here the tongue-warrior lies, disabled now,
Disarm'd, dishonour'd, like a wretch that's gagg'd,
And cannot tell his ails to passers-by.
Great man of language!——whence this mighty change,
This dumb despair, and drooping of the head?   301
Though strong persuasion hung upon thy lip,
And sly insinuation's softer arts
In ambush lay about thy flowing tongue;
Alas, how chop-fallen now!   Thick mists and silence
Rest, like a weary cloud, upon thy breast
Unceasing.——Ah! where is the lifted arm,
The strength of action, and the force of words,
The well-turn'd period, and the well-tuned voice,
With all the lesser ornaments of phrase?   310
Ah! fled for ever, as they ne'er had been;
Razed from the book of fame; or, more provoking,
Perchance some hackney hunger-bitten scribbler
Insults thy memory, and blots thy tomb
With long flat narrative, or duller rhymes,
With heavy halting pace that drawl along;
Enough to rouse a dead man into rage,
And warm with red resentment the wan cheek.
  Here the great masters of the healing art,
These mighty mock defrauders of the tomb,   320
Spite of their juleps and catholicons,
Resign to fate.——Proud Æsculapius' son!

Where are thy boasted implements of art,   323
And all thy well-cramm'd magazines of health ?
Nor hill nor vale, as far as ship could go,
Nor margin of the gravel-bottom'd brook,
Escaped thy rifling hand ;——from stubborn shrubs
Thou wrung'st their shy retiring virtues out,
And vex'd them in the fire : nor fly, nor insect,
Nor writhy snake, escaped thy deep research.   330
But why this apparatus ?   Why this cost ?
Tell us, thou doughty keeper from the grave,
Where are thy recipes and cordials now,
With the long list of vouchers for thy cures ?
Alas ! thou speakest not.——The bold impostor
Looks not more silly when the cheat's found out.
    Here the lank-sided miser, worst of felons,
Who meanly stole (discreditable shift !)
From back, and belly too, their proper cheer,
Eased of a tax it irk'd the wretch to pay   340
To his own carcase, now lies cheaply lodged.
By clamorous appetites no longer teased,
Nor tedious bills of charges and repairs.
But, ah ! where are his rents, his comings-in ?
Ay ! now you've made the rich man poor indeed ;
Robb'd of his gods, what has he left behind ?
O cursed lust of gold ! when for thy sake
The fool throws up his interest in both worlds ;
First starved in this, then damn'd in that to come.
    How shocking must thy summons be, O Death !   350
To him that is at ease in his possessions ;
Who, counting on long years of pleasure here,
Is quite unfurnish'd for that world to come !
In that dread moment, how the frantic soul
Raves round the walls of her clay tenement,
Runs to each avenue, and shrieks for help,

But shrieks in vain !—How wishfully she looks   357
On all she's leaving, now no longer her's!
A little longer, yet a little longer,
Oh! might she stay, to wash away her stains,
And fit her for her passage.——Mournful sight!
Her very eyes weep blood;—and every groan
She heaves is big with horror: but the foe,
Like a staunch murderer, steady to his purpose,
Pursues her close through every lane of life,
Nor misses once the track, but presses on;
Till, forced at last to the tremendous verge,
At once she sinks to everlasting ruin.
   Sure 'tis a serious thing to die! My soul,
What a strange moment it must be, when near   370
Thy journey's end, thou hast the gulf in view!
That awful gulf no mortal e'er repass'd
To tell what's doing on the other side.
Nature runs back and shudders at the sight,
And every life-string bleeds at thoughts of parting;
For part they must: body and soul must part;
Fond couple! link'd more close than wedded pair.
This wings its way to its Almighty Source,
The witness of its actions, now its judge:
That drops into the dark and noisome grave,   380
Like a disabled pitcher of no use.
   If death were nothing, and nought after death;
If when men died, at once they ceased to be,
Returning to the barren womb of nothing,
Whence first they sprung; then might the debauchee
Untrembling mouth the heavens:—then might the drunkard
Reel over his full bowl, and, when 'tis drain'd,
Fill up another to the brim, and laugh
At the poor bugbear Death: then might the wretch
That's weary of the world, and tired of life,   390

At once give each inquietude the slip, 391
By stealing out of being when he pleased,
And by what way, whether by hemp, or steel.
Death's thousand doors stand open.——Who could force
The ill pleased guest to sit out his full time,
Or blame him if he goes ?   Sure he does well,
That helps himself, as timely as he can,
When able.——But if there's an Hereafter;
And that there is, conscience, uninfluenced,
And suffer'd to speak out, tells every man ; 400
Then must it be an awful thing to die :
More horrid yet to die by one's own hand.
Self-murder !——name it not : our island's shame,
That makes her the reproach of neighbouring states.
Shall nature, swerving from her earliest dictate,
Self-preservation, fall by her own act ?
Forbid it, Heaven !——Let not upon disgust
The shameless hand be foully crimson'd o'er
With blood of its own lord.——Dreadful attempt !
Just reeking from self-slaughter, in a rage 410
To rush into the presence of our Judge;
As if we challenged him to do his worst,
And matter'd not his wrath !——Unheard-of tortures
Must be reserved for such : these herd together;
The common damn'd shun their society,
And look upon themselves as fiends less foul.
Our time is fix'd; and all our days are number'd;
How long, how short, we know not :——this we know,
Duty requires we calmly wait the summons,
Nor dare to stir till Heaven shall give permission : 420
Like sentries that must keep their destined stand,
And wait the appointed hour, till they 're relieved.
Those only are the brave who keep their ground,
And keep it to the last.   To run away

K

Is but a coward's trick: to run away   425
From this world's ills, that at the very worst
Will soon blow o'er, thinking to mend ourselves,
By boldly venturing on a world unknown,
And plunging headlong in the dark;—'tis mad!
No frenzy half so desperate as this.   430
   Tell us, ye dead! will none of you, in pity
To those you left behind, disclose the secret?
Oh! that some courteous ghost would blab it out;
What 'tis you are, and we must shortly be.
I 've heard that souls departed have sometimes
Forewarn'd men of their death:—'twas kindly done
To knock, and give the alarm.—But what means
This stinted charity?—'Tis but lame kindness
That does its work by halves.—Why might you not
Tell us what 'tis to die? do the strict laws   440
Of your society forbid your speaking
Upon a point so nice?—I 'll ask no more:
Sullen, like lamps in sepulchres, your shine
Enlightens but yourselves.   Well, 'tis no matter;
A very little time will clear up all,
And make us learn'd as you are, and as close.
   Death's shafts fly thick!—Here falls the village-swain,
And there his pamper'd lord!—The cup goes round;
And who so artful as to put it by?
'Tis long since death had the majority;   450
Yet, strange! the living lay it not to heart.
See yonder maker of the dead man's bed,
The Sexton, hoary-headed chronicle;
Of hard, unmeaning face, down which ne'er stole
A gentle tear; with mattock in his hand
Digs through whole rows of kindred and acquaintance,
By far his juniors.—Scarce a skull's cast up,
But well he knew its owner, and can tell

Some passage of his life.——Thus hand in hand   459
The sot has walk'd with death twice twenty years ;
And yet ne'er younker on the green laughs louder,
Or clubs a smuttier tale : when drunkards meet,
None sings a merrier catch, or lends a hand
More willing to his cup.——Poor wretch ! he minds not,
That soon some trusty brother of the trade
Shall do for him what he has done for thousands.

On this side, and on that, men see their friends
Drop off, like leaves in autumn ; yet launch out
Into fantastic schemes, which the long livers
In the world's hale and undegenerate days   470
Could scarce have leisure for.——Fools that we are !
Never to think of death and of ourselves
At the same time : as if to learn to die
Were no concern of ours.——O more than sottish,
For creatures of a day, in gamesome mood,
To frolic on eternity's dread brink
Unapprehensive ; when, for aught we know,
The very first swoln surge shall sweep us in !
Think we, or think we not, time hurries on
With a resistless, unremitting stream ;   480
Yet treads more soft than e'er did midnight thief,
That slides his hand under the miser's pillow,
And carries off his prize.——What is this world ?
What but a spacious burial-field unwall'd,
Strew'd with death's spoils, the spoils of animals
Savage and tame, and full of dead men's bones !
The very turf on which we tread once lived ;
And we that live must lend our carcases
To cover our own offspring : in their turns
They too must cover theirs.——'Tis here all meet !   490
The shivering Icelander, and sun-burnt Moor ;
Men of all climes, that never met before ;

And of all creeds, the Jew, the Turk, the Christian. 493
Here the proud prince, and favourite yet prouder,
His sovereign's keeper, and the people's scourge,
Are huddled out of sight.——Here lie abash'd
The great negotiators of the earth,
And celebrated masters of the balance,
Deep read in stratagems, and wiles of courts.
Now vain their treaty skill : death scorns to treat. 500
Here the o'er-loaded slave flings down his burden
From his gall'd shoulders ;——and when the cruel tyrant,
With all his guards and tools of power about him,
Is meditating new unheard-of hardships,
Mocks his short arm,——and, quick as thought, escapes
Where tyrants vex not, and the weary rest.
Here the warm lover, leaving the cool shade,
The tell-tale echo, and the babbling stream
(Time out of mind the favourite seats of love),
Fast by his gentle mistress lays him down, 510
Unblasted by foul tongue.——Here friends and foes
Lie close ; unmindful of their former feuds.
The lawn-robed prelate and plain presbyter,
Erewhile that stood aloof, as shy to meet,
Familiar mingle here, like sister streams
That some rude interposing rock had split.
Here is the large-limb'd peasant ;——here the child
Of a span long, that never saw the sun,
Nor press'd the nipple, strangled in life's porch.
Here is the mother, with her sons and daughters ; 520
The barren wife ; the long-demurring maid,
Whose lonely unappropriated sweets
Smiled like yon knot of cowslips on the cliff,
Not to be come at by the willing hand.
Here are the prude severe, and gay coquette,
The sober widow, and the young green virgin,

Cropp'd like a rose before 'tis fully blown,   527
Or half its worth disclosed.   Strange medley here !
Here garrulous old age winds up his tale ;
And jovial youth, of lightsome vacant heart,
Whose every day was made of melody,
Hears not the voice of mirth.——The shrill-tongued shrew,
Meek as the turtle-dove, forgets her chiding.
Here are the wise, the generous, and the brave ;
The just, the good, the worthless, the profane ;
The downright clown, and perfectly well-bred ;
The fool, the churl, the scoundrel, and the mean ;
The supple statesman, and the patriot stern ;
The wrecks of nations, and the spoils of time,
With all the lumber of six thousand years.   540
    Poor man !——how happy once in thy first state !
When yet but warm from thy great Maker's hand,
He stamp'd thee with his image, and, well pleased,
Smiled on his last fair work.——Then all was well.
Sound was the body, and the soul serene ;
Like two sweet instruments, ne'er out of tune,
That play their several parts.——Nor head, nor heart,
Offer'd to ache : nor was there cause they should ;
For all was pure within : no fell remorse,
Nor anxious casting-up of what might be,   550
Alarm'd his peaceful bosom.——Summer seas
Show not more smooth, when kiss'd by southern winds
Just ready to expire.——Scarce importuned,
The generous soil, with a luxuriant hand,
Offer'd the various produce of the year,
And everything most perfect in its kind.
Blessed ! thrice-blessed days !——But ah, how short !
Blest as the pleasing dreams of holy men ;
But fugitive like those, and quickly gone.
O slippery state of things !——What sudden turns !   560

What strange vicissitudes in the first leaf   561
Of man's sad history !——To-day most happy,
And ere to-morrow's sun has set, most abject !
How scant the space between these vast extremes !
Thus fared it with our sire :——not long he enjoy'd
His paradise.——Scarce had the happy tenant
Of the fair spot due time to prove its sweets,
Or sum them up, when straight he must be gone,
Ne'er to return again.——And must he go ?
Can nought compound for the first dire offence   570
Of erring man ?   Like one that is condemn'd,
Fain would he trifle time with idle talk,
And parley with his fate.   But 'tis in vain ;
Not all the lavish odours of the place,
Offer'd in incense, can procure his pardon,
Or' mitigate his doom.   A mighty angel,
With flaming sword, forbids his longer stay,
And drives the loiterer forth ; nor must he take
One last and farewell round.   At once he lost
His glory and his God.   If mortal now,   580
And sorely maim'd, no wonder !——Man has sinn'd.
Sick of his bliss, and bent on new adventures,
Evil he needs would try : nor tried in vain.
(Dreadful experiment ! destructive measure !
Where the worst thing could happen is success.)
Alas ! too well he sped :——the good he scorn'd
Stalk'd off reluctant, like an ill-used ghost,
Not to return ; or if it did, its visits,
Like those of angels, short and far between :
Whilst the black Demon, with his hell-scaped train, 590
Admitted once into its better room,
Grew loud and mutinous, nor would be gone ;
Lording it o'er the man : who now too late
Saw the rash error which he could not mend :

An error fatal not to him alone, 595
But to his future sons, his fortune's heirs.
Inglorious bondage !   Human nature groans
Beneath a vassalage so vile and cruel,
And its vast body bleeds through every vein.
    What havoc hast thou made, foul monster, Sin ! 600
Greatest and first of ills : the fruitful parent
Of woes of all dimensions : but for thee
Sorrow had never been,——All-noxious thing,
Of vilest nature !   Other sorts of evils
Are kindly circumscribed, and have their bounds.
The fierce volcano, from his burning entrails
That belches molten stone and globes of fire,
Involved in pitchy clouds of smoke and stench,
Mars the adjacent fields for some leagues round,
And there it stops.   The big-swoln inundation, 610
Of mischief more diffusive, raving loud,
Buries whole tracts of country, threatening more ;
But that too has its shore it cannot pass.
More dreadful far than these ! Sin has laid waste,
Not here and there a country, but a world :
Despatching, at a wide-extended blow,
Entire mankind ; and for their sakes defacing
A whole creation's beauty with rude hands ;
Blasting the foodful grain, the loaded branches ;
And marking all along its way with ruin. 620
Accursed thing !——Oh ! where shall fancy find
A proper name to call thee by, expressive
Of all thy horrors ?——Pregnant womb of ills !
Of tempers so transcendantly malign,
That toads and serpents of most deadly kind
Compared to thee are harmless.——Sicknesses
Of every size and symptom, racking pains,
And bluest plagues, are thine.——See how the fiend

Profusely scatters the contagion round !   629
Whilst deep-mouth'd slaughter, bellowing at her heels,
Wades deep in blood new-spilt ; yet for to-morrow
Shapes out new work of great uncommon daring,
And inly pines till the dread blow is struck.
 But, hold ! I 've gone too far ; too much discover'd
My father's nakedness, and nature's shame.
Here let me pause, and drop an honest tear,
One burst of filial duty and condolence,
O'er all those ample deserts Death hath spread,
This chaos of mankind.——O great man-eater !
Whose every day is carnival, not sated yet !   640
Unheard-of epicure, without a fellow !
The veriest gluttons do not always cram ;
Some intervals of abstinence are sought
To edge the appetite : Thou seekest none.
Methinks the countless swarms thou hast devour'd,
And thousands at each hour thou gobblest up,
This, less than this, might gorge thee to the full !
But, ah ! rapacious still, thou gap'st for more :
Like one, whole days defrauded of his meals,
On whom lank Hunger lays her skinny hand,   650
And whets to keenest eagerness his cravings :
As if diseases, massacres, and poison,
Famine, and war, were not thy caterers.
 But know that thou must render up thy dead,
And with high interest too.——They are not thine,
But only in thy keeping for a season,
Till the great promised day of restitution ;
When loud-diffusive sound from brazen trump
Of strong-lung'd cherub shall alarm thy captives,
And rouse the long, long sleepers into life,   660
Day-light, and liberty.——
Then must thy gates fly open, and reveal

The mines that lay long forming under ground,   663
In their dark cells immured; but now full ripe,
And pure as silver from the crucible,
That twice has stood the torture of the fire
And inquisition of the forge.   We know,
The illustrious Deliverer of mankind,
The Son of God, thee foil'd.   Him in thy power
Thou couldst not hold : self-vigorous he rose,   670
And, shaking off thy fetters, soon retook
Those spoils his voluntary yielding lent :'
(Sure pledge of our releasement from thy thrall !)
Twice twenty days he sojourn'd here on earth,
And show'd himself alive to chosen witnesses,
By proofs so strong, that the most slow-assenting
Had not a scruple left.   This having done,
He mounted up to heaven.   Methinks I see him
Climb the aërial heights, and glide along
Athwart the severing clouds : but the faint eye,   680
Flung backwards in the chase, soon drops its hold ;
Disabled quite, and jaded with pursuing.
Heaven's portals wide expand to let him in ;
Nor are his friends shut out : as some great prince
Not for himself alone procures admission,
But for his train.   It was his royal will
That where he is, there should his followers be.
Death only lies between: a gloomy path,
Made yet more gloomy by our coward fears ;
But not untrod, nor tedious : the fatigue   690
Will soon go off.   Besides, there's no bye-road
To bliss.   Then why, like ill-condition'd children,
Start we at transient hardships in the way
That leads to purer air, and softer skies,
And a ne'er-setting sun ?—Fools that we are !
We wish to be where sweets unwithering bloom ;

But straight our wish revoke, and will not go.   697
So have I seen, upon a summer's even,
Fast by the rivulet's brink a youngster play:
How wishfully he looks to stem the tide!
This moment resolute, next unresolved:
At last he dips his foot; but as he dips,
His fears redouble, and he runs away
From the inoffensive stream, unmindful now
Of all the flowers that paint the further bank,
And smiled so sweet of late.——Thrice welcome death!
That after many a painful bleeding step
Conducts us to our home, and lands us safe
On the long-wish'd-for shore.——Prodigious change!
Our bane turn'd to a blessing!——Death, disarm'd,   71(
Loses his fellness quite.——All thanks to him
Who scourged the venom out!——Sure the last end
Of the good man is peace!——How calm his exit!
Night dews fall not more gently to the ground,
Nor weary, worn-out winds expire so soft.
Behold him in the evening-tide of life,
A life well spent, whose early care it was
His riper years should not upbraid his green:
By unperceived degrees he wears away;
Yet, like the sun, seems larger at his setting.   72
High in his faith and hopes, look how he reaches
After the prize in view! and, like a bird
That's hamper'd, struggles hard to get away:
Whilst the glad gates of sight are wide expanded
To let new glories in, the first fair fruits
Of the fast-coming harvest.——Then, oh then!
Each earth-born joy grows vile, or disappears,
Shrunk to a thing of nought.——Oh! how he longs
To have his passport sign'd, and be dismiss'd!
'Tis done! and now he's happy!   The glad soul   73

Has not a wish uncrown'd.——Even the lag flesh   731
Rests, too, in hope of meeting once again
Its better half, never to sunder more.
Nor shall it hope in vain :——the time draws on,
When not a single spot of burial earth,
Whether on land, or in the spacious sea,
But must give back its long-committed dust
Inviolate !——and faithfully shall these
Make up the full account ; not the least atom
Embezzled, or mislaid, of the whole tale.   740
Each soul shall have a body ready furnish'd ;
And each shall have his own.——Hence, ye profane !
Ask not how this can be ?——Sure the same power
That rear'd the piece at first, and took it down,
Can re-assemble the loose scatter'd parts,
And put them as they were.——Almighty God
Has done much more ; nor is his arm impair'd
Through length of days : and what he can, he will :
His faithfulness stands bound to see it done.
When the dread trumpet sounds, the slumbering dust, 750
Not unattentive to the call, shall wake ;
And every joint possess its proper place,
With a new elegance of form, unknown
To its first state. Nor shall the conscious soul
Mistake its partner, but, amidst the crowd,
Singling its other half, into its arms
Shall rush, with all the impatience of a man
That's new come home ; and, having long been absent,
With haste runs over every different room,
In pain to see the whole. Thrice happy meeting !   760
Nor time, nor death, shall ever part them more.
'Tis but a night, a long and moonless night ;
We make the grave our bed, and then are gone.
    Thus, at the shut of even, the weary bird

Leaves the wide air, and in some lonely brake   765
Cowers down, and dozes till the dawn of day,
Then claps his well-fledged wings, and bears away.

A POEM,

DEDICATED TO THE MEMORY OF THE LATE LEARNED AND
EMINENT MR WILLIAM LAW, PROFESSOR OF PHILO-
SOPHY IN THE UNIVERSITY OF EDINBURGH.

IN silence to suppress my griefs I've tried,
And kept within its banks the swelling tide !
But all in vain : unbidden numbers flow ;
Spite of myself my sorrows vocal grow.
This be my plea.——Nor thou, dear Shade, refuse
The well-meant tribute of the willing muse,
Who trembles at the greatness of its theme,
And fain would say what suits so high a name.
    Which, from the crowded journal of thy fame,——
Which of thy many titles shall I name ?   10
For, like a gallant prince, that wins a crown,
By undisputed right before his own,
Variety thou hast : our only care
Is what to single out, and what forbear.
    Though scrupulously just, yet not severe ;
Though cautious, open ; courteous, yet sincere ;
Though reverend, yet not magisterial ;
Though intimate with few, yet loved by all ;
Though deeply read, yet absolutely free
From all the stiffnesses of pedantry ;   20
Though circumspectly good, yet never sour ;
Pleasant with innocence, and never more.

Religion, worn by thee, attractive show'd,   2£
And with its own unborrow'd beauty glow'd:
Unlike the bigot, from whose watery eyes
Ne'er sunshine broke, nor smile was seen to rise;
Whose sickly goodness lives upon grimace,
And pleads a merit from a blubber'd face.
Thou kept thy raiment for the needy poor,
And taught the fatherless to know thy door;   3(
From griping hunger set the needy free;
That they were needy, was enough to thee.
    Thy fame to please, whilst others restless be,
Fame laid her shyness by, and courted thee;
And though thou bade the flattering thing give o'er,
Yet, in return, she only woo'd thee more.
    How sweet thy accents! and how mild thy look!
What smiling mirth was heard in all thou spoke;
Manhood and grizzled age were fond of thee,
And youth itself sought thy society.   4(
The aged thou taught, descended to the young,
Clear'd up the irresolute, confirm'd the strong;
To the perplex'd thy friendly counsel lent,
And gently lifted up the diffident;
Sigh'd with the sorrowful, and bore a part
In all the anguish of a bleeding heart;
Reclaim'd the headstrong; and, with sacred skill,
Committed hallow'd rapes upon the will;
Soothed our affections; and, with their delight,
To gain our actions, bribed our appetite.   5(
    Now, who shall, with a greatness like thy own,
Thy pulpit dignify, and grace thy gown?
Who, with pathetic energy like thine,
The head enlighten, and the heart refine?
Learn'd were thy lectures, noble the design,
The language *Roman*, and the action fine;

The heads well ranged, the inferences clear, 57
And strong and solid thy deductions were:
Thou mark'd the boundaries out 'twixt right and wrong,
And show'd the land-marks as thou went along.
Plain were thy reasonings, or, if perplex'd,
Thy life was the best comment on thy text;
For, if in darker points we were deceived,
'Twas only but observing how thou lived.
  Bewilder'd in the greatness of thy fame,
What shall the Muse, what next in order name?
Which of thy social qualities commend—
Whether of husband, father, or of friend?
A husband soft, beneficent, and kind,
As ever virgin wish'd, or wife could find; 70
A father indefatigably true
To both a father's trust and tutor's too;
A friend affectionate and staunch to those
Thou wisely singled out; for few thou chose:
Few, did I say, that word we must recall;
A friend, a willing friend, thou wast to all.
Those properties were thine, nor could we know
Which rose the uppermost, so all wast thou.
So have I seen the many-colour'd mead,
Brush'd by the vernal breeze, its fragrance shed: 80
Though various sweets the various field exhaled,
Yet could we not determine which prevail'd,
Nor this part *rose*, that *honey-suckle* call
But a rich bloomy aggregate of all.
  And thou, the once glad partner of his bed,
But now by sorrow's weeds distinguished,
Whose busy memory thy grief supplies,
And calls up all thy husband to thine eyes;
Thou must not be forgot. How alter'd now!
How thick thy tears! How fast thy sorrows flow! 90

The well known voice that cheer'd thee heretofore,   91
These soothing accents thou must hear no more.
Untold be all the tender sighs thou drew,
When on thy cheek he fetch'd a long adieu.
Untold be all thy faithful agonies,
At the last anguish of his closing eyes;
For thou, and only such as thou, can tell
The killing anguish of a last farewell.
 This earth, yon sun, and these blue-tinctured skies,
Through which it rolls, must have their obsequies: 100
Pluck'd from their orbits, shall the planets fall,
And smoke and conflagration cover all:
What, then, is man? The creature of a day,
By moments spent, and minutes borne away.
Time, like a raging torrent, hurries on;
Scarce can we say *it is*, but that 'tis gone.
 Whether, fair shade! with social spirits, tell
(Whose properties thou once described so well),
Familiar now thou hearest them relate
The rites and methods of their happy state: 110
Or if, with forms more fleet, thou roams abroad,
And views the great magnificence of God,
Points out the courses of the orbs on high,
And counts the silver wonders of the sky!
Or if, with glowing seraphim, thou greets
Heaven's King, and shoutest through the golden streets,
That crowds of white-robed choristers display,
Marching in triumph through the pearly way?
 Now art thou raised beyond this world of cares,
This weary wilderness, this vale of tears;   120
Forgetting all thy toils and labours past,
No gloom of sorrow stains thy peaceful breast.
Now, 'midst seraphic splendours shalt thou dwell,
And be what only these pure forms can tell.

How cloudless now, and cheerful is thy day !   12
What joys, what raptures, in thy bosom play !
How bright the sunshine, and how pure the air !
There's no difficulty of breathing there.
     With willing steps a pilgrim at thy shrine,
To dew it with my tears the task be mine ;   13
In lonely dirge, to murmur o'er thy urn
And with new-gather'd flowers thy turf adorn :
Nor shall thy image from my bosom part ;
No force shall rip thee from this bleeding heart.
Oft shall I think o'er all I've left in thee,
Nor shall oblivion blot thy memory ;
But grateful love its energy express
(The father gone) now to the fatherless.

END OF BLAIR'S POEMS.

POETICAL WORKS

OF

WILLIAM FALCONER.

L

THE LIFE AND POETRY OF
WILLIAM FALCONER.

IT may seem singular how the life of a sailor—a life so full of vicissitude and enterprise, of hair's-breadth escapes, of contact with wild men and wild usages, and of intercourse with a form of nature so vast, so fluctuating, so mysterious, and so terribly sublime as the ocean, which, in its calm and silence, forms an emblem of all that is peaceful and profound, and, in its tempestuous rage, of all that is unreconciled and anarchical in the mind of man, now comparable to a

"Cradled child in dreamless slumber bound !"

and now to a mad sister of the earth, screaming and foaming in fierce and aimless antagonism to her brother—should have reared so few poets. This may arise either from the uncultivated and careless character of sailors as a class, or from the influence of habit in deadening the effect of the grandest objects. It is the same with other modes of life equally romantic. What more so than that of a shepherd among the Grampian Mountains, constantly living between the everlasting hills and the silent sun and stars, surrounded by streams, cataracts, deep dun moorlands, and the wild-eyed and wild-winged creatures which dwell in them alone, their life hid in Nature, and their cries of rude praise going up continually to Nature's God? And yet the Highlands of Scotland have not hitherto produced one great rural poet, except Macpherson, who did not belong to the peasantry. And so of the seafaring class; two only, so far as we remember, have expressed, the one in verse, and the other in prose, the *poetry* of their calling,—namely, Cooper and Falconer, both of whose descriptions of sea storms and scenery have been equalled, if not surpassed, however, by such landsmen as Byron and Scott. A poetic mind, which comes in contact with strange and wonderful events or scenery only at intervals, often carries away a much more vivid idea of their striking features than those who reside constantly in their midst. It must be a very rough rope, to borrow an image from the theme, which does not feel softer after long handling. It is the short and sudden impression, made in the twinkling of an eye, which is at once the most lively and the most lasting. When, however, enthusiasm continues, as in some favoured cases, unabated by familiarity, and is united to thorough technical knowledge, then the professional man may be nearly as successful as the amateur, or if there be any deficiency in freshness of feeling, it is made up for by accuracy of knowledge. It was so in the case of James Hogg, the poet of the shepherd life of Southern Scotland, and in William Falconer, the poet of British shipwreck. We shall afterwards show how his knowledge of his profession partly helped and partly hindered him in his poem.

William Falconer was born in Edinburgh in the year 1736. He was the son of a poor barber in the Netherbow, who had two other children, both deaf and dumb, who ended their days in a poor-house. He early, through frequent visits to Leith, came in contact with that tremendous element which he was to sing so powerfully, and in which he was to sink at last—which was to give him at once his glory and his grave. While a mere boy, he went, by his own account, reluctantly on board a Leith merchant ship, and was afterwards in the Royal Navy. Of his early education or habits very little is known. He had all his scholarship from one Webster. We figure him (after the similitude of a dear lost sailor boy, a relative of our own) as a stripling, with curling hair, ruddy cheek, form prematurely developed into round robustness, frank, free, and manly bearing, returning ever and anon from his ocean wanderings, and bearing to his friends some rare bird or shell of the tropics as a memorial of his labours and his love. Before he was eighteen years of age, Providence supplied him with the materials whence he was to pile up the monument of his future fame. He became second mate in the ship *Britannia*, a vessel trading in the Levant. This vessel was shipwrecked off Cape Colonna, exactly in the manner described in the poem, which is just a coloured photograph of the adventures, difficulties, dangers, and disastrous result of the voyage. In 1751 we find him living in Edinburgh, and publishing his first poem. This was an elegy on the death of Frederick, Prince of Wales. It was followed by other pieces, which appeared in the *Gentleman's Magazine,* and which will be found in this volume. Some have claimed for him the authorship of the favourite sea song, "Cease, Rude Boreas," but this seems uncertain.

Falconer is supposed to have continued in the merchant service (one of his biographers maintains that he was for some time in the *Ramilies*, a man-of-war, which suffered shipwreck in the Channel) till 1762, when he published his "Shipwreck." This poem was dedicated to the Duke of York, who had newly become Rear-Admiral of the Blue on board the *Princess Amelia*, attached to the fleet under Sir Edward Hawke. The Duke was not a Solomon, but he had sense enough to perceive, that the sailor who could produce such a poem was no ordinary man, and generous enough to offer him promotion, if he should leave the merchant service for the Royal Navy. Falconer, accordingly, was promoted to be a midshipman on board the *Royal George* (Sir Edward Hawke's ship) ; the same, we believe, which afterwards went down in such a disastrous manner, and furnished a subject for one of Cowper's boldest little poems. "The Shipwreck" was highly commended by the *Monthly Review,*—then the leading literary organ,—and became widely popular.

While in the *Royal George*, Falconer contrived to find time for his poetical studies. Retiring sometimes from his messmates, into a small space between the cable-trees and the ship's side, he wrote his Ode on "the Duke of York's Second Departure from England, as Rear-Admiral." This poem was severely criticised in the *Critical Review.* It has certainly much pomp, and thundering sound of language and versification, but wants the genuine Pindaric inspiration.

At the peace of 1763 the *Royal George* was paid off, and Falconer became purser of the *Glory*, frigate of 32 guns. About this time he married a young lady named Hicks, daughter of a surgeon in Sheerness-yard—a lady more distinguished by her mental than her physical qualities. The poet dubbed her in his verses, " Miranda." It is hinted that he had some difficulty in procuring her consent to marry him, and was forced to lay regular siege to her in rhyme. At length she capitulated, and the marriage was eminently happy. She survived her husband many years ; lived at Bath, and enjoyed a comfortable livelihood on the proceeds of her husband's " Marine Dictionary."

When the *Glory* was laid up at Chatham, Commissioner Hanway, brother of the once celebrated Jonas Hanway (whom Dr Johnson so justly chastised for his diatribe against Tea), showed much interest in the pursuits and person of our poet. He even ordered the captain's cabin to be fitted up with every comfort, that Falconer might pursue his studies without expense, and with all convenience. Here he brought his " Marine Dictionary " to a conclusion—a work which had occupied him for years, and which supplied a desideratum in the literature of the profession. The design had been suggested by one Scott, and approved of by Sir Edward Hawke ; and the book, when it appeared in 1769, was greatly commended by Dr Hamel, the Frenchman, who had gained note himself, by producing some works on naval architecture. From the *Glory* Falconer received an appointment in the *Swift-sure*. In 1764 he issued a new edition of " The Shipwreck," carefully corrected, and with considerable additions. The next year he issued a political poem, in which, like a true tar of the *Royal George*, he took the King's side, and emitted much dull and drivelling bile against Lord Chatham, Wilkes, and Churchill. The satire proved that, though at home on the ocean, he was utterly " at sea " in land-politics.

Falconer had now left his cabin study with its many pleasant accommodations, and become a scribbler of all work in a

London garret. Here his existence ran on for a while in an obscure and probably miserable current. It is said that Murray, the bookseller, the father of *the* John Murray, of Albemarle Street, wished to take the poet into partnership,— upon terms of great advantage,—but that Falconer, for reasons which are not known, declined the offer. "My Murray," as Byron calls him, was destined instead to have his name connected with a grander and ghastlier shipwreck than it lay in the brain of the projected partner of his firm to conceive, or in his genius to execute—that, namely, described in the ever-detestable, yet ever-memorable, second canto of "Don Juan."

In 1769, a third edition of his poem was called for, and he was employed in making improvements and additions when he was again summoned to sea. In his hurry of departure, he is said to have committed these to the care of the notorious David Mallett, the son of a Crieff innkeeper, the friend of Thomson, the biographer of Bacon, and, as Johnson called him, the "beggarly Scotchman, who drew the trigger of Bolingbroke's blunderbuss of infidelity," who seems to have paid no manner of attention to his trust, as mistakes in the nautical terms and a frequent inferiority in execution manifest.

Falconer had undoubtedly thought the sea a hard and sickening profession; but latterly found that writing for the booksellers was a slavery still more abject and unendurable. He resolved once more to embark upon the "melancholy main." Often as he had hugged its horrors, laid his hand on its mane, and narrowly escaped its devouring jaws, he was drawn in again as by the fatal suction of a whirlpool into its power. Perhaps he had imbibed a passion for the sea. At all events, he accepted the office of purser to the Aurora frigate, which was going out to India, and on the 30th of September 1769, he left England for ever. The Aurora was never heard of more! Some vague rumours, indeed, prevailed of a contradictory character — that she had been burned—that she had foundered in the Mozambique Channel—that she had been cast away on a reef of rocks near Macao — that five persons had been saved from her wreck, but nothing certain transpired, except that she was lost; and this fine singer of the sea, along with her. Unfortunate Aurora! dawn soon overcast! Unfortunate poet, so speedily removed!

> " It was that fatal and perfidious bark,
> Built i' the eclipse, and rigg'd with curses dark,
> That laid so low that sacred head of thine."

The drowning of one poet of far loftier genius in the Bay of Spezia, latterly proved that the offering up of Falconer's life had not fully appeased the wrath of old Neptune, and that bards may still entertain, in the lines of Wordsworth,

> " Of the old sea some reverential fear."

Burns heard of and deplored the loss of the Poet of the Shipwreck. In one of his letters to Mrs Dunlop, he mentions the fact, and adds the beautiful words, " He was one of those daring, adventurous spirits which Scotland beyond any other country is remarkable for producing. Little does the fond mother think, as she hangs delighted over the sweet little leech at her bosom, where the poor fellow may hereafter wander, and what may be his fate. I remember a stanza in an old Scottish ballad, which speaks feelingly to the heart—

> ' Little did my mother think,
> That day she cradled me,
> What land I was to travel on,
> Or what death I should die.' "

Falconer is represented as a bluff, blunt, but cheerful sailor— fond of amusing his shipmates with acrostics on the names of their mistresses—with little learning except in seamanship, and what he had picked up in his travels. His smaller pieces scarcely deserve criticsm. His whole reputation now reposes on the one pillar of his one poem, " The Shipwreck."

This poem was greatly overrated when it first appeared. It was by some critics preferred to Virgil's " Eneid," and compared to the " Odyssey." It is now, we think, as unjustly depreciated. That there is a good deal of swollen commonplace in the diction and sentiments, must be admitted. Falconer arose in a bad age in respect of poetry. The terseness of Pope was gone, and in his imitators only his tinkle remained. His exquisite sense and trembling finish had vanished, and only his conventional diction—the ghost of his greatness—was to be found in the poets of the time. It was extremely natural that a half-taught mind like Falconer's should be captivated by what was the mode of the day. Indeed, Burns himself was only saved from the same error by continuing to write in Scotch; many of his English verses and his letters are marred by more or less of the disgusting and vicious affectation of style which then prevailed; and in parts of Campbell's "Pleasures of Hope," we find the last modified specimen of the evil. Hence, in Falconer the obsolete mythological allusions—the names with classical terminations—the perpetual apostrophes—the set and stilted speeches he puts into the mouths of heroes—the bombast, verbiage, and sounding sameness of much of his verse. Nor do we greatly admire the story which he introduces with the poem, nor the discrimination of his characters, nor, what may be called strictly, the pathos of the piece. Indeed, considering the size of the poem, there is so much that is vapid and common, that the counterbalancing excellences must be great ere they could have floated it so long. To use an expression suitable to the theme, the vessel which has sailed so far, notwithstanding its numerous leaks, must be of a strong and sturdy build.

And this is the main merit of "The Shipwreck." It has in most of its descriptive passages a certain rugged strength and truth, which prove at once the perspicacity and the poetic vision of the author, who, while he sees all the minute details of his subject, sees also the glory of imagination shining around them. A ship appears before his view, with its every spar and yard, clear and distinct as if seen in meridian sunshine, and yet with a radiance of poetry around it all, as if he were looking at it by moonlight, or in the magical light of a dream. Take the following lines, for instance:—

> " Up-torn reluctant from its oozy cave,
> The ponderous anchor rises o'er the wave.
> High on the slipp'ry masts the yards ascend,
> And far abroad the canvas wings extend.

> Along the glassy plain the vessel glides,
> While azure radiance trembles on her sides."

We grant, indeed, that sometimes his technical lore rises up, as it were, and drowns the poetry. What imaginative quality, for example, have we in the following verses?

> " The mainsail, by the squall so lately rent,
> In streaming pendants flying, is unbent ;
> With brails refixed, another soon prepared,
> Ascending spreads along beneath the yard ;
> To each yard-arm the head-rope they extend,
> And soon their ear-rings and their robans bend.
> That task perform'd, they first the braces slack,
> Then to the chess-tree drag the unwilling tack ;
> And, while the lee clue-garnet's lower'd away,
> Taught aft the sheet they tally, and belay."

This is mere log-book ; and such passages are common in the poem. But frequently he bathes the web of the shrouds and ship-rigging in rich ideal gold. Take the following :—

> " With equal sheets restrain'd, the bellying sail
> Spreads a broad concave to the sweeping gale ;
> While o'er the foam the ship impetuous flies,
> The helm the attentive timoneer applies :
> As in pursuit along the aërial way,
> With ardent eye the falcon marks his prey,
> Each motion watches of the doubtful chase,
> Obliquely wheeling through the fluid space ;
> So, govern'd by the steersman's GLOWING hands,
> The regent helm her motion still commands."

Falconer may in some points be likened to Crabbe. Like him, he excels in minute and patient painting. Like him he is capable at times of extracting the imaginative element from the barest and simplest details. And, like him, he sometimes sets before us, mere dry inventories or invoices, instead of such poetical catalogues as Homer gives of ships, and Milton of devils. It is remarkable that Falconer never shines at all except when he is describing ships or sea scenery.

> " His path is on the mountain waves,
> His home is on the deep."

No words in Scripture are so strange to him as these,

" There shall be no more sea." The course of his voyage in the Shipwreck, brings him past lands the most famous in the ancient world for arts and arms, for philosophy, patriotism, and poetry. And sore does he labour to lash himself into inspiration as he apostrophizes them ; but in vain—the result is little else than furious feebleness and stilted bombast. But when he returns to the element, the impatient, irregular, changeful, treacherous, terrible ocean—and watches the night, winged with black storm and red lightning, sinking down over the Mediterranean, and the devoted bark which is helplessly struggling with its billows, then his blood rises, his verse heaves, and hurries on, and you see the full-born poet—

> " High o'er the poop the audacious seas aspire,
> Uproll'd in hills of fluctuating fire :
> With labouring throes she rolls on either side,
> And dips her gunnells in the yawning tide.
> Her joints unhinged in palsied langour play,
> As ice-flakes part beneath the noontide ray ;
> The gale howls doleful through the blocks and shrouds,
> And big rain pours a deluge from the clouds.
> From wintry magazines that sweep the sky,
> Descending globes of hail incessant fly ;
> High on the masts with pale and lurid rays,
> Amid the gloom portentous meteors blaze !
> The ethereal dome in mournful pomp array'd,
> Now buried lies beneath impervious shade,—
> Now flashing round intolerable light,
> Redoubles all the horrors of the night.
> Such terror Sinai's trembling hill o'erspread,
> When Heaven's loud trumpet sounded o'er its head.
> It seem'd the wrathful angel of the wind,
> Had all the horrors of the skies combined ;
> And here to one ill-fated ship opposed,
> At once the dreadful magazine disclosed."

This is noble writing. " Deep calleth unto deep." It reminds us of Pope's translation of that tremendous passage in the 8th Book of the Iliad, where Jove comes forth, and darts his angry lightnings in the eyes of the Grecians, and repels and appals their mightiest ; Nestor alone, but with his horse wounded by the dart of Paris, sustaining the divine assault.

Lord Byron, in his letter to Bowles in defence of Pope,

alludes to Falconer's Shipwreck, and cites it in proof of the poetical use which may be made of the works of art.   But it has justly been remarked by Hazlitt, in his very masterly reply, published in the *London Magazine*, that the finest parts of the Shipwreck are not those in which he appears to versify parts of his own Marine Dictionary, or in which he makes vain efforts to describe the vestiges of Grecian grandeur, but those in which, as in the above passage, he mates with the sublime and terrible *natural* phenomena he meets in his voyage—the gathering of the storm—the treacherous lull of the sea, breathing itself like a tiger for its fatal spring—the ship, now walking the calm waters of the glassy sea, and now wrestling like a demon of kindred power and fury with the angry billows—the last fearful onset of the maddened surge—and the secret stab given by the assassin rock from below, which completes the ruin of the doomed vessel, and scatters its fragments o'er the tide, growling in joy—these, as the poet describes them, constitute the poetical glory of " The Shipwreck," and these have little connexion with art, and much with nature.

Lord Byron was better at emulating than at criticising Falconer's *chef-d'œuvre*.   We have already once or twice alluded to *his* Shipwreck—surely the grandest and most characteristic effort of his genius, in its demoniac force, and demoniac spirit.   As we have elsewhere said, " he describes the horrors of a shipwreck, like a fiend who had, invisible, sat amid the shrouds, choked with laughter—with immeasurable glee had heard the wild farewell rising from sea to sky—had leaped into the long-boat as it put off with its pale crew—had gloated o'er the cannibal repast—had leered, unseen, into the ' dim eyes of those shipwreck'd men '— and with a loud and savage burst of derision had seen them at length sinking into the waves."   The superiority of his picture over Falconer's, lies in the simplicity and strength of the style, in the ease of the narrative, in the variety of the incidents and characters, and in certain short masterly touches, now of pathos, now of infernal humour, and now of description, competent only to Byron and to Shakspeare.   Such are,—

> " Then shriek'd the timid and stood still the brave."
>> " The bubbling cry
> Of some strong swimmer in his agony."
>> " For he, poor fellow, had a wife and children,
>> Two things to dying people quite bewildering,"—

and the inimitable description of the rainbow, closing with,—

>> " Then changed like to a bow that 's bent, and then—
>> Forsook the dim eyes of these shipwreck'd men."

The technicalities introduced are fewer ; and are handled with greater force, and made to tell more on the general effect. You marvel, too, at the versatility of the writer, who seems this moment to be looking at the scene with the eye of the melancholy Jacques ; the next, with the philosophical aspect of the moralizing Hamlet ; the next, with the rage of a misanthropical Timon ; and the next, with the bitter sneer of a malignant Iago : and yet, who, amidst all these disguises, leaves on you the impression that he is throughout acting the part, and displaying the spirit, of a demon—a deep current of mockery at man's miseries, and at God's providence, running under all his moods and imitations. We read it once, when recovering from an illness, and shall never forget the withering horror, and the shock of disgust and loathing, which it gave to our weakened nerves.

Since Falconer's time, besides Byron, Scott, in the Pirate, and Cooper, there has not, as we hinted, been much of the poetical extracted from the sea. The subject suggested in Boswell's Johnson, by General Oglethorpe, as a noble theme for a poem—namely, " The Mediterranean," is still unsung, at least by any competent bard. Mrs Hemans has one sweet strain on the " Treasures of the Deep." Allan Cunningham's " Wet Sheet and Flowing Sea," and Barry Cornwall's " The Sea, the Sea," are in everybody's mouth. We remember a young student at Glasgow College, long since dead—George Gray by name—a thin lame lad, with dark mild eyes, and a fine spiritual expression on his pale face, handing in to Professor Milne of the Moral Philosophy class, some lines which he read to his class, and by which they, as well as the old, arid, although profound and ingenious philosopher, were perfectly electrified. We shall quote all we remember of them, and it will be thought much, when we state that twenty-five years have elapsed since we read them. They began—

> " The storm is up ; the anchor spring,
> And man the sails, my merry men ;
> I must not lose the carolling
> Of ocean in a hurricane ;
> My soul mates with the mountain storm,
> The cooing gale disdains.
> Bring Ocean in his wildest form,
> All booming thunder-strains ;
> I 'll bid him welcome, clap his mane ;
> I 'll dip my temples in his yeast,
> And hug his breakers to my breast ;
> And bid them hail ! all hail, I cry,
> My younger brethren hail !
>
> > The sea shall be my cemetery
> > Unto eternity.
>
> How glorious 'tis to have the wave
> For ever dashing o'er thee ;—
> Besides that dull and lonesome grave,
> Where worms and earth devour thee.
>
> My messmates, when ye drink my dirge,
> Go, fill the cup from ocean's surge ;
> And when ye drain the beverage up,
> Remember Neptune in the cup.
> For he has been my *brawling host,*
> Since first I roam'd from coast to coast ;
> And he my *brawling* host shall be—
> I love his ocean courtesy—
> His *boisterous* hospitality."

These lines, to us at least, seem to echo the rough roar of the breakers, as they rush upon an iron-bound coast. Poor G. Gray ! He now sleeps, not in the bosom of that old Ocean he loved so dearly, but, we think, in the kirkyard of Douglas, in the Upper Ward of Lanarkshire,—a light early quenched,— but whose memory this notice and these lines may, perhaps, for a season, preserve ! The SEA still lies over, after all written in prose or rhyme regarding it, as the subject for a great poem ; and it will task all the energies of even the truest poet.

FALCONER'S POEMS.

THE SHIPWRECK.

IN THREE CANTOS.

THE TIME EMPLOYED IN THIS POEM IS ABOUT SIX DAYS.

Quæque ipse miserrima vidi,
Et quorum pars magna fui.—VIRG. ÆN. lib. ii.

INTRODUCTION TO THE POEM.

WHILE jarring interests wake the world to arms,
And fright the peaceful vale with dire alarms,
While Albion bids the avenging thunder roll
Along her vassal deep from pole to pole ;
Sick of the scene, where War with ruthless hand
Spreads desolation o'er the bleeding land ;
Sick of the tumult, where the trumpet's breath
Bids ruin smile, and drowns the groan of death ;
'Tis mine, retired beneath this cavern hoar,
That stands all lonely on the sea-beat shore,   10
Far other themes of deep distress to sing
Than ever trembled from the vocal string :

A scene from dumb oblivion to restore,   13
To fame unknown, and new to epic lore ;
Where hostile elements conflicting rise,
And lawless surges swell against the skies,
Till hope expires, and peril and dismay
Wave their black ensigns on the watery way.
    Immortal train ! who guide the maze of song,
To whom all science, arts, and arms belong ;   20
Who bid the trumpet of eternal fame
Exalt the warrior's and the poet's name,
Or in lamenting elegies express
The varied pang of exquisite distress ;
If e'er with trembling hope I fondly stray'd
In life's fair morn beneath your hallow'd shade,
To hear the sweetly-mournful lute complain,
And melt the heart with ecstasy of pain,
Or listen to the enchanting voice of love,
While all Elysium warbled through the grove :   30
Oh ! by the hollow blast that moans around,
That sweeps the wild harp with a plaintive sound ;
By the long surge that foams through yonder cave,
Whose vaults remurmur to the roaring wave ;
With living colours give my verse to glow,
The sad memorial of a tale of woe !
The fate in lively sorrow to deplore
Of wanderers shipwreck'd on a leeward shore.
    Alas ! neglected by the sacred Nine,
Their suppliant feels no genial ray divine :   40
Ah ! will they leave Pieria's happy shore
To plough the tide where wintry tempests roar ?
Or shall a youth approach their hallow'd fane,
Stranger to Phœbus, and the tuneful train ?
Far from the Muses' academic grove
'Twas his the vast and trackless deep to rove ;

Alternate change of climates has he known,   47
And felt the fierce extremes of either zone :
Where polar skies congeal the eternal snow,
Or equinoctial suns for ever glow,
Smote by the freezing, or the scorching blast,
' A ship-boy on the high and giddy mast,' [1]
From regions where Peruvian billows roar,
To the bleak coasts of savage Labrador ;
From where Damascus, pride of Asian plains,
Stoops her proud neck beneath tyrannic chains,
To where the Isthmus,[2] laved by adverse tides,
Atlantic and Pacific seas divides :
But while he measured o'er the painful race
In fortune's wild illimitable chase,   60
Adversity, companion of his way,
Still o'er the victim hung with iron sway,
Bade new distresses every instant grow,
Marking each change of place with change of woe :
In regions where the Almighty's chastening hand
With livid pestilence afflicts the land,
Or where pale famine blasts the hopeful year,
Parent of want and misery severe ;
Or where, all-dreadful in the embattled line,
The hostile ships in flaming combat join,   70
Where the torn vessel wind and waves assail,
Till o'er her crew distress and death prevail.
Such joyless toils in early youth endured,
The expanding dawn of mental day obscured,
Each genial passion of the soul oppress'd,
And quench'd the ardour kindling in his breast.
Then censure not severe the native song,
Though jarring sounds the measured verse prolong,

[1] ' A ship-boy,' &c. = Shakspeare's 'Henry the Fourth,' act iii. — [2] ' Isthmus : ' of Darien.

M

Though terms uncouth offend the softer ear,   79
Yet truth and human anguish deign to hear :
No laurel wreath these lays attempt to claim,
Nor sculptured brass to tell the poet's name.
    And, lo ! the power that wakes the eventful song
Hastes hither from Lethean banks along :
She sweeps the gloom, and rushing on the sight,
Spreads o'er the kindling scene propitious light.
In her right hand an ample roll appears,
Fraught with long annals of preceding years,
With every wise and noble art of man,
Since first the circling hours their course began :   90
Her left a silver wand on high display'd,
Whose magic touch dispels oblivion's shade :
Pensive her look ; on radiant.wings that glow
Like Juno's birds, or Iris' flaming bow,
She sails ; and swifter than the course of light
Directs her rapid intellectual flight :
The fugitive ideas she restores,
And calls the wandering thought from Lethe's shores ;
To things long past a second date she gives,
And hoary time from her fresh youth receives ;   100
Congenial sister of immortal Fame,
She shares her power, and Memory is her name.
    O first-born daughter of primeval time !
By whom transmitted down in every clime
The deeds of ages long elapsed are known,
And blazon'd glories spread from zone to zone ;
Whose magic breath dispels the mental night,
And o'er the obscured idea pours the light :
Say on what seas, for thou alone canst tell,
What dire mishap a fated ship befell,   110
Assail'd by tempests, girt with hostile shores ?
Arise ! approach ! unlock thy treasured stores !

Full on my soul the dreadful scene display,   113
And give its latent horrors to the day.

CANTO I.

THE SCENE OF WHICH LIES NEAR THE CITY OF CANDIA.   TIME, ABOUT FOUR
DAYS AND A HALF.

THE ARGUMENT.

I. Retrospect of the voyage.   Arrival at Candia.   State of that island.
Season of the year described.— II. Character of the master, and his officers, Albert, Rodmond, and Arion.   Palemon, son to the owner of the
ship.   Attachment of Palemon to Anna, the daughter of Albert.—III.
Noon.   Palemon's history.—IV. Sunset.   Midnight.   Arion's dream.
Unmoor by moonlight.   Morning.   Sun's azimuth taken.   Beautiful appearance of the ship, as seen by the natives from the shore.

I. A SHIP from Egypt, o'er the deep impell'd
By guiding winds, her course for Venice held :
Of famed Britannia were the gallant crew,
And from that isle her name the vessel drew.
The wayward steps of fortune they pursued,
And sought in certain ills imagined good :
Though caution'd oft her slippery path to shun,
Hope still with promised joys allured them on ;
And, while they listen'd to her winning lore,
The softer scenes of peace could please no more.   10
Long absent they from friends and native home
The cheerless ocean were inured to roam ;
Yet Heaven, in pity to severe distress,
Had crown'd each painful voyage with success ;
Still, to compensate toils and hazards past,
Restored them to maternal plains at last.
   Thrice had the sun, to rule the varying year,
Across the equator roll'd his flaming sphere,

Since last the vessel spread her ample sail   19
From Albion's coast, obsequious to the gale ;
She o'er the spacious flood, from shore to shore
Unwearying wafted her commercial store ;
The richest ports of Afric she had view'd,
Thence to fair Italy her course pursued ;
Had left behind Trinacria's burning isle,
And visited the margin of the Nile.
And now that winter deepens round the pole,
The circling voyage hastens to its goal :
They, blind to fate's inevitable law,
No dark event to blast their hope foresaw ;   30
But from gay Venice soon expect to steer
For Britain's coast, and dread no perils near :
Inflamed by hope, their throbbing hearts, elate,
Ideal pleasures vainly antedate,
Before whose vivid intellectual ray
Distress recedes, and danger melts away.
Already British coasts appear to rise,
The chalky cliffs salute their longing eyes ;
Each to his breast, where floods of rapture roll,
Embracing strains the mistress of his soul ;   40
Nor less o'erjoy'd, with sympathetic truth,
Each faithful maid expects the approaching youth.
In distant souls congenial passions glow,
And mutual feelings mutual bliss bestow :
Such shadowy happiness their thoughts employ,
Illusion all, and visionary joy !
      Thus time elapsed, while o'er the pathless tide
Their ship through Grecian seas the pilots guide.
Occasion call'd to touch at Candia's shore,
Which, blest with favouring winds, they soon explore ;
The haven enter, borne before the gale,   5:
Despatch their commerce, and prepare to sail.

Eternal powers ! what ruins from afar
Mark the fell track of desolating war :
Here arts and commerce with auspicious reign
Once breathed sweet influence on the happy plain :
While o'er the lawn, with dance and festive song,
Young Pleasure led the jocund hours along :
In gay luxuriance Ceres too was seen
To crown the valleys with eternal green :
For wealth, for valour, courted and revered,
What Albion is, fair Candia then appear'd.
Ah ! who the flight of ages can revoke ?
The free-born spirit of her sons is broke,
They bow to Ottoman's imperious yoke.
No longer fame their drooping heart inspires,
For stern oppression quench'd its genial fires :
Though still her fields, with golden harvests crown'd,
Supply the barren shores of Greece around,
Sharp penury afflicts these wretched isles,
There hope ne'er dawns, and pleasure never smiles :
The vassal wretch contented drags his chain,
And hears his famish'd babes lament in vain.
These eyes have seen the dull reluctant soil
A seventh year mock the weary labourer's toil.
No blooming Venus, on the desert shore,
Now views with triumph captive gods adore ;
No lovely Helens now with fatal charms
Excite the avenging chiefs of Greece to arms ;
No fair Penelopes enchant the eye,
For whom contending kings were proud to die :
Here sullen beauty sheds a twilight ray,
While sorrow bids her vernal bloom decay :
Those charms, so long renown'd in classic strains,
Had dimly shone on Albion's happier plains !

Now in the southern hemisphere the sun   86
Through the bright Virgin, and the Scales, had run,
And on the Ecliptic wheel'd his winding way,
Till the fierce Scorpion felt his flaming ray.
Four days becalm'd the vessel here remains,   90
And yet no hopes of aiding wind obtains ;
For sickening vapours lull the air to sleep,
And not a breeze awakes the silent deep :
This, when the autumnal equinox is o'er,
And Phœbus in the north declines no more,
The watchful mariner, whom Heaven informs,
Oft deems the prelude of approaching storms.
No dread of storms the master's soul restrain,
A captive fetter'd to the oar of gain :
His anxious heart, impatient of delay,   100
Expects the winds to sail from Candia's bay,
Determined, from whatever point they rise,
To trust his fortune to the seas and skies.
     Thou living ray of intellectual fire,
Whose voluntary gleams my verse inspire,
Ere yet the deepening incidents prevail,
Till roused attention feel our plaintive tale ;
Record whom chief among the gallant crew
The unblest pursuit of fortune hither drew !
Can sons of Neptune, generous, brave, and bold,   110
In pain and hazard toil for sordid gold ?
     They can ! for gold too oft with magic art
Can rule the passions, and corrupt the heart :
This crowns the prosperous villain with applause,
To whom in vain sad merit pleads her cause ;
This strews with roses life's perplexing road,
And leads the way to pleasure's soft abode ;
This spreads with slaughter'd heaps the bloody plain,
And pours adventurous thousands o'er the main.

II. The stately ship with all her daring band   120
To skilful Albert own'd the chief command :
Though train'd in boisterous elements, his mind
Was yet by soft humanity refined ;
Each joy of wedded love at home he knew ;
Aboard, confest the father of his crew!
Brave, liberal, just, the calm domestic scene
Had o'er his temper breathed a gay serene :
Him Science taught by mystic lore to trace
The planets wheeling in eternal race ;
To mark the ship in floating balance held,   130
By earth attracted, and by seas repell'd ;
Or point her devious track through climes unknown
That leads to every shore and every zone.
He saw the moon through heaven's blue concave glide,
And into motion charm the expanding tide,
While earth impetuous round her axle rolls,
Exalts her watery zone, and sinks the poles ;
Light and attraction, from their genial source,
He saw still wandering with diminish'd force ;
While on the margin of declining day   140
Night's shadowy cone reluctant melts away—
Inured to peril, with unconquer'd soul,
The chief beheld tempestuous oceans roll :
O'er the wild surge when dismal shades preside,
His equal skill the lonely bark could guide ;
His genius, ever for the event prepared,
Rose with the storm, and all its dangers shared.
  Rodmond the next degree to Albert bore,
A hardy son of England's farthest shore,
Where bleak Northumbria pours her savage train   150
In sable squadrons o'er the northern main ;
That, with her pitchy entrails stored, resort,
A sooty tribe, to fair Augusta's port :

Where'er in ambush lurk the fatal sands,   154
They claim the danger, proud of skilful bands ;
For while with darkling course their vessels sweep
The winding shore, or plough the faithless deep,
O'er bar and shelf the watery path they sound
With dexterous arm, sagacious of the ground :
Fearless they combat every hostile wind,   160
Wheeling in mazy tracks, with course inclined :
Expert to moor where terrors line the road,
Or win the anchor from its dark abode ;
But drooping, and relax'd, in climes afar,
Tumultuous and undisciplined in war.
Such Rodmond was ; by learning unrefined,
That oft enlightens to corrupt the mind—
Boisterous of manners ; train'd in early youth
To scenes that shame the conscious cheek of truth ;
To scenes that nature's struggling voice control,   170
And freeze compassion rising in the soul :
Where the grim hell-hounds, prowling round the shore,
With foul intent the stranded bark explore :
Deaf to the voice of woe, her decks they board,
While tardy justice slumbers o'er her sword.
The indignant Muse, severely taught to feel,
Shrinks from a theme she blushes to reveal.
Too oft example, arm'd with poisons fell,
Pollutes the shrine where mercy loves to dwell :
Thus Rodmond, train'd by this unhallow'd crew,   180
The sacred social passions never knew.
Unskill'd to argue, in dispute yet loud,
Bold without caution, without honours proud ;
In art unschool'd, each veteran rule he prized,
And all improvement haughtily despised.
Yet, though full oft to future perils blind,
With skill superior glow'd his daring mind,

Through snares of death the reeling bark to guide,   188
When midnight shades involve the raging tide.
     To Rodmond, next in order of command,
Succeeds the youngest[1] of our naval band :
But what avails it to record a name
That courts no rank among the sons of fame ;
Whose vital spring had just begun to bloom,
When o'er it sorrow spread her sickening gloom ?
While yet a stripling, oft with fond alarms
His bosom danced to nature's boundless charms ;
On him fair science dawn'd in happier hour,
Awakening into bloom young fancy's flower :
But soon adversity, with freezing blast,   200
The blossom wither'd, and the dawn o'ercast.
Forlorn of heart, and by severe decree
Condemn'd reluctant to the faithless sea,
With long farewell he left the laurel grove,
Where science and the tuneful sisters rove—
Hither he wander'd, anxious to explore
Antiquities of nations now no more ;
To penetrate each distant realm unknown,
And range excursive o'er the untravell'd zone.
In vain—for rude adversity's command   210
Still on the margin of each famous land,
With unrelenting ire his steps opposed,
And every gate of hope against him closed.
Permit my verse, ye blest Pierian train !
To call Arion this ill-fated swain ;
For, like that bard unhappy, on his head
Malignant stars their hostile influence shed :
Both, in lamenting numbers, o'er the deep
With conscious anguish taught the harp to weep ;

[1] ' The youngest : ' Falconer himself.

And both the raging surge in safety bore   220
Amid destruction, panting to the shore :
This last, our tragic story from the wave
Of dark oblivion haply yet may save ;
With genuine sympathy may yet complain,
While sad remembrance bleeds at every vein.
    These, chief among the ship's conducting train,
Her path explored along the deep domain ;
Train'd to command, and range the swelling sail,
Whose varying force conforms to every gale.
Charged with the commerce, hither also came   230
A gallant youth, Palemon was his name :
A father's stern resentment doom'd to prove,
He came the victim of unhappy love !
His heart for Albert's beauteous daughter bled,
For her a sacred flame his bosom fed :
Nor let the wretched slaves of folly scorn
This genuine passion, nature's eldest born !
'Twas his with lasting anguish to complain,
While blooming Anna mourn'd the cause in vain.
    Graceful of form, by nature taught to please,   240
Of power to melt the female breast with ease ;
To her Palemon told his tender tale,
Soft as the voice of summer's evening gale :
His soul, where moral truth spontaneous grew,
No guilty wish, no cruel passion knew :
Though tremblingly alive to nature's laws,
Yet ever firm to honour's sacred cause ;
O'erjoy'd he saw her lovely eyes relent,
The blushing maiden smiled with sweet consent.
Oft in the mazes of a neighbouring grove   250
Unheard they breathed alternate vows of love :
By fond society their passion grew,
Like the young blossom fed with vernal dew ;

While their chaste souls possess'd the pleasing pains 254
That truth improves, and virtue ne'er restrains.
In evil hour the officious tongue of fame
Betray'd the secret of their mutual flame.
With grief and anger struggling in his breast,
Palemon's father heard the tale confest :
Long had he listen'd with suspicion's ear,   260
And learn'd, sagacious, this event to fear.
Too well, fair youth ! thy liberal heart he knew,
A heart to nature's warm impressions true :
Full oft his wisdom strove with fruitless toil
With avarice to pollute that generous soil :
That soil, impregnated with nobler seed,
Refused the culture of so rank a weed.
Elate with wealth in active commerce won,
And basking in the smile of fortune's sun ;
For many freighted ships from shore to shore,   270
Their wealthy charge by his appointment bore :
With scorn the parent eyed the lowly shade
That veil'd the beauties of this charming maid.
He, by the lust of riches only moved,
Such mean connexions haughtily reproved :
Indignant he rebuked the enamour'd boy,
The flattering promise of his future joy :
He soothed and menaced, anxious to reclaim
This hopeless passion, or divert its aim :
Oft led the youth where circling joys delight   280
The ravish'd sense, or beauty charms the sight.
With all her powers enchanting music fail'd,
And pleasure's syren voice no more prevail'd :
Long with unequal art, in vain he strove
To quench the ethereal flame of ardent love.
The merchant, kindling then with proud disdain,
In look and voice assumed a harsher strain.

In absence now his only hope remain'd ;   288
And such the stern decree his will ordain'd :
Deep anguish, while Palemon heard his doom,
Drew o'er his lovely face a saddening gloom;
High beat his heart, fast flow'd the unbidden tear,
His bosom heaved with agony severe :
In vain with bitter sorrow he repined,
No tender pity touch'd that sordid mind—
To thee, brave Albert ! was the charge consign'd.
The stately ship, forsaking England's shore,
To regions far remote Palemon bore.
Incapable of change, the unhappy youth
Still loved fair Anna with eternal truth;   300
Still Anna's image swims before his sight
In fleeting vision through the restless night;
From clime to clime an exile doom'd to roam,
His heart still panted for its secret home.
     The moon had circled twice her wayward zone,
To him since young Arion first was known ;
Who, wandering here through many a scene renown'd,
In Alexandria's port the vessel found;
Where, anxious to review his native shore,
He on the roaring wave embark'd once more.   310
Oft by pale Cynthia's melancholy light
With him Palemon kept the watch of night,
In whose sad bosom many a sigh suppress'd
Some painful secret of the soul confess'd :
Perhaps Arion soon the cause divined,
Though shunning still to probe a wounded mind;
He felt the chastity of silent woe,
Though glad the balm of comfort to bestow.
He with Palemon oft recounted o'er
The tales of hapless love in ancient lore,   320
Recall'd to memory by the adjacent shore :

The scene thus present, and its story known,   322
The lover sigh'd for sorrows not his own.
Thus, though a recent date their friendship bore,
Soon the ripe metal own'd the quickening ore;
For in one tide their passions seem'd to roll,
By kindred age and sympathy of soul.
  These o'er the inferior naval train preside,
The course determine, or the commerce guide :
O'er all the rest an undistinguish'd crew,   330
Her wing of deepest shade oblivion drew.
  A sullen languor still the skies oppress'd,
And held the unwilling ship in strong arrest:
High in his chariot glow'd the lamp of day,
O'er Ida flaming with meridian ray;
Relax'd from toil the sailors range the shore,
Where famine, war, and storm are felt no more;
The hour to social pleasure they resign,
And black remembrance drown in generous wine.
On deck, beneath the shading canvas spread,   340
Rodmond a rueful tale of wonders read
Of dragons roaring on the enchanted coast;
The hideous goblin, and the yelling ghost :
But with Arion, from the sultry heat
Of noon, Palemon sought a cool retreat.
And, lo ! the shore with mournful prospects crown'd,[1]
The rampart torn with many a fatal wound,
The ruin'd bulwark tottering o'er the strand,
Bewail the stroke of war's tremendous hand :
What scenes of woe this hapless isle o'erspread !   350
Where late thrice fifty thousand warriors bled.

[1] ' Mournful prospects crown'd,' &c.: these remarks allude to the ever-
memorable siege of Candia, which was taken from the Venetians by the Turks
in 1669; being then considered as impregnable, and esteemed the most for-
midable fortress in the universe.

Full twice twelve summers were yon towers assail'd, 352
Till barbarous Ottoman at last prevail'd;
While thundering mines the lovely plains o'erturn'd,
While heroes fell, and domes and temples burn'd.
 III. But now before them happier scenes arise,
Elysian vales salute their ravish'd eyes;
Olive and cedar form'd a grateful shade,
Where light with gay romantic error stray'd :
The myrtles here with fond caresses twine,   360
There, rich with nectar, melts the pregnant vine :
And, lo! the stream renown'd in classic song,
Sad Lethe, glides the silent vale along.
On mossy banks, beneath the citron grove,
The youthful wanderers found a wild alcove;
Soft o'er the fairy region languor stole,
And with sweet melancholy charm'd the soul.
Here first Palemon, while his pensive mind
For consolation on his friend reclined,
In pity's bleeding bosom pour'd the stream 370
Of love's soft anguish, and of grief supreme :
" Too true thy words! by sweet remembrance taught,
My heart in secret bleeds with tender thought;
In vain it courts the solitary shade,
By every action, every look betray'd :
The pride of generous woe disdains appeal
To hearts that unrelenting frosts congeal;
Yet sure, if right Palemon can divine,
The sense of gentle pity dwells in thine :
Yes! all his cares thy sympathy shall know, 380
And prove the kind companion of his woe.
 " Albert thou know'st with skill and science graced,
In humble station though by fortune placed,
Yet never seaman more serenely brave
Led Britain's conquering squadrons o'er the wave :

Where full in view Augusta's spires are seen,   386
With flowery lawns and waving woods between,
An humble habitation rose, beside
Where Thames meandering rolls his ample tide :
There live the hope and pleasure of his life,
A pious daughter, and a faithful wife :
For his return with fond officious care,
Still every grateful object these prepare :
Whatever can allure the smell or sight,
Or wake the drooping spirits to delight.
" This blooming maid in virtue's path to guide
The admiring parents all their care applied ;
Her spotless soul to soft affection train'd,
No voice untuned, no sickening folly stain'd !
Not fairer grows the lily of the vale,   400
Whose bosom opens to the vernal gale :
Her eyes, unconscious of their fatal charms,
Thrill'd every heart with exquisite alarms :
Her face, in beauty's sweet attraction dress'd,
The smile of maiden innocence express'd ;
While health, that rises with the new-born day,
Breathed o'er her cheek the softest blush of May :
Still in her look complacence smiled serene ;
She moved the charmer of the rural scene !
" 'Twas at that season when the fields resume   410
Their loveliest hues, array'd in vernal bloom :
Yon ship, rich freighted from the Italian shore,
To Thames' fair banks her costly tribute bore :
While thus my father saw his ample hoard,
From this return, with recent treasures stored,
Me, with affairs of commerce charged, he sent
To Albert's humble mansion—soon I went !
Too soon, alas ! unconscious of the event.

There, struck with sweet surprise and silent awe,   419
The gentle mistress of my hopes I saw;
There, wounded first by love's resistless arms,
My glowing bosom throbb'd with strange alarms:
My ever charming Anna! who alone
Can all the frowns of cruel fate atone;
Oh! while all-conscious memory holds her power,
Can I forget that sweetly-painful hour,
When from those eyes, with lovely lightning fraught,
My fluttering spirits first the infection caught?
When as I gazed, my faltering tongue betray'd
The heart's quick tumults, or refused its aid;   430
While the dim light my ravish'd eyes forsook,
And every limb, unstrung with terror, shook;
With all her powers dissenting reason strove
To tame at first the kindling flame of love:
She strove in vain; subdued by charms divine,
My soul a victim fell at beauty's shrine.
Oft from the din of bustling life I stray'd,
In happier scenes to see my lovely maid;
Full oft, where Thames his wandering current leads,
We roved at evening hour through flowery meads;   440
There, while my heart's soft anguish I reveal'd,
To her with tender sighs my hope appeal'd.
While the sweet nymph my faithful tale believed,
Her snowy breast with secret tumult heaved;
For, train'd in rural scenes from earliest youth,
Nature was hers, and innocence and truth:
She never knew the city damsel's art,
Whose frothy pertness charms the vacant heart.
My suit prevail'd! for love inform'd my tongue,
And on his votary's lips persuasion hung.   450
Her eyes with conscious sympathy withdrew,
And o'er her cheek the rosy current flew.

Thrice happy hours ! where with no dark allay   4.
Life's fairest sunshine gilds the vernal day;
For here the sigh that soft affection heaves,
From stings of sharper woe the soul relieves:
Elysian scenes ! too happy long to last,
Too soon a storm the smiling dawn o'ercast;
Too soon some demon to my father bore
The tidings that his heart with anguish tore.   4.
My pride to kindle, with dissuasive voice
Awhile he labour'd to degrade my choice:
Then, in the whirling wave of pleasure, sought
From its loved object to divert my thought.
With equal hope he might attempt to bind
In chains of adamant the lawless wind;
For love had aim'd the fatal shaft too sure,
Hope fed the wound, and absence knew no cure.
With alienated look, each art he saw
Still baffled by superior nature's law.   4.
His anxious mind on various schemes revolved,
At last on cruel exile he resolved;
The rigorous doom was fix'd; alas, how vain
To him of tender anguish to complain!
His soul, that never love's sweet influence felt,
By social sympathy could never melt:
With stern command to Albert's charge he gave
To waft Palemon o'er the distant wave.
   " The ship was laden and prepared to sail,
And only waited now the leading gale: 4.
'Twas ours, in that sad period, first to prove
The poignant torments of despairing love,
The impatient wish that never feels repose,
Desire that with perpetual current flows,
The fluctuating pangs of hope and fear,
Joy distant still, and sorrow ever near.

                     N

Thus, while the pangs of thought severer grew,   487
The western breezes inauspicious blew,
Hastening the moment of our last adieu.
The vessel parted on the falling tide,
Yet time one sacred hour to love supplied:
The night was silent, and advancing fast,
The moon o'er Thames her silver mantle cast;
Impatient hope the midnight path explored,
And led me to the nymph my soul adored.
Soon her quick footsteps struck my listening ear;
She came confest! the lovely maid drew near!
But, ah! what force of language can impart
The impetuous joy that glow'd in either heart?
O ye! whose melting hearts are form'd to prove   500
The trembling ecstasies of genuine love;
When, with delicious agony, the thought
Is to the verge of high delirium wrought:
Your secret sympathy alone can tell
What raptures then the throbbing bosom swell:
O'er all the nerves what tender tumults roll,
While love with sweet enchantment melts the soul.
    " In transport lost, by trembling hope imprest,
The blushing virgin sunk upon my breast,
While hers congenial beat with fond alarms;   510
Dissolving softness! Paradise of charms!
Flash'd from our eyes, in warm transfusion flew
Our blending spirits that each other drew!
O bliss supreme! where virtue's self can melt
With joys that guilty pleasure never felt;
Form'd to refine the thought with chaste desire,
And kindle sweet affection's purest fire.
Ah! wherefore should my hopeless love, she cries,—
While sorrow bursts with interrupting sighs,—

For ever destined to lament in vain,   52
Such flattering, fond ideas entertain?
My heart through scenes of fair illusion stray'd,
To joys decreed for some superior maid.
'Tis mine, abandon'd to severe distress,
Still to complain, and never hope redress—
Go then, dear youth! thy father's rage atone,
And let this tortured bosom beat alone.
The hovering anger yet thou mayst appease:
Go then, dear youth! nor tempt the faithless seas.
Find out some happier maid, whose equal charms   53
With fortune's fairer joys may bless thy arms:
Where, smiling o'er thee with indulgent ray,
Prosperity shall hail each new-born day:
Too well thou know'st good Albert's niggard fate
Ill fitted to sustain thy father's hate.
Go then, I charge thee by thy generous love,
That fatal to my father thus may prove;
On me alone let dark affliction fall,
Whose heart for thee will gladly suffer all.
Then haste thee hence, Palemon, ere too late,   .   54
Nor rashly hope to brave opposing fate.
   "She ceased: while anguish in her angel-face
O'er all her beauties shower'd celestial grace:
Not Helen, in her bridal charms array'd,
Was half so lovely as this gentle maid.—
O soul of all my wishes! I replied,
Can that soft fabric stem affliction's tide?
Canst thou, bright pattern of exalted truth,
To sorrow doom the summer of thy youth,
And I, ingrateful! all that sweetness see   5£
Consign'd to lasting misery for me?
Sooner this moment may the eternal doom
Palemon in the silent earth entomb:

Attest, thou moon, fair regent of the night!   554
Whose lustre sickens at this mournful sight:
By all the pangs divided lovers feel,
Which sweet possession only knows to heal;
By all the horrors brooding o'er the deep,
Where fate, and ruin, sad dominion keep;
Though tyrant duty o'er me threatening stands,   560
And claims obedience to her stern commands,
Should fortune cruel or auspicious prove,
Her smile or frown shall never change my love:
My heart, that now must every joy resign,
Incapable of change, is only thine.
    " Oh, cease to weep, this storm will yet decay,
And the sad clouds of sorrow melt away:
While through the rugged path of life we go,
All mortals taste the bitter draught of woe:
The famed and great, decreed to equal pain,   570
Full oft in splendid wretchedness complain:
For this, prosperity, with brighter ray,
In smiling contrast gilds our vital day.
Thou, too, sweet maid! ere twice ten months are o'er,
Shalt hail Palemon to his native shore,
Where never interest shall divide us more.——
    " Her struggling soul, o'erwhelm'd with tender grief,
Now found an interval of short relief:
So melts the surface of the frozen stream
Beneath the wintry sun's departing beam.   580
With cruel haste the shades of night withdrew,
And gave the signal of a sad adieu.
As on my neck the afflicted maiden hung,
A thousand racking doubts her spirit wrung:
She wept the terrors of the fearful wave,
Too oft, alas! the wandering lover's grave:

With soft persuasion I dispell'd her fear,
And from her cheek beguiled the falling tear,
While dying fondness languish'd in her eyes,
She pour'd her soul to heaven in suppliant sighs !
' Look down with pity, O ye powers above !
Who hear the sad complaint of bleeding love ;
Ye, who the secret laws of fate explore,
Alone can tell if he returns no more ;
Or if the hour of future joy remain,
Long-wish'd atonement of long-suffer'd pain ;
Bid every guardian minister attend,
And from all ill the much-loved youth defend !'
With grief o'erwhelm'd we parted twice in vain,
And, urged by strong attraction, met again.
At last, by cruel fortune torn apart,
While tender passion beat in either heart,
Our eyes transfix'd with agonizing look,
One sad farewell, one last embrace, we took.
Forlorn of hope the lovely maid I left,
Pensive and pale, of every joy bereft :
She to her silent couch retired to weep,
Whilst I embark'd, in sadness, on the deep."
　　His tale thus closed, from sympathy of grief
Palemon's bosom felt a sweet relief :
To mutual friendship thus sincerely true,
No secret wish, or fear their bosoms knew ;
In mutual hazards oft severely tried,
Nor hope, nor danger, could their love divide.
　　Ye tender maids ! in whose pathetic souls
Compassion's sacred stream impetuous rolls,
Whose warm affections exquisitely feel
The secret wound you tremble to reveal ;
Ah! may no wanderer of the stormy main
Pour through your breasts the soft delicious bane ;

May never fatal tenderness approve   621
The fond effusions of their ardent love :
Oh ! warn'd, avoid the path that leads to woe,
Where thorns and baneful weeds alternate grow :
Let them severer stoic nymphs possess,
Whose stubborn passions feel no soft distress.
   Now, as the youths returning o'er the plain
Approach'd the lonely margin of the main,
First, with attention roused, Arion eyed
The graceful lover, form'd in nature's pride.   630
His frame the happiest symmetry display'd,
And locks of waving gold his neck array'd ;
In every look the Paphian graces shine,
Soft breathing o'er his cheek their bloom divine ;
With lighten'd heart he smiled serenely gay,
Like young Adonis, or the son of May.
Not Cytherea from a fairer swain
Received her apple on the Trojan plain.
   IV. The sun's bright orb, declining all serene,
Now glanced obliquely o'er the woodland scene ;   640
Creation smiles around ; on every spray
The warbling birds exalt their evening lay ;
Blithe skipping o'er yon hill, the fleecy train
Join the deep chorus of the lowing plain ;
The golden lime and orange there were seen
On fragrant branches of perpetual green ;
The crystal streams that velvet meadows lave,
To the green ocean roll with chiding wave.
The glassy ocean, hush'd, forgets to roar,
But trembling murmurs on the sandy shore ;   650
And, lo ! his surface lovely to behold,
Glows in the west, a sea of living gold !
While all above a thousand liveries gay
The skies with pomp ineffable array.

Arabian sweets perfume the happy plains ;   €
Above, beneath, around, enchantment reigns !
While glowing Vesper leads the starry train,
And night slow draws her veil o'er land and main,
Emerging clouds the azure east invade,
And wrap the lucid spheres in gradual shade ;   €
While yet the songsters of the vocal grove,
With dying numbers tune the soul to love :
With joyful eyes the attentive master sees
The auspicious omens of an eastern breeze.
Round the charged bowl the sailors form a ring ;
By turns recount the wondrous tale, or sing,
As love, or battle, hardships of the main,
Or genial wine, awake the homely strain.
Then some the watch of night alternate keep :
The rest lie buried in oblivious sleep.   €
     Deep midnight now involves the livid skies,
When eastern breezes, yet enervate, rise :
The waning moon behind a watery shroud
Pale glimmer'd o'er the long protracted cloud ;
A mighty halo round her silver throne,
With parting meteors cross'd, portentous shone :
This in the troubled sky full oft prevails,
Oft deem'd a signal of tempestuous gales.
     While young Arion sleeps, before his sight
Tumultuous swim the visions of the night :   (
Now blooming Anna with her happy swain
Approach'd the sacred hymeneal fane ;
Anon tremendous lightnings flash between,
And funeral pomp, and weeping loves are seen :
Now with Palemon, up a rocky steep,
Whose summit trembles o'er the roaring deep,
With painful step he climb'd ; while far above
Sweet Anna charm'd them with the voice of love :

Then sudden from the slippery height they fell,   689
While dreadful yawn'd beneath the jaws of hell.
Amid this fearful trance, a thundering sound
He hears, and thrice the hollow decks rebound:
Upstarting from his couch, on deck he sprung,
Thrice with shrill note the boatswain's whistle rung:
All hands unmoor! proclaims a boisterous cry;
All hands unmoor! the cavern'd rocks reply.
Roused from repose, aloft the sailors swarm,
And with their levers soon the windlass arm:
The order given, up-springing with a bound,
They fix the bars, and heave the windlass[1] round;   700
At every turn the clanging pauls resound:
Up-torn reluctant from its oozy cave,
The ponderous anchor rises o'er the wave.
High on the slippery masts the yards ascend,
And far abroad the canvas wings extend.
Along the glassy plain the vessel glides,
While azure radiance trembles on her sides;
The lunar rays in long reflection gleam,
With silver deluging the fluid stream.
Levant and Thracian gales alternate play,   710
Then in the Egyptian quarter die away.
A calm ensues; adjacent shores they dread;
The boats, with rowers mann'd, are sent ahead;
With cordage fasten'd to the lofty prow,
Aloof to sea the stately ship they tow;[2]
The nervous crew their sweeping oars extend,
And pealing shouts the shore of Candia rend:

---

[1] 'Windlass:' the windlass is a sort of large roller, used to wind in the
cable, or heave up the anchor. It is turned about vertically, by a number of
long bars or levers; in which operation it is prevented from recoiling, by the
'pauls,' ver. 701.—[2] 'Ship they tow:' towing is the operation of drawing a
ship forward by means of ropes, extending from her fore-part to one or more
of the boats rowing before her.

Success attends their skill! the danger's o'er! 718
The port is doubled, and beheld no more.
　　Now morn with gradual pace advanced on high,
Whitening with orient beam the twilight sky:
She comes not in refulgent pomp array'd,
But frowning stern, and wrapt in sullen shade.
Above incumbent mists, tall Ida's height,
Tremendous rock! emerges on the sight;
North-east a league, the Isle of Standia bears,
And westward, Freschin's woody Cape appears.
　　In distant angles while the transient gales
Alternate blow, they trim the flagging sails;
The drowsy air attentive to retain, 730
As from unnumber'd points it sweeps the main.
Now swelling stud-sails[1] on each side extend,
Then stay-sails[2] sidelong to the breeze ascend;
While all to court the veering winds are placed
With yards alternate square, and sharply braced.
　　The dim horizon lowering vapours shroud,
And blot the sun yet struggling in the cloud;
Through the wide atmosphere, condensed with haze,
His glaring orb emits a sanguine blaze.
The pilots now their azimuth attend, 740
On which all courses duly form'd depend:
The compass placed to catch the rising ray,[3]
The quadrant's shadows studious they survey;
Along the arch the gradual index slides,
While Phœbus down the vertic-circle glides;

[1] 'Stud-sails:' studding-sails are long, narrow sails, which are only used in fine weather and fair winds, on the outside of the larger square sails.— [2] 'Stay-sails,' are three-cornered sails, which are hoisted up on the stays, when the wind crosses the ship's course, either directly or obliquely.— [3] 'Catch the rising ray:' the operation of taking the sun's azimuth, in order to discover the eastern or western variation of the magnetical needle.

Now seen on ocean's utmost verge to swim,   746
He sweeps it vibrant with his nether limb.
Thus height and polar distance are obtain'd,
Then latitude and declination gain'd ;
In chiliads next the analogy is sought,
And on the sinical triangle wrought :
By this magnetic variance is explored,
Just angles known, and polar truth restored.
    The natives, while the ship departs their land,
Ashore with admiration gazing stand.
Majestically slow, before the breeze
She moved triumphant o'er the yielding seas ;
Her bottom through translucent waters shone,
White as the clouds beneath the blaze of noon;
The bending wales[1] their contrast next display'd,   760
All fore and aft in polish'd jet array'd.
Britannia, riding awful on the prow,
Gazed o'er the vassal waves that roll'd below :
Where'er she moved the vassal waves were seen
To yield obsequious, and confess their queen.
The imperial trident graced her dexter hand,
Of power to rule the surge, like Moses' wand;
The eternal empire of the main to keep,
And guide her squadrons o'er the trembling deep.
Her left, propitious, bore a mystic shield,   770
Around whose margin rolls the watery field ;
There her bold genius in his floating car
O'er the wild billow, hurls the storm of war :
And, lo ! the beasts[2] that oft with jealous rage
In bloody combat met, from age to age,

---

[1] ' Bending wales : ' the wales, here alluded to, are an assemblage of strong planks which envelop the lower part of the ship's side, wherein they are broader and thicker than the rest, and appear somewhat like a range of hoops which separates the bottom from the upper works. — [2] ' Beasts : ' the lion and unicorn.

Tamed into union, yoked in friendship's chain,   776
Draw his proud chariot round the vanquish'd main ;
From the proud margin to the centre grew
Shelves, rocks, and whirlpools, hideous to the view.
The immortal shield from Neptune she received,
When first her head above the waters heaved ;
Loose floated o'er her limbs an azure vest,
A figured 'scutcheon glitter'd on her breast ;
There from one parent soil for ever young,
The blooming rose and hardy thistle sprung :
Around her head an oaken wreath was seen,
Inwove with laurels of unfading green.
    Such was the sculptured prow ; from van to rear
The artillery frown'd, a black tremendous tier !
Embalm'd with orient gum, above the wave   790
The swelling sides a yellow radiance gave.
On the broad stern, a pencil warm and bold,
That never servile rules of art controll'd,
An allegoric tale on high portray'd ;
There a young hero, here a royal maid :
Fair England's genius in the youth express'd,
Her ancient foe, but now her friend confess'd,
The warlike nymph with fond regard survey'd ;
No more his hostile frown her heart dismay'd :
His look, that once shot terror from afar,   800
Like young Alcides, or the god of war,
Serene as summer's evening skies she saw ;
Serene, yet firm ; though mild, impressing awe :
Her nervous arm, inured to toils severe,
Brandish'd the unconquer'd Caledonian spear :
The dreadful falchion of the hills she wore,
Sung to the harp in many a tale of yore,
That oft her rivers dyed with hostile gore.

Blue was her rocky shield; her piercing eye   809
Flash'd like the meteors of her native sky;
Her crest high-plumed, was rough with many a scar,
And o'er her helmet gleam'd the Northern Star.
The warrior youth appear'd of noble fràme,
The hardy offspring of some Runic dame :
Loose o'er his shoulders hung the slacken'd bow,
Renown'd in song, the terror of the foe !
The sword that oft the barbarous north defied,
The scourge of tyrants ! glitter'd by his side :
Clad in refulgent arms in battle won,
The George emblazon'd on his corslet shone ;   820
Fast by his side was seen a golden lyre,
Pregnant with numbers of eternal fire ;
Whose strings unlock the witches' midnight spell,
Or waft rapt fancy through the gulfs of hell :
Struck with contagion, kindling fancy hears
The songs of heaven, the music of the spheres !
Borne on Newtonian wing, through air she flies,
Where other suns to other systems rise.
    These front the scene conspicuous ; overhead
Albion's proud oak his filial branches spread :   830
While on the sea-beat shore obsequious stood,
Beneath their feet, the father of the flood :
Here the bold native of her cliffs above,
Perch'd by the martial maid the bird of Jove ;
There on the watch, sagacious of his prey,
With eyes of fire, an English mastiff lay :
Yonder fair Commerce stretch'd her wingèd sail,
Here frown'd the God that wakes the living gale.
High o'er the poop the flattering winds unfurl'd
The imperial flag that rules the watery world.   840
Deep blushing armors all the tops invest,
And warlike trophies either quarter dress'd ;

Then tower'd the masts, the canvas swell'd on high,   843
And waving streamers floated in the sky.
Thus the rich vessel moves in trim array,
Like some fair virgin on her bridal day;
Thus, like a swan, she cleaved the watery plain,
The pride and wonder of the Ægean main.

CANTO II.

THE SCENE LIES AT SEA, BETWEEN CAPE FRESCHIN IN CANDIA, AND THE
ISLAND OF FALCONERA, WHICH IS NEARLY TWELVE LEAGUES NORTH-
WARD OF CAPE SPADO.   TIME, FROM NINE IN THE MORNING UNTIL
ONE O'CLOCK OF THE NEXT DAY AT NOON.

THE ARGUMENT.

I. Reflections on leaving shore.—II. Favourable breeze.   Water-spout.   The
dying dolphin.   Breeze freshens.   Ship's rapid progress along the coast.
Top-sails reefed.   Gale of wind.   Last appearance, bearing, and distance
of Cape Spado.   A squall.   Top-sails double-reefed.   Main-sail split.
The ship bears up; again hauls upon the wind.   Another main-sail bent,
and set.   Porpoises.—III. The ship driven out of her course from Candia.
Heavy gale.   Top-sails furled.   Top-gallant-yards lowered.   Heavy
sea.   Threatening sun-set.   Difference of opinion respecting the mode of
taking in the main-sail.   Courses reefed.   Four seamen lost off the lee
mainyard-arm.   Anxiety of the master, and his mates, on being near a
lee-shore.   Mizen reefed.—IV. A tremendous sea bursts over the deck;
its consequences.   The ship labours in great distress.   Guns thrown over-
board.   Dismal appearance of the weather.   Very high and dangerous
sea.   Storm of lightning.   Severe fatigue of the crew at the pumps.
Critical situation of the ship near the Island of Falconera.   Consultation
and resolution of the officers.   Speech and advice of Albert; his devout
address to heaven.   Order given to scud.   The fore stay-sail hoisted and
split.   The head yards braced aback.   The mizen-mast cut away.

I. ADIEU! ye pleasures of the sylvan scene,
Where peace and calm contentment dwell serene:
To me, in vain, on earth's prolific soil,
With summer crown'd, the Elysian valleys smile:

To me those happier scenes no joy impart,
But tantalize with hope my aching heart.
Ye tempests! o'er my head congenial roll,
To suit the mournful music of my soul;
In black progression, lo, they hover near!
Hail, social horrors! like my fate severe:
Old Ocean hail! beneath whose azure zone
The secret deep lies unexplored, unknown.
Approach, ye brave companions of the sea!
And fearless view this awful scene with me.
Ye native guardians of your country's laws!
Ye brave assertors of her sacred cause!
The Muse invites you, judge if she depart,
Unequal, from the thorny rules of art.
In practice train'd, and conscious of her power,
She boldly moves to meet the trying hour:
Her voice attempting themes, before unknown
To music, sings distresses all her own.
    II. O'er the smooth bosom of the faithless tides,
Propell'd by flattering gales, the vessel glides:
Rodmond, exulting, felt the auspicious wind,
And by a mystic charm its aim confined.
The thoughts of home that o'er his fancy roll,
With trembling joy dilate Palemon's soul;
Hope lifts his heart, before whose vivid ray
Distress recedes, and danger melts away.
Tall Ida's summit now more distant grew,
And Jove's high hill[1] was rising to the view;
When on the larboard quarter they descry
A liquid column towering shoot on high;
The foaming base the angry whirlwinds sweep,
Where curling billows rouse the fearful deep:

---

[1] ' Jove's high hill: ' Dicte.

Still round and round the fluid vortex flies,   37
Diffusing briny vapours o'er the skies.
This vast phenomenon, whose lofty head,
In heaven immersed, embracing clouds o'erspread,
In spiral motion first, as seamen deem,
Swells, when the raging whirlwind sweeps the stream.
The swift volution, and the enormous train,
Let sages versed in nature's lore explain.
The horrid apparition still draws nigh,
And white with foam the whirling billows fly.
The guns were primed; the vessel northward veers,
Till her black battery on the column bears:
The nitre fired; and, while the dreadful sound,
Convulsive shook the slumbering air around,   50
The watery volume, trembling to the sky,
Burst down, a dreadful deluge, from on high!
The expanding ocean trembled as it fell,
And felt with swift recoil her surges swell;
But soon, this transient undulation o'er,
The sea subsides, the whirlwinds rage no more.
While southward now the increasing breezes veer,
Dark clouds incumbent on their wings appear:
Ahead they see the consecrated grove
Of Cyprus, sacred once to Cretan Jove.   60
The ship beneath her lofty pressure reels,
And to the freshening gale still deeper heels.
    But now, beneath the lofty vessel's stern,
A shoal of sportive dolphins they discern,
Beaming from burnish'd scales refulgent rays,
Till all the glowing ocean seems to blaze:
In curling wreaths they wanton on the tide,
Now bound aloft, now downward swiftly glide;
Awhile beneath the waves their tracks remain,
And burn in silver streams along the liquid plain.   70

Soon to the sport of death the crew repair,
Dart the long lance, or spread the baited snare.
One in redoubling mazes wheels along,
And glides unhappy near the triple prong:
Rodmond, unerring, o'er his head suspends
The barbed steel, and every turn attends;
Unerring aim'd, the missile weapon flew,
And, plunging, struck the fated victim through:
The upturning points his ponderous bulk sustain,
On deck he struggles with convulsive pain.
But while his heart the fatal javelin thrills,
And flitting life escapes in sanguine rills,
What radiant changes strike the astonish'd sight !
What glowing hues of mingled shade and light !
Not equal beauties gild the lucid west
With parting beams all o'er profusely drest;
Not lovelier colours paint the vernal dawn,
When orient dews impearl the enamell'd lawn,
Than from his sides in bright suffusion flow,
That now with gold empyreal seem to glow;
Now in pellucid sapphires meet the view,
And emulate the soft celestial hue;
Now beam a flaming crimson on the eye,
And now assume the purple's deeper dye:
But here description clouds each shining ray;
What terms of art can nature's powers display !
  The lighter sails, for summer winds and seas,
Are now dismiss'd, the straining masts to ease;
Swift on the deck the stud-sails all descend,
Which ready seamen from the yards unbend;
The boats then hoisted in are fix'd on board,
And on the deck with fastening gripes secured.
The watchful ruler of the helm no more
With fix'd attention eyes the adjacent shore,

But by the oracle of truth below,   105
The wondrous magnet guides the wayward prow.
The powerful sails, with steady breezes swell'd,
Swift and more swift the yielding bark impell'd :
Across her stem the parting waters run,
As clouds, by tempests wafted, pass the sun.   110
Impatient thus she darts along the shore,
Till Ida's mount, and Jove's, are seen no more ;
And, while aloof from Retimo she steers,
Maleca foreland full in front appears.
Wide o'er yon Isthmus stands the cypress grove,
That once enclosed the hallow'd fane of Jove :
Here, too, memorial of his name! is found
A tomb in marble ruins on the ground.
This gloomy tyrant, whose despotic sway
Compell'd the trembling nations to obey,   120
Through Greece for murder, rape, and incest known,
The Muses raised to high Olympus' throne ;
For oft, alas! their venal strains adorn
The prince whom blushing virtue holds in scorn :
Still Rome and Greece record his endless fame,
And hence yon mountain yet retains his name.
    But see! in confluence borne before the blast,
Clouds roll'd on clouds the dusky noon o'ercast :
The blackening ocean curls, the winds arise,
And the dark scud [1] in swift succession flies.   130
While the swoln canvas bends the masts on high,
Low in the wave the leeward [2] cannon lie.

[1] 'Dark scud:' scud is a name given by seamen to the lowest clouds,
which are driven with great rapidity along the atmosphere, in squally or tempestuous weather. — [2] 'Leeward:' When the wind crosses a ship's course
either directly or obliquely, that side of the ship, upon which it acts, is called
the weather-side ; and the opposite one, which is then pressed downwards, is
called the lee-side.   Hence all the rigging and furniture of the ship are, at
this time, distinguished by the side on which they are situated ; as the lee-
cannon, the lee-braces, the weather-braces, &c.

The master calls to give the ship relief,   133
The top-sails[1] lower, and form a single reef ![2]
Each lofty yard with slacken'd cordage reels ;
Rattle the creaking blocks and ringing wheels.
Down the tall masts the top-sails sink amain,
Are mann'd and reef'd, then hoisted up again.
More distant grew receding Candia's shore,
And southward of the west. Cape Spado bore.   140
    Four hours the sun his high meridian throne
Had left, and o'er Atlantic regions shone ;
Still blacker clouds, that all the skies invade,
Draw o'er his sullied orb a dismal shade :
A lowering squall obscures the southern sky,
Before whose sweeping breath the waters fly ;
Its weight the top-sails can no more sustain—
Reef top-sails, reef ! the master calls again.
The halyards and top-bow-lines[3] soon are gone,
To clue-lines and reef-tackles[4] next they run :   150
The shivering sails descend ; the yards are square ;
Then quick aloft the ready crew repair :
The weather-earings[5] and the lee they past,
The reefs enroll'd, and every point made fast.

---

[1] ' Top-sails : ' the top-sails are large square sails of the second degree in
height and magnitude. — [2] ' Reef : ' reefs are certain divisions or spaces by
which the principal sails are reduced when the wind increases ; and again enlarged proportionally when its force abates. — [3] ' Halyards and top-bow-
lines : ' halyards are either single ropes or tackles, by which the sails are
hoisted up and lowered when the sail is to be extended or reduced. Bow-
lines are ropes intended to keep the windward-edge of the sail steady, and
prevent it from shaking in an unfavourable wind. — [4] ' Clue-lines and reef-
tackles : ' clue-lines are ropes used to truss up the clues, or lower corners, of
the principal sails to their respective yards, particularly when the sail is to be
close-reefed or furled. Reef-tackles are ropes employed to facilitate the operation of reefing, by confining the extremities of the reef close up to the yard,
so that the interval becomes slack, and is therefore easily rolled up and fastened to the yard by the points employed for this purpose, ver. 154.— [5] ' Earings : ' small cords, by which the upper corners of the principal sails, and
also the extremities of the reefs, are fastened to the yard-arms.

Their task above thus finish'd, they descend,   155
And vigilant the approaching squall attend.
It comes resistless! and with foaming sweep
Upturns the whitening surface of the deep :
In such a tempest, borne to deeds of death,
The wayward sisters scour the blasted heath.   160
The clouds, with ruin pregnant, now impend ;
And storm, and cataracts, tumultuous blend.
Deep on her side the reeling vessel lies :
Brail up the mizen ¹ quick! the master cries,
Man the clue-garnets !² let the main-sheet fly!
It rends in thousand shivering shreds on high!
The main-sail all in streaming ruins tore,
Loud fluttering, imitates the thunder's roar :
The ship still labours in the oppressive strain,
Low bending, as if ne'er to rise again.   170
Bear up the helm a-weather !³ Rodmond cries :
Swift at the word the helm a-weather flies ;
She feels its guiding power, and veers apace,
And now the fore-sail right athwart they brace :
With equal sheets restrain'd, the bellying sail
Spreads a broad concave to the sweeping gale.
While o'er the foam the ship impetuous flies,
The helm the attentive timoneer⁴ applies :

¹ ' Mizen :' the mizen is a large sail of an oblong figure extended upon the
mizen-mast. — ² ' Clue-garnets,' are employed for the same purposes on the
main-sail and fore-sail as the clue-lines are upon all other square sails ; see
the note on ver. 150.   It is necessary in this place to remark, that the sheets,
which are universally mistaken by the English poets and their readers, for the
sails themselves, are no other than the ropes used to extend the clues, or lower
corners of the sails to which they are attached.   To the main-sail and fore-
sail there is a sheet and tack on each side ; the latter of which is a thick rope
serving to confine the weather-clue of the sail down to the ship's side, whilst
the former draws out the lee-clue or lower-corner on the opposite side.   Tacks
are only used in a side-wind. — ³ ' Helm a-weather :' the helm is said to be
a-weather when the bar by which it is managed is turned to the side of the
ship next the wind. — ⁴ ' Timoneer :' (from *timonnier*, Fr.) the helmsman,
or steersman.

As in pursuit along the aërial way   179
With ardent eye the falcon marks his prey,
Each motion watches of the doubtful chase,
Obliquely wheeling through the fluid space ;
So, govern'd by the steersman's glowing hands,
The regent helm her motion still commands.
    But now the transient squall to leeward past,
Again she rallies to the sullen blast :
The helm to starboard[1] moves ; each shivering sail
Is sharply trimm'd to clasp the augmenting gale.
The mizen draws ; she springs aloof once more,
While the fore stay-sail[2] balances before.   190
The fore-sail braced obliquely to the wind,
They near the prow the extended tack confined ;
Then on the leeward sheet the seamen bend,
And haul the bow-line to the bowsprit-end.
To top-sails next they haste ; the bunt-lines gone !
Through rattling blocks the clue-lines swiftly run ;
The extending sheets on either side are mann'd,
Abroad they come ! the fluttering sails expand ;
The yards again ascend each comrade mast.
The leeches taught, the halyards are made fast,   200
The bow-lines haul'd, and yards to starboard braced,[3]
And straggling ropes in pendent order placed.
    The main-sail, by the squall so lately rent,
In streaming pendants flying, is unbent :

---

[1] ' Helm to starboard : ' the helm, being turned to starboard, or to the right
side of the ship, directs the prow to the left, or to port, and *vice versâ.*
Hence the helm being put a-starboard, when the ship is running northward,
directs her prow towards the west. — [2] ' Fore stay-sail : ' this sail, which is
with more propriety called the fore topmast-stay-sail, is a triangular sail that
runs upon the fore topmast-stay, over the bowsprit. It is used to command
the fore-part of the ship, and counterbalance the sails extended towards the
stern. — [3] ' Yards to starboard braced : ' a yard is said to be braced when it
is turned about the mast horizontally, either to the right or left ; the ropes
employed in this service are accordingly called braces.

With brails[1] refix'd, another soon prepared,   205
Ascending, spreads along beneath the yard.
To each yard-arm the head-rope[2] they extend,
And soon their earings and their robans[3] bend.
That task perform'd, they first the braces slack,[4]
Then to the chesstree drag the unwilling tack.   210
And, while the lee clue-garnet's lower'd away,
Taught aft the sheet they tally, and belay.[5]
　　Now to the north from Afric's burning shore,
A troop of porpoises their course explore :
In curling wreaths they gambol on the tide,
Now bound aloft, now down the billow glide :
Their tracks awhile the hoary waves retain,
That burn in sparkling trails along the main——
These fleetest coursers of the finny race,
When threatening clouds the ethereal vault deface,   220
Their route to leeward still sagacious form,
To shun the fury of the approaching storm.
　　III. Fair Candia now no more, beneath her lee,
Protects the vessel from the insulting sea ;
Round her broad arms, impatient of control,
Roused from the secret deep, the billows roll :
Sunk were the bulwarks of the friendly shore,
And all the scene an hostile aspect wore.
The flattering wind, that late with promised aid
From Candia's bay the unwilling ship betray'd,   230

---

[1] ' Brails : ' the ropes used to truss up a sail to the yard or mast whereto it is attached, are in a general sense called brails. — [2] ' Head-rope : ' the head-rope is a cord to which the upper part of the sail is sewed. — [3] ' Robans : ' rope-bands, pronounced roebins, are small cords, used to fasten the upper edge of any sail to its respective yard. — [4] ' Braces slack : ' because the lee-brace confines the yard so that the tack will not come down to its place till the braces are cast loose. — [5] ' Taught,' ' tally,' and ' belay : ' taught implies stiff, tense, or extended straight ; and tally is a phrase particularly applied to the operation of hauling aft the sheets, or drawing them towards the ship's stern ; to belay, is to fasten.

No longer fawns beneath the fair disguise,   231
But like a ruffian on his quarry flies.
Tost on the tide she feels the tempest blow,
And dreads the vengeance of so fell a foe—
As the proud horse, with costly trappings gay,
Exulting, prances to the bloody fray;
Spurning the ground he glories in his might,
But reels tumultuous in the shock of fight :
Even so, caparison'd in gaudy pride,
The bounding vessel dances on the tide.   240
    Fierce and more fierce the gathering tempest grew,
South and by west the threatening demon blew ;
Auster's resistless force all air invades,
And every rolling wave more ample spreads :
The ship no longer can her top-sails bear ;
No hopes of milder weather now appear.
Bow-lines and halyards are cast off again,
Clue-lines haul'd down, and sheets let fly amain :
Embrail'd each top-sail, and by braces squared,
The seamen climb aloft, and man each yard :   250
They furl'd the sails, and pointed to the wind
The yards, by rolling tackles[1] then confined,
While o'er the ship the gallant boatswain flies;
Like a hoarse mastiff through the storm he cries—
Prompt to direct the unskilful still appears,
The expert he praises, and the timid cheers.
Now some, to strike top-gallant-yards[2] attend,
Some, travellers up the weather-back-stays[3] send,

[1] ' Rolling-tackles : ' the rolling-tackle is an assemblage of pulleys, used to confine the yard to the weather-side of the mast, and prevent the former from rubbing against the latter by the fluctuating motion of the ship in a turbulent sea. — [2] ' Strike top-gallant-yards : ' it is usual to send down the top-gallant yards on the approach of a storm ; they are the highest yards that are rigged in a ship. — [3] ' Travellers ' and ' back-stays : ' travellers are slender iron rings, encircling the back-stays, and used to facilitate the hoisting or lowering of the top-gallant-yards, by confining them to the backstays, in their ascent

At each mast-head the top-ropes[1] others bend :   259
The parrels, lifts,[2] and clue-lines soon are gone,
Topp'd and unrigg'd, they down the backstays run ;
The yards secure along the booms[3] were laid,
And all the flying ropes aloft belay'd :
Their sails reduced, and all the rigging clear,
Awhile the crew relax from toils severe ;
Awhile their spirits with fatigue opprest,
In vain expect the alternate hour of rest—
But with redoubling force the tempests blow,
And watery hills in dread succession flow :
A dismal shade o'ercasts the frowning skies ;   270
New troubles grow ; fresh difficulties rise ;
No season this from duty to descend,
All hands on deck must now the storm attend.
　　His race perform'd, the sacred lamp of day
Now dipt in western clouds his parting ray !
His languid fires, half lost in ambient haze,
Refract along the dusk a crimson blaze ;
Till deep immerged the sickening orb descends,
And cheerless night o'er heaven her reign extends.
Sad evening's hour, how different from the past !   280
No flaming pomp, no blushing glories cast,
No ray of friendly light is seen around ;
The moon and stars in hopeless shade are drown'd.

or descent, so as to prevent them from swinging about by the agitation of the vessel.   Back-stays are long ropes, extending from the right and left side of the ship to the topmast-heads, which they are intended to secure, by counter-acting the effort of the wind upon the sails. — [1] ' Top-ropes : ' cords by which the top-gallant-yards are hoisted up from the deck, or lowered again in stormy weather. — [2] ' Parrels,' and ' lifts : ' the parrel, which is usually a moveable band of rope, is employed to confine the yard to its respective mast. Lifts are ropes extending from the head of any mast to the extremities of its particular yard, to support the weight of the latter ; to retain it in balance ; or to raise one yard-arm higher than the other, which is accordingly called ' topping,' ver. 261. — [3] ' Booms : ' the booms in this place imply any masts or yards lying on the deck in reserve, to supply the place of others which may be carried away by distress of weather, &c.

The ship no longer can whole courses[1] bear,   284
To reef them now becomes the master's care;
The sailors summon'd aft all ready stand,
And man the enfolding brails at his command:
But here the doubtful officers dispute,
Till skill and judgment prejudice confute:
For Rodmond, to new methods still a foe,   290
Would first, at all events, the sheet let go;
To long-tried practice obstinately warm,
He doubts conviction, and relies on form.
This Albert and Arion disapprove,
And first to brail the tack up firmly move:
" The watchful seaman, whose sagacious eye
On sure experience may with truth rely,
Who from the reigning cause foretells the effect,
This barbarous practice ever will reject;
For, fluttering loose in air, the rigid sail   300
Soon flits to ruins in the furious gale;
And he, who strives the tempest to disarm,
Will never first embrail the lee yard-arm."
So Albert spoke; to windward, at his call,
Some seamen the clue-garnet stand to haul—
The tack's eased off,[2] while the involving clue
Between the pendent blocks ascending flew;
The sheet and weather-brace they now stand by,[3]
The lee clue-garnet and the bunt-lines ply:

[1] ' Courses:' the courses are generally understood to be the mainsail, fore-sail, and mizen, which are the largest and lowest sails on their several masts: the term is however sometimes taken in a larger sense.— [2] ' Tack's eased off:' it has been remarked before, in note to ver. 165, p. 211, that the tack is always fastened to windward; accordingly, as soon as it is cast loose, and the clue-garnet hauled up, the weather-clue of the sail immediately mounts to the yard; and this operation must be carefully performed in a storm, to prevent the sail from splitting, or being torn to pieces by shivering. — [3] ' Sheet and weather-brace they now stand by:' it is necessary to pull in the weather-brace, whenever the sheet is cast off, to preserve the sail from shaking violently.

Then, all prepared, Let go the sheet! he cries——   310
Loud rattling, jarring, through the blocks it flies!
Shivering at first, till by the blast impell'd,
High o'er the lee yard-arm the canvas swell'd;
By spilling lines[1] embraced, with brails confined,
It lies at length unshaken by the wind.
The fore-sail then secured with equal care,
Again to reef the mainsail they repair;
While some above the yard o'erhaul the tye,
Below the down-haul tackle[2] others ply;
Jears,[3] lifts, and brails, a seaman each attends,   320
And down the mast its mighty yard descends:
When lower'd sufficient they securely brace,
And fix the rolling tackle in its place;
The reef-lines[4] and their earings now prepared,
Mounting on pliant shrouds[5] they man the yard:
Far on the extremes appear two able hands,
For no inferior skill this task demands——
To wind, foremost, young Arion strides;
The lee yard-arm the gallant boatswain rides:
Each earing to its cringle first they bend,   330

---

[1] ' Spilling-lines : ' the spilling-lines, which are only used on particular occasions in tempestuous weather, are employed to draw together and confine
the belly of the sail, when it is inflated by the wind over the yard.— [2] ' Down-
haul-tackle : ' the violence of the wind forces the yard so much outward from
the mast on these occasions, that it cannot easily be lowered so as to reef the
sail, without the application of a tackle to haul it down on the mast.   This is
afterwards converted into rolling-tackle ; see the note on ver. 252, p. 214.—
[3] ' Jears ' are the same to the mainsail, foresail, and mizen, as the halyards
(note to ver. 149, p. 210), are to all the inferior sails.   The tye is the upper
part of the jears. — [4] ' Reef-lines ' are only used to reef the mainsail and
foresail; they are passed in spiral turns through the eye-let holes of the reef,
and over the head of the sails between the rope-band legs, till they reach the
extremities of the reef to which they are firmly extended, so as to lace the reef
close up to the yard. — [5] ' Shrouds ' are thick ropes, stretching from the mast-
heads downwards to the outside of the ship, serving to support the masts ;
they are also used as a range of rope-ladders by which the seamen ascend or
descend to perform whatever is necessary about the sails and rigging.

The reef-band[1] then along the yard extend;   331
The circling earings[2] round the extremes entwined,
By outer and by inner turns they bind;
The reef-lines next from hand to hand received,
Through eyelet-holes and roban-legs were reeved;
The folding reefs in plaits inroll'd they lay,
Extend the worming lines, and ends belay.

  Hadst thou, Arion! held the leeward post
While on the yard by mountain billows tost,
Perhaps oblivion o'er our tragic tale   340
Had then for ever drawn her dusky veil;
But ruling Heaven prolong'd thy vital date,
Severer ills to suffer and relate.

  For, while aloft the order those attend
To furl the main-sail, or on deck descend;
A sea,[3] up-surging with stupendous roll,
To instant ruin seems to doom the whole:
O friends, secure your hold! Arion cries—
It comes all dreadful! down the vessel lies
Half buried sideways; while, beneath it tost,   350
Four seamen off the lee yard-arm are lost:
Torn with resistless fury from their hold,
In vain their struggling arms the yard enfold;
In vain to grapple flying ropes they try,
The ropes, alas! a solid gripe deny:
Prone on the midnight surge with panting breath
They cry for aid, and long contend with death;
High o'er their heads the rolling billows sweep,
And down they sink in everlasting sleep.

[1] 'Reef-band:' the reef-band is a long piece of canvas sewed across the sail, to strengthen the canvas in the place where the eyelet-holes of the reef are formed. — [2] 'Circling earings:' the outer turns of the earing serve to extend the sail along the yard, and the inner turns are employed to confine its head-rope close to its surface; see note to ver. 207, p. 213. — [3] 'A sea' is the general name given by sailors to a single wave, or billow; hence when a wave bursts over the deck, the vessel is said to have 'shipped a sea.'

Bereft of power to help, their comrades see   360
The wretched victims die beneath the lee ;
With fruitless sorrow their lost state bemoan,
Perhaps a fatal prelude to their own !
    In dark suspense on deck the pilots stand,
Nor can determine on the next command :
Though still they knew the vessel's armed side
Impenetrable to the clasping tide ;
Though still the waters by no secret wound
A passage to her deep recesses found ;
Surrounding evils yet they ponder o'er,   370
A storm, a dangerous sea, and leeward shore !
" Should they, though reef'd, again their sails extend,
Again in shivering streamers they may rend ;
Or, should they stand, beneath the oppressive strain,
The down-press'd ship may never rise again ;
Too late to weather now Morea's land,[1]
And drifting fast on Athens' rocky strand."——
Thus they lament the consequence severe,
Where perils unallay'd by hope appear :
Long pondering in their minds each fear'd event,   380
At last to furl the courses they consent ;
That done, to reef the mizen next agree,
And try[2] beneath it sidelong in the sea.
    Now down the mast the yard they lower away,
Then jears and topping-lift[3] secure belay ;

---

[1] ' To weather ' a shore, is to pass to the windward of it, which at this time
is prevented by the violence of the storm. — [2] ' Try : ' to try, is to lay the ship
with her side nearly in the direction of the wind and sea, with the head somewhat inclined to the windward ; the helm being laid a-lee to retain her in
that position. — [3] ' Topping-lift : ' the topping-lift, which tops the upper end
of the mizen-yard (see note to ver. 260, p. 215) ; this line and the six following describe the operation of reefing and balancing the mizen. The reef of
this sail is towards the lower end, the knittles being small short lines used in
the room of points for this purpose (see notes to ver. 134, 150, p. 210) ; they
are accordingly knotted under the foot-rope, or lower edge of the sail.

The head, with doubling canvas fenced around,   386
In balance near the lofty peak they bound ;
The reef enwrapp'd, the inserting knittles tied,
The halyards throat and peak are next applied —
The order given, the yard aloft they sway'd,   390
The brails relax'd, the extended sheet belay'd ;
The helm its post forsook, and, lash'd a-lee,[1]
Inclined the wayward prow to front the sea.
    IV. When sacred Orpheus on the Stygian coast,
With notes divine deplored his consort lost ;
Though round him perils grew in fell array,
And Fates and Furies stood to bar his way ;
Not more adventurous was the attempt to move
The infernal powers with strains of heavenly love,
Than mine, in ornamental verse to dress   400
The harshest sounds that terms of art express :
Such arduous toil sage Dædalus endured
In mazes, self-invented, long immured,
Till genius her superior aid bestow'd,
To guide him through that intricate abode—
Thus, long imprison'd in a rugged way
Where Phœbus' daughters never aim'd to stray,
The Muse, that tuned to barbarous sounds her string,
Now spreads, like Dædalus, a bolder wing ;
The verse begins in softer strains to flow,   410
Replete with sad variety of woe.
    As yet, amid this elemental war,
Where Desolation in his gloomy car
Triumphant rages round the starless void,
And Fate on every billow seems to ride ;
Nor toil, nor hazard, nor distress appear
To sink the seamen with unmanly fear.

---

[1] ' Lash'd a-lee : ' fastened to the lee-side ; see note to ver. 132, p. 209.

Though their firm hearts no pageant-honour boast,   418
They scorn the wretch that trembles at his post;
Who from the face of danger strives to turn,
Indignant from the social hour they spurn:
Though now full oft they felt the raging tide
In proud rebellion climb the vessel's side;
Though every rising wave more dreadful grows,
And in succession dire the deck o'erflows;
No future ills unknown their souls appal,
They know no danger, or they scorn it all:
But even the generous spirits of the brave,
Subdued by toil, a friendly respite crave;
They, with severe fatigue alone opprest,   430
Would fain indulge an interval of rest.·
    Far other cares the master's mind employ;
Approaching perils all his hopes destroy.
In vain he spreads the graduated chart,
And bounds the distance by the rules of art;
Across the geometric plane expands
The compasses to circumjacent lands:
Ungrateful task! for, no asylum found,
Death yawns on every leeward shore around.——
While Albert thus, with horrid doubts dismay'd,   440
The geometric distances survey'd;
On deck the watchful Rodmond cries aloud,
Secure your lives! grasp every man a shroud—
Roused from his trance, he mounts with eyes aghast;
When o'er the ship, in undulation vast,
A giant surge down rushes from on high,
And fore and aft dissever'd ruins lie.
As when, Britannia's empire to maintain,
Great Hawke descends in thunder on the main,
Around the brazen voice of battle roars,   450
And fatal lightnings blast the hostile shores;

Beneath the storm their shatter'd navies groan ;   452
The trembling deep recoils from zone to zone—
Thus the torn vessel felt the enormous stroke,
The boats beneath the thundering deluge broke ;
Torn from their planks the cracking ring-bolts drew,
And gripes and lashings all asunder flew ;
Companion, binnacle, in floating wreck,
With compasses and glasses strew'd the deck ;
The balanced mizen, rending to the head,   460
In fluttering fragments from its bolt-rope fled ;
The sides convulsive shook on groaning beams,
And, rent with labour, yawn'd their pitchy seams.
    They sound the well,[1] and, terrible to hear !
Five feet immersed along the line appear :
At either pump they ply the clanking brake,[2]
And, turn by turn, the ungrateful office take :
Rodmond, Arion, and Palemon here
At this sad task all diligent appear.
As some strong citadel, begirt with foes,   470
Tries long the tide of ruin to oppose,
Destruction near her spreads his black array,
And death and sorrow mark his horrid way ;
Till, in some destined hour, against her wall
In tenfold rage the fatal thunders fall :
It breaks ! it bursts before the cannonade !
And following hosts the shatter'd domes invade :
Her inmates long repel the hostile flood,
And shield their sacred charge in streams of blood :
So the brave mariners their pumps attend,   480
And help incessant, by rotation, lend ;

---

[1] ' The well ' is an apartment in a ship's hold, serving to inclose the pumps ; it is sounded by dropping a measured iron rod down into it by a long line ; hence the increase or diminution of the leaks is easily discovered.—[2] ' Brake : ' the brake is the lever or handle of the pump, by which it is wrought.

But all in vain! for now the sounding cord, 482
Updrawn, an undiminish'd depth explored.
Nor this severe distress is found alone,
The ribs opprest by ponderous cannon groan;
Deep rolling from the watery volume's height,
The tortured sides seem bursting with their weight—
So reels Pelorus with convulsive throes,
When in his veins the burning earthquake glows;
Hoarse through his entrails roars the infernal flame, 490
And central thunders rend his groaning frame—
Accumulated mischiefs thus arise,
And fate, vindictive, all their skill defies:
For this, one remedy is only known,
From the torn ship her metal must be thrown;
Eventful task! which last distress requires,
And dread of instant death alone inspires:
For, while intent the yawning decks to ease,
Fill'd ever and anon with rushing seas,
Some fatal billow with recoiling sweep 500
May whirl the helpless wretches in the deep.
    No season this for counsel or delay;
Too soon the eventful moments haste away!
Here perseverance, with each help of art,
Must join the boldest efforts of the heart:
These only now their misery can relieve,
These only now a dawn of safety give.
While o'er the quivering deck, from van to rear,
Broad surges roll in terrible career,
Rodmond, Arion, and a chosen crew, 510
This office in the face of death pursue:
The wheel'd artillery o'er the deck to guide,
Rodmond descending claim'd the weather-side;
Fearless of heart the chief his orders gave,
Fronting the rude assaults of every wave—

Like some strong watch-tower nodding o'er the deep,
Whose rocky base the foaming waters sweep,   517
Untamed he stood ; the stern aërial war,
Had mark'd his honest face with many a scar :
Meanwhile Arion, traversing the waist,[1]
The cordage of the leeward guns unbraced,
And pointed crows beneath the metal placed.
Watching the roll, their forelocks they withdrew,
And from their beds the reeling cannon threw ;
Then, from the windward battlements unbound,
Rodmond's associates wheel'd the artillery round ;
Pointed with iron fangs, their bars beguile
The ponderous arms across the steep defile ;
Then, hurl'd from sounding hinges o'er the side
Thundering they plunge into the flashing tide.   530
　　The ship, thus eased, some little respite finds
In this rude conflict of the seas and winds—
Such ease Alcides felt, when, clogg'd with gore,
The envenom'd mantle from his side he tore ;
When, stung with burning pain, he strove too late
To stop the swift career of cruel fate ;
Yet then his heart one ray of hope procured,
Sad harbinger of sevenfold pangs endured—
Such, and so short, the pause of woe she found !
Cimmerian darkness shades the deep around,   540
Save when the lightnings in terrific blaze
Deluge the cheerless gloom with horrid rays :
Above, all ether, fraught with scenes of woe,
With grim destruction threatens all below ;
Beneath, the storm-lash'd surges furious rise,
And wave uproll'd on wave assails the skies ;

---

[1] ' The waist ' of a ship of this kind is a hollow space, of about five feet in depth, contained between the elevations of the quarter-deck and forecastle, and having the upper-deck for its base or platform.

With ever-floating bulwarks they surround   547
The ship, half-swallow'd in the black profound.
    With ceaseless hazard and fatigue oppress'd,
Dismay and anguish every heart possess'd ;
For while, with sweeping inundation, o'er
The sea-beat ship the booming waters roar,
Displaced beneath by her capacious womb,
They rage their ancient station to resume ;
By secret ambushes, their force to prove,
Through many a winding channel first they rove ;
Till gathering fury, like the fever'd blood,
Through her dark veins they roll a rapid flood :
When unrelenting thus the leaks they found,
The clattering pumps with clanking strokes resound ; 560
Around each leaping valve, by toil subdued,
The tough bull-hide must ever be renew'd :
Their sinking hearts unusual horrors chill,
And down their weary limbs thick dews distil ;
No ray of light their dying hope redeems,
Pregnant with some new woe each moment teems.
    Again the chief the instructive chart extends,
And o'er the figured plane attentive bends ;
To him the motion of each orb was known,
That wheels around the sun's refulgent throne.   570
But here, alas! his science nought avails,
Skill droops unequal, and experience fails.
The different traverses, since twilight made.
He on the hydrographic circle laid ;
Then, in the graduated arch contain'd,
The angle of lee-way,[1] seven points, remain'd—

---

[1] ' Lee-way : ' the lee-way, or drift, which in this place are synonymous terms, is the movement by which a ship is driven sideways at the mercy of the wind and sea, when she is deprived of the government of the sails and helm.

P

Her place discover'd by the rules of art,   577
Unusual terrors shook the master's heart,
When, on the immediate line of drift, he found
The rugged isle, with rocks and breakers bound,
Of Falconera ; distant only now
Nine lessening leagues beneath the leeward bow :
For, if on those destructive shallows tost,
The helpless bark with all her crew are lost :
As fatal still appears, that danger o'er,
The steep St George, and rocky Gardalor.
With him the pilots, of their hopeless state,
In mournful consultation, long debate—
Not more perplexing doubts her chiefs appal,
When some proud city verges to her fall,   590
While ruin glares around, and pale affright
Convenes her councils in the dead of night.
No blazon'd trophies o'er their concave spread,
Nor storied pillars raised aloft their head :
But here the Queen of shade around them threw
Her dragon wing, disastrous to the view !
Dire was the scene with whirlwind, hail, and shower ;
Black melancholy ruled the fearful hour :
Beneath, tremendous roll'd the flashing tide,
Where fate on every billow seem'd to ride—   600
Enclosed with ills, by peril unsubdued,
Great in distress the master-seaman stood !
Skill'd to command ; deliberate to advise ;
Expert in action ; and in council wise—
Thus to his partners, by the crew unheard,
The dictates of his soul the chief referr'd :
    " Ye faithful mates ! who all my troubles share,
Approved companions of your master's care !
To you, alas! 'twere fruitless now to tell
Our sad distress, already known too well :   610

This morn with favouring gales the port we left,　6
Though now of every flattering hope bereft :
No skill nor long experience could forecast
The unseen approach of this destructive blast :
These seas, where storms at various seasons blow,
No reigning winds nor certain omens know——
The hour, the occasion, all your skill demands,
A leaky ship, embay'd by dangerous lands !
Our bark no transient jeopardy surrounds,
Groaning she lies beneath unnumber'd wounds :　6
'Tis ours the doubtful remedy to find,
To shun the fury of the seas and wind ;
For in this hollow swell, with labour sore,
Her flank can bear the bursting floods no more.
One only shift, though desperate, we must try,
And that before the boisterous storm to fly :
Then less her sides will feel the surges' power,
Which thus may soon the foundering hull devour.
'Tis true the vessel and her costly freight
To me consign'd, my orders only wait ;　6
Yet, since the charge of every life is mine,
To equal votes our counsels I resign——
Forbid it, Heaven ! that in this dreadful hour
I claim the dangerous reins of purblind power !
But should we now resolve to bear away,
Our hopeless state can suffer no delay :
Nor can we, thus bereft of every sail,
Attempt to steer obliquely on the gale ;
For then, if broaching sideway to the sea,
Our dropsied ship may founder by the lee ;　6
Vain all endeavours then to bear away,
Nor helm, nor pilot, would she more obey."
　He said, the listening mates with fix'd regard
And silent reverence his opinion heard.

Important was the question in debate,   645
And o'er their counsels hung impending fate :
Rodmond, in many a scene of peril tried,
Had oft the master's happier skill descried,
Yet now, the hour, the scene, the occasion known,
Perhaps with equal right preferr'd his own :   650
Of long experience in the naval art,
Blunt was his speech and naked was his heart ;
Alike to him each climate, and each blast,
The first in danger, in retreat the last :
Sagacious, balancing the opposed events,
From Albert his opinion thus dissents :—
   " Too true the perils of the present hour,
Where toils succeeding toils our strength o'erpower !
Our bark, 'tis true, no shelter here can find,
Sore shatter'd by the ruffian seas and wind :   660
Yet where with safety can we dare to scud
Before this tempest and pursuing flood ?
At random driven, to present death we haste,
And one short hour perhaps may be our last.
Though Corinth's gulf extend along the lee,
To whose safe ports appears a passage free,
Yet think ! this furious unremitting gale
Deprives the ship of every ruling sail ;
And if before it she directly flies,
New ills enclose us, and new dangers rise :   670
Here Falconera spreads her lurking snares,
There distant Greece her rugged shelves prepares :
Our hull, if once it strikes that iron coast,
Asunder bursts, in instant ruin lost ;
Nor she alone, but with her all the crew,
Beyond relief, are doom'd to perish too :
Such mischiefs follow if we bear away ;
O safer that sad refuge—to delay !

" Then of our purpose this appears the scope,   679
To weigh the danger with the doubtful hope :
Though sorely buffeted by every sea,
Our hull unbroken long may try a-lee ;
The crew, though harass'd much with toils severe,
Still at their pumps, perceive no hazards near :
Shall we, incautious, then the danger tell,
At once their courage and their hope to quell ?
Prudence forbids ! this southern tempest soon
May change its quarter with the changing moon ;
Its rage, though terrible, may soon subside,
Nor into mountains lash the unruly tide ;   690
These leaks shall then decrease——the sails once more
Direct our course to some relieving shore."
      Thus while he spoke, around from man to man
At either pump a hollow murmur ran ;
For, while the vessel through unnumber'd chinks,
Above, below, the invading water drinks,
Sounding her depth they eyed the wetted scale,
And lo ! the leaks o'er all their powers prevail :
Yet at their post, by terrors unsubdued,
They with redoubling force their task pursued.   700
      And now the senior pilots seem'd to wait
Arion's voice, to close the dark debate.
Not o'er his vernal life the ripening sun
Had yet progressive twice ten summers run ;
Slow to debate, yet eager to excel,
In thy sad school, stern Neptune ! taught too well :
With lasting pain to rend his youthful heart,
Dire fate in venom dipp'd her keenest dart ;
Till his firm spirit, temper'd long to ill,
Forgot her persecuting scourge to feel ;   710
But now the horrors, that around him roll,
Thus rouse to action his rekindling soul :

" Can we, delay'd in this tremendous tide,   713
A moment pause what purpose to decide ?
Alas ! from circling horrors thus combined,
One method of relief alone we find :
Thus water-logg'd, thus helpless to remain
Amid this hollow, how ill judged ! how vain !
Our sea-breach'd vessel can no longer bear
The floods that o'er her burst in dread career ;   720
The labouring hull already seems half-fill'd
With water through a hundred leaks distill'd ;
Thus drench'd by every wave, her riven deck,
Stript and defenceless, floats a naked wreck ;
At every pitch the o'erwhelming billows bend
Beneath their load the quivering bowsprit's end ;
A fearful warning ! since the masts on high
On that support with trembling hope rely ;
At either pump our seamen pant for breath,
In dire dismay anticipating death ;   730
Still all our powers the increasing leaks defy,
We sink at sea, no shore, no haven nigh.
One dawn of hope yet breaks athwart the gloom,
To light and save us from a watery tomb ;
That bids us shun the death impending here,
Fly from the following blast, and shoreward steer.
    " 'Tis urged indeed, the fury of the gale
Precludes the help of every guiding sail ;
And, driven before it on the watery waste,
To rocky shores and scenes of death we haste ;   740
But haply Falconera we may shun,
And long to Grecian coasts is yet the run :
Less harass'd then, our scudding ship may bear
The assaulting surge repell'd upon her rear ;
And since as soon that tempest may decay
When steering shoreward—wherefore thus delay ?

Should we at last be driven by dire decree
Too near the fatal margin of the sea,
The hull dismasted there awhile may ride
With lengthen'd cables, on the raging tide ;
Perhaps kind Heaven, with interposing power,
May curb the tempest ere that dreadful hour ;
But here, ingulf'd and foundering, while we stay,
Fate hovers o'er, and marks us for her prey."
  He said : Palemon saw with grief of heart
The storm prevailing o'er the pilot's art ;
In silent terror and distress involved,
He heard their last alternative resolved :
High beat his bosom.   With such fear subdued,
Beneath the gloom of some enchanted wood,
Oft in old time the wandering swain explored
The midnight wizards' breathing rites abhorr'd ;
Trembling, approach'd their incantations fell,
And, chill'd with horror, heard the songs of hell.
Arion saw, with secret anguish moved,
The deep affliction of the friend he loved,
And, all awake to friendship's genial heat,
His bosom felt consenting tremors beat :
Alas ! no season this for tender love,
Far hence the music of the myrtle grove—
He tried with soft persuasion's melting lore
Palemon's fainting courage to restore ;
His wounded spirit heal'd with friendship's balm,
And bade each conflict of the mind be calm.
  Now had the pilots all the events revolved,
And on their final refuge thus resolved—
When, like the faithful shepherd who beholds
Some prowling wolf approach his fleecy folds,
To the brave crew, whom racking doubts perplex,
The dreadful purpose Albert thus directs :

" Unhappy partners in a wayward fate !   781
Whose courage now is known perhaps too late ;
Ye ! who unmoved behold this angry storm
In conflict all the rolling deep deform :
Who, patient in adversity, still bear
The firmest front when greatest ills are near ;
The truth, though painful, I must now reveal,
That long in vain I purposed to conceal :
Ingulf'd, all help of art we vainly try,
To weather leeward shores, alas ! too nigh :   790
Our crazy bark no longer can abide ·
The seas, that thunder o'er her batter'd side ;
And while the leaks a fatal warning give
That in this raging sea she cannot live,
One only refuge from despair we find——
At once to wear, and scud before the wind.
Perhaps even then to ruin we may steer,
For rocky shores beneath our lee appear ;
But that 's remote, and instant death is here :
Yet there, by Heaven's assistance, we may gain   800
Some creek or inlet of the Grecian main ;
Or, shelter'd by some rock, at anchor ride
Till with abating rage the blast subside :
But if, determined by the will of Heaven,
Our helpless bark at last ashore is driven,
These councils, follow'd, from a watery grave
Our crew perhaps amid the surf may save :——
" And first, let all our axes be secured,
To cut the masts and rigging from aboard ;
Then to the quarters bind each plank and oar,   810
To float between the vessel and the shore :
The longest cordage too must be convey'd
On deck, and to the weather-rails belay'd :

So they who haply reach alive the land,   814
The extended lines may fasten on the strand,
Whene'er, loud thundering on the leeward shore,
While yet aloof, we hear the breakers roar :
Thus for the terrible event prepared,
Brace fore and aft to starboard every yard ;
So shall our masts swim lighter on the wave,   820
And from the broken rocks our seamen save ;
Then westward turn the stem, that every mast
May shoreward fall as from the vessel cast.
When o'er her side once more the billows bound,
Ascend the rigging till she strikes the ground ;
And, when you hear aloft the dreadful shock
That strikes her bottom on some pointed rock,
The boldest of our sailors must descend,
The dangerous business of the deck to tend :
Then burst the hatches off, and every stay   830
And every fastening laniard cut away ;
Planks, gratings, booms, and rafts to leeward cast ;
Then with redoubled strokes attack each mast,
That buoyant lumber may sustain you o'er
The rocky shelves and ledges to the shore :
But, as your firmest succour, till the last
O cling securely on each faithful mast !
Though great the danger, and the task severe,
Yet bow not to the tyranny of fear ;
If once that slavish yoke your souls subdue,   840
Adieu to hope ! to life itself adieu !
    " I know among you some have oft beheld
A bloodhound train, by rapine's lust impell'd,
On England's cruel coast impatient stand,
To rob the wanderers wreck'd upon their strand !
These, while their savage office they pursue,
Oft wound to death the helpless plunder'd crew,

Who, 'scaped from every horror of the main,   848
Implored their mercy, but implored in vain :
Yet dread not this, a crime to Greece unknown,
Such bloodhounds all her circling shores disown ;
Who, though by barbarous tyranny oppress'd,
Can share affliction with the wretch distress'd :
Their hearts, by cruel fate inured to grief,
Oft to the friendless stranger yield relief."
    With conscious horror struck, the naval band
Detested for a while their native land ;
They cursed the sleeping vengeance of the laws,
That thus forgot her guardian sailors' cause.
    Meanwhile the master's voice again they heard,   860
Whom, as with filial duty, all revered :
" No more remains—but now a trusty band
Must ever at the pumps industrious stand ;
And, while with us the rest attend to wear,
Two skilful seamen to the helm repair—
And thou, Eternal Power ! whose awful sway
The storms revere, and roaring seas obey !
On thy supreme assistance we rely ;
Thy mercy supplicate, if doom'd to die !
Perhaps this storm is sent with healing breath   870
From neighbouring shores to scourge disease and death :
'Tis ours on thine unerring laws to trust ;
With thee, great Lord ! 'whatever is, is just.'"
    He said : and, with consenting reverence fraught,
The sailors join'd his prayer in silent thought :
His intellectual eye, serenely bright,
Saw distant objects with prophetic light.
Thus, in a land that lasting wars oppress,
That groans beneath misfortune and distress ;
Whose wealth to conquering armies falls a prey,   880
Till all her vigour, pride, and fame decay ;

Some bold sagacious statesman, from the helm, 882
Sees desolation gathering o'er his realm;
He darts around his penetrating eyes
Where dangers grow, and hostile unions rise;
With deep attention marks the invading foe,
Eludes their wiles and frustrates every blow,
Tries his last art the tottering state to save,
Or in its ruins find a glorious grave.
　　Still in the yawning trough the vessel reels, 890
Ingulf'd beneath two fluctuating hills;
On either side they rise, tremendous scene!
A long dark melancholy vale between:
The balanced ship, now forward, now behind,
Still felt the impression of the waves and wind,
And to the right and left by turns inclined;
But Albert from behind the balance drew,
And on the prow its double efforts threw,
The order now was given to bear away!
The order given, the timoneers obey: 900
Both stay-sail sheets to mid-ships were convey'd,
And round the foremast on each side belay'd:
Thus ready, to the halyards they apply——
They hoist! away the flitting ruins fly:
Yet Albert new resources still prepares,
Conceals his grief, and doubles all his cares——
" Away there! lower the mizen-yard on deck,"
He calls, "and brace the foremost yards aback!"
His great example every bosom fires,
New life rekindles and new hope inspires: 910
While to the helm unfaithful still she lies,
One desperate remedy at last he tries——
" Haste! with your weapons cut the shrouds and stay,
And hew at once the mizen-mast away!"

He said : to cut the girding stay they run,   915
Soon on each side the sever'd shrouds are gone :
Fast by the fated pine bold Rodmond stands,
The impatient axe hung gleaming in his hands ;
Brandish'd on high, it fell with dreadful sound,
The tall mast, groaning, felt the deadly wound ;   920
Deep gash'd beneath, the tottering structure rings,
And crashing, thundering, o'er the quarter swings.
Thus, when some limb, convulsed with pangs of death,
Imbibes the gangrene's pestilential breath,
The experienced artist from the blood betrays
The latent venom, or its course delays ;
But if the infection triumphs o'er his art,
Tainting the vital stream that warms the heart,
To stop the course of death's inflaming tides,
The infected member from the trunk divides.   930

CANTO III.

THE SCENE IS EXTENDED FROM THAT PART OF THE ARCHIPELAGO WHICH
LIES TEN MILES TO THE NORTHWARD OF FALCONERA, TO CAPE COLONNA
IN ATTICA.   THE TIME, ABOUT SEVEN HOURS ; FROM ONE UNTIL EIGHT
IN THE MORNING.

THE ARGUMENT.

I. The beneficial influence of poetry in the civilisation of mankind. Diffidence of the author.—II. Wreck of the mizen-mast cleared away. Ship
put before the wind—labours much. Different stations of the officers.
Appearance of the island of Falconera.—III. Excursion to the adjacent
nations of Greece renowned in antiquity. Athens. Socrates, Plato, Aristides, Solon. Corinth—its architecture. Sparta. Leonidas. Invasion by
Xerxes. Lycurgus. Epaminondas. Present state of the Spartans.
Arcadia. Former happiness, and fertility. Its present distress the effect
of slavery. Ithaca. Ulysses and Penelope. Argos and Mycæne. Aga-
memnon. Macronisi. Lemnos. Vulcan. Delos. Apollo and Diana.
Troy. Sestos. Leander and Hero. Delphos. Temple of Apollo. Parnassus.

The Muses.—IV. Subject resumed. Address to the spirits of the storm. A tempest, accompanied with rain, hail, and meteors. Darkness of the night, lightning and thunder. Daybreak. St George's cliffs open upon them. The ship, in great danger, passes the island of St George.—V. Land of Athens appears. Helmsman struck blind by lightning. Ship laid broadside to the shore. Bowsprit, foremast, and main top-mast carried away. Albert, Rodmond, Arion, and Palemon strive to save themselves on the wreck of the foremast. The ship parts asunder. Death of Albert and Rodmond. Arion reaches the shore. Finds Palemon expiring on the beach. His dying address to Arion, who is led away by the humane natives.

I. When, in a barbarous age, with blood defiled,
The human savage roam'd the gloomy wild ;
When sullen ignorance her flag display'd,
And rapine and revenge her voice obey'd ;
Sent from the shores of light, the Muses came
The dark and solitary race to tame,
The war of lawless passions to control,
To melt in tender sympathy the soul ;
The heart's remote recesses to explore,
And touch its springs, when prose avail'd no more : 10
The kindling spirit caught the empyreal ray,
And glow'd congenial with the swelling lay ;
Roused from the chaos of primeval night,
At once fair truth and reason sprung to light.
When great Mæonides, in rapid song,
The thundering tide of battle rolls along,
Each ravish'd bosom feels the high alarms,
And all the burning pulses beat to arms ;
Hence, war's terrific glory to display,
Became the theme of every epic lay : 20
But when his strings with mournful magic tell
What dire distress Laertes' son befell,
The strains, meandering through the maze of woe
Bid sacred sympathy the heart o'erflow :
Far through the boundless realms of thought he springs,
From earth upborne on Pegasean wings,

While distant poets, trembling as they view
His sunward flight, the dazzling track pursue ;
His magic voice, that rouses and delights,
Allures and guides to climb Olympian heights.
But I, alas ! through scenes bewilder'd stray,
Far from the light of his unerring ray ;
While, all unused the wayward path to tread,
Darkling I wander with prophetic dread.
To me in vain the bold Mæonian lyre
Awakes the numbers fraught with living fire ;
Full oft indeed that mournful harp of yore
Wept the sad wanderer lost upon the shore ;
'Tis true he lightly sketch'd the bold design,
But toils more joyless, more severe are mine ;
Since o'er that scene his genius swiftly ran,
Subservient only to a nobler plan :
But I, perplex'd in labyrinths of art,
Anatomize and blazon every part ;
Attempt with plaintive numbers to display,
And chain the events in regular array ;
Though hard the task to sing in varied strains,
When still unchanged the same sad theme remains :
O could it draw compassion's melting tear
For kindred miseries, oft beheld too near !
For kindred wretches, oft in ruin cast
On Albion's strand beneath the wintry blast ;
For all the pangs, the complicated woe,
Her bravest sons, her guardian sailors know ;
Then every breast should sigh at our distress—
This were the summit of my hoped success !
For this, my theme through mazes I pursue,
Which nor Mæonides, nor Maro knew.

    II. Awhile the mast, in ruins dragg'd behind,
Balanced the impression of the helm and wind ;

The wounded serpent, agonized with pain,   61
Thus trails his mangled volume on the plain :
But now, the wreck, dissever'd from the rear,
The long reluctant prow began to veer ;
While round before the enlarging wind it falls,
"Square fore and aft the yards," the master calls,
" You, timoneers, her motion still attend,
For on your steerage all our lives depend :
So, steady !¹ meet her ! watch the curving prow,
And from the gale directly let her go."   70
"Starboard again !" the watchful pilot cries,
"Starboard !" the obedient timoneer replies :
Then back to port, revolving at command,
The wheel² rolls swiftly through each glowing hand.
The ship no longer, foundering by the lee,
Bears on her side the invasions of the sea ;
All lonely o'er the desert waste she flies,
Scourged on by surges, storms, and bursting skies.
As when enclosing harpooneers assail
In Hyperborean seas the slumbering whale,   80
Soon as their javelins pierce his scaly side,
He groans, he darts impetuous down the tide ;
And rack'd all o'er with lacerating pain,
He flies remote beneath the flood in vain—
So with resistless haste the wounded ship
Scuds from pursuing waves along the deep ;
While, dash'd apart by her dividing prow,
Like burning adamant the waters glow ;
Her joints forget their firm elastic tone,
Her long keel trembles, and her timbers groan :   90
Upheaved behind her in tremendous height
The billows frown, with fearful radiance bright ;

¹ ' Steady : ' the order to steer the ship according to the line on which she
advances at that instant, without deviating to the right or left thereof.—
² ' The wheel : ' in all large ships the helm is managed by a wheel.

Now quivering o'er the topmost waves she rides,   95
While deep beneath the enormous gulf divides;
Now launching headlong down the horrid vale,
Becalm'd she hears no more the howling gale;
Till up the dreadful height again she flies,
Trembling beneath the current of the skies.
As that rebellious angel, who, from heaven,   100
To regions of eternal pain was driven,
When dreadless he forsook the Stygian shore
The distant realms of Eden to explore;
Here, on sulphureous clouds sublime upheaved,
With daring wing the infernal air he cleaved;
There, in some hideous gulf descending prone,
Far in the void abrupt of night was thrown—
Even so she climbs the briny mountain's height,
Then down the black abyss precipitates her flight:
The mast, about whose tops the whirlwinds sing,   110
With long vibration round her axle swing.
    To guide her wayward course amid the gloom,
The watchful pilots different posts assume:
Albert and Rodmond on the poop appear,
There to direct each guiding timoneer;
While at the bow the watch Arion keeps,
To shun what cruisers wander o'er the deeps:
Where'er he moves Palemon still attends,
As if on him his only hope depends;
While Rodmond, fearful of some neighbouring shore, 120
Cries, ever and anon, Look out afore!
    Thus o'er the flood four hours she scudding flew,
When Falconera's rugged cliffs they view
Faintly along the larboard bow descried,
As o'er its mountain tops the lightnings glide;
High o'er its summit, through the gloom of night,
The glimmering watch-tower casts a mournful light:

In dire amazement riveted they stand,   128
And hear the breakers lash the rugged strand ;
But scarce perceived, when past the beam it flies,
Swift as the rapid eagle cleaves the skies :
That danger past reflects a feeble joy,
But soon returning fears their hope destroy.
As in the Atlantic ocean, when we find
Some Alp of ice driven southward by the wind,
The sultry air all sickening pants around,
In deluges of torrid ether drown'd ;
Till when the floating isle approaches nigh,
In cooling tides the aërial billows fly :
Awhile deliver'd from the scorching heat,   140
In gentler tides our feverish pulses beat :
Such transient pleasure, as they pass'd this strand,
A moment bade their throbbing hearts expand ;
The illusive meteors of a lifeless fire,
Too soon they kindle, and too soon expire.
    III. Say, Memory! thou, from whose unerring tongue
Instructive flows the animated song,
What regions now the scudding ship surround ?
Regions of old through all the world renown'd ;
That, once the poet's theme, the Muses' boast,   150
Now lie in ruins, in oblivion lost !
Did they whose sad distress these lays deplore,
Unskill'd in Grecian or in Roman lore,
Unconscious pass along each famous shore ?
They did : for in this desert, joyless soil,
No flowers of genial science deign to smile ;
Sad Ocean's genius, in untimely hour,
Withers the bloom of every springing flower ;
For native tempests here, with blasting breath,
Despoil, and doom the vernal buds to death ;   160

Q

Here fancy droops, while sullen clouds and storm,   161
The generous temper of the soul deform :
Then if, among the wandering naval train,
One stripling, exiled from the Aonian plain,
Had e'er, entranced in fancy's soothing dream,
Approach'd to taste the sweet Castalian stream
(Since those salubrious streams, with power divine,
To purer sense the soften'd soul refine) ;
Sure he, amid unsocial mates immured,
To learning lost, severer grief endured ;   170
In vain might Phœbus' ray his mind inspire,
Since fate with torrents quench'd the kindling fire :
If one this pain of living death possess'd,
It dwelt supreme, Arion ! in thy breast ;
When, with Palemon, watching in the night
Beneath pale Cynthia's melancholy light,
You oft recounted those surrounding states,
Whose glory Fame with brazen tongue relates.
    Immortal Athens first, in ruin spread,
Contiguous lies at Port Liono's head ;   180
Great source of science ! whose immortal name
Stands foremost in the glorious roll of fame.
Here godlike Socrates and Plato shone,
And, firm to truth, eternal honour won :
The first in virtue's cause his life resign'd,
By Heaven pronounced the wisest of mankind :
The last proclaim'd the spark of vital fire,
The soul's fine essence, never could expire :
Here Solon dwelt, the philosophic sage
That fled Pisistratus' vindictive rage :
Just Aristides here maintain'd the cause,   190
Whose sacred precepts shine through Solon's laws.
Of all her towering structures, now alone
Some columns stand, with mantling weeds o'ergrown ;

The wandering stranger near the port descries   194
A milk-white lion of stupendous size,
Of antique marble ; hence the haven's name.
Unknown to modern natives whence it came.
   Next, in the gulf of Engia, Corinth lies,
Whose gorgeous fabrics seem'd to strike the skies ;
Whom, though by tyrant victors oft subdued,   200
Greece, Egypt, Rome, with admiration view'd :
Her name, for architecture long renown'd,
Spread like the foliage which her pillars crown'd ;
But now, in fatal desolation laid,
Oblivion o'er it draws a dismal shade.
   Then further westward, on Morea's land,
Fair Misitra ! thy modern turrets stand :
Ah ! who, unmoved with secret woe, can tell
That here great Lacedæmon's glory fell ?
Here once she flourish'd, at whose trumpet's sound   210
War burst his chains, and nations shook around ;
Here brave Leonidas from shore to shore
Through all Achaia bade her thunders roar :
He, when imperial Xerxes from afar
Advanced with Persia's sumless hosts to war,
Till Macedonia shrunk beneath his spear,
And Greece all shudder'd as the chief drew near ;
He, at Thermopylæ's decisive plain,
Their force opposed with Sparta's glorious train ;
Tall Œta saw the tyrant's conquer'd bands   220
In gasping millions bleed on hostile lands :
Thus vanquish'd, haughty Asia heard thy name,
And Thebes and Athens sicken'd at thy fame :
Thy state, supported by Lycurgus' laws,
Gain'd, like thine arms, superlative applause ;
Even great Epaminondas strove in vain
To curb thy spirit with a Theban chain.

But ah! how low that free-born spirit now!   228
Thy abject sons to haughty tyrants bow;
A false, degenerate, superstitious race
Invest thy region, and its name disgrace.
  Not distant far, Arcadia's blest domains
Peloponnesus' circling shore contains:
Thrice happy soil! where, still serenely gay,
Indulgent Flora breathed perpetual May;
Where buxom Ceres bade each fertile field
Spontaneous gifts in rich profusion yield:
Then, with some rural nymph supremely blest,
While transport glow'd in each enamour'd breast,
Each faithful shepherd told his tender pain,   240
And sung of sylvan sports in artless strain;
Soft as the happy swain's enchanting lay
That pipes among the shades of Endermay.
Now, sad reverse! oppression's iron hand
Enslaves her natives, and despoils her land;
In lawless rapine bred, a sanguine train,
With midnight ravage, scour the uncultured plain.
  Westward of these, beyond the Isthmus, lies
The long-sought isle of Ithacus the wise;
Where fair Penelope, of him deprived,   250
To guard her honour endless schemes contrived:
She, only shielded by a stripling son,
Her lord Ulysses long to Ilion gone,
Each bold attempt of suitor-kings repell'd,
And undefiled her nuptial contract held;
True to her vows, and resolutely chaste,
Met arts with art, and triumph'd at the last.
  Argos, in Greece forgotten and unknown,
Still seems her cruel fortune to bemoan;
Argos, whose monarch led the Grecian hosts   260
Across the Ægean main to Dardan coasts:

Unhappy prince ! who, on a hostile shore,   262
Fatigue and danger ten long winters bore ;
And when to native realms restored at last,
To reap the harvest of thy labours past,
There found a perjured friend, and faithless wife,
Who sacrificed to impious lust thy life ;
Fast by Arcadia stretch these desert plains,
And o'er the land a gloomy tyrant reigns.
   Next, Macronisi is adjacent seen,   270
Where adverse winds detain'd the Spartan queen ;
For whom, in arms combined, the Grecian host,
With vengeance fired, invaded Phrygia's coast ;
For whom so long they labour'd to destroy
The lofty turrets of imperial Troy ;
Here, driven by Juno's rage, the hapless dame,
Forlorn of heart, from ruin'd Ilion came :
The port an image bears of Parian stone,
Of ancient fabric, but of date unknown.
   Due east from this appears the immortal shore,   280
That sacred Phœbus and Diana bore——
Delos ! through all the Ægean seas renown'd,
Whose coast the rocky Cyclades surround ;
By Phœbus honour'd, and by Greece revered,
Her hallow'd groves even distant Persia fear'd :
But now a desert unfrequented land,
No human footstep marks the trackless sand.
   Thence to the north, by Asia's western bound,
Fair Lemnos stands, with rising marble crown'd ;
Where, in her rage, avenging Juno hurl'd   290
Ill-fated Vulcan from the ethereal world.
There his eternal anvils first he rear'd ;
Then, forged by Cyclopean art, appear'd
Thunders that shook the skies with dire alarms,
And form'd, by skill divine, immortal arms ;

There, with this crippled wretch, the foul disgrace   296
And living scandal of the empyreal race,
In wedlock lived the beauteous queen of love ;
Can such sensations heavenly bosoms move ?

  Eastward of this appears the Dardan shore,   300
That once the imperial towers of Ilium bore—
Illustrious Troy ! renown'd in every clime
Through the long records of succeeding time ;
Who saw protecting gods from heaven descend
Full oft, thy royal bulwarks to defend :
Though chiefs unnumber'd in her cause were slain,
With fate the gods and heroes fought in vain !
That refuge of perfidious Helen's shame
At midnight was involved in Grecian flame ;
And now, by time's deep ploughshare harrow'd o'er,   310
The seat of sacred Troy is found no more :
No trace of her proud fabrics now remains,
But corn and vines enrich her cultured plains ;
Silver Scamander laves the verdant shore,
Scamander, oft o'erflow'd with hostile gore.

  Not far removed from Ilion's famous land,
In counter-view appears the Thracian strand,
Where beauteous Hero, from the turret's height,
Display'd her cresset each revolving night ;
Whose gleam directed loved Leander o'er   320
The rolling Hellespont from Asia's shore ;
Till, in a fated hour, on Thracia's coast,
She saw her lover's lifeless body toss'd :
Then felt her bosom agony severe,
Her eyes, sad gazing, pour'd the incessant tear ;
O'erwhelm'd with anguish, frantic with despair,
She beat her swelling breast, and tore her hair ;
On dear Leander's name in vain she cried,
Then headlong plunged into the parting tide :

The exulting tide received the lovely maid,   330
And proudly from the strand its freight convey'd.
  Far west of Thrace, beyond the Ægean main,
Remote from ocean lies the Delphic plain :
The sacred oracle of Phœbus there
High o'er the mount arose, divinely fair !
Achaian marble form'd the gorgeous pile,
August the fabric ! elegant in style !
On brazen hinges turn'd the silver doors,
And chequer'd marble paved the polish'd floors ;
The roof, where storied tablature appear'd,   340
On columns of Corinthian mould was rear'd ;
Of shining porphyry the shafts were framed,
And round the hollow dome bright jewels flamed :
Apollo's priests before the holy shrine
Suppliant pour'd forth their orisons divine ;
To front the sun's declining ray 'twas placed,
With golden harps and branching laurels graced :
Around the fane, engraved by Vulcan's hand,
The sciences and arts were seen to stand ;
Here Æsculapius' snake display'd his crest,   350
And burning glories sparkled on his breast ;
While from his eye's insufferable light,
Disease and death recoil'd in headlong flight :
Of this great temple, through all time renown'd,
Sunk in oblivion, no remains are found.
  Contiguous here, with hallow'd woods o'erspread,
Renown'd Parnassus lifts its honour'd head ;
There roses blossom in eternal spring,
And strains celestial feather'd warblers sing ;
Apollo here bestows the unfading wreath ;   360
Here Zephyrs aromatic odours breathe ;
They o'er Castalian plains diffuse perfume,
Where round the scene perennial laurels bloom :

Fair daughters of the sun, the sacred Nine !   364
Here wake to ecstasy their harps divine,
Or bid the Paphian lute mellifluous play,
And tune to plaintive love the liquid lay :
Their numbers every mental storm control,
And lull to harmony the afflicted soul ;
With heavenly balm the tortured breast compose,   370
And soothe the agony of latent woes :
The verdant shades that Helicon surround,
On rosy gales seraphic tunes resound !
Perpetual summers crown the happy hours,
Sweet as the breath that fans Elysian flowers :
Hence pleasure dances in an endless round,
And love and joy, ineffable, abound.
    IV. Stop, wandering thought! methinks I feel their strains
Diffuse delicious languor through my veins.
Adieu, ye flowery vales, and fragrant scenes,   380
Delightful bowers, and ever vernal greens !
Adieu, ye streams ! that o'er enchanted ground
In lucid maze the Aonian hill surround ;
Ye fairy scenes ! where fancy loves to dwell,
And young delight, for ever, oh, farewell !
The soul with tender luxury you fill,
And o'er the sense Lethean dews distil—
Awake, O memory ! from the inglorious dream,
With brazen lungs resume the kindling theme ;
Collect thy powers, arouse thy vital fire,   390
Ye spirits of the storm my verse inspire !
Hoarse as the whirlwinds that enrage the main,
In torrents pour along the swelling strain.
    Now, through the parting wave impetuous bore,
The scudding vessel stemm'd the Athenian shore ;
The pilots, as the waves behind her swell,
Still with the wheeling stern their force repel ;

For this assault should either quarter[1] feel,   398
Again to flank the tempest she might reel !
The steersmen every bidden turn apply,
To right and left the spokes alternate fly——
Thus, when some conquer'd host retreats in fear,
The bravest leaders guard the broken rear;
Indignant they retire, and long oppose
Superior armies that around them close:
Still shield the flanks, the routed squadrons join,
And guide the flight in one continued line.
Thus they direct the flying bark before
The impelling floods, that lash her to the shore :
High o'er the poop the audacious seas aspire,   410
Uproll'd in hills of fluctuating fire;
With labouring throes she rolls on either side,
And dips her gunnels in the yawning tide;
Her joints, unhinged, in palsied languors play,
As ice-flakes part beneath the noontide ray.
The gale howls doleful through the blocks and shrouds,
And big rain pours a deluge from the clouds;
From wintry magazines that sweep the sky,
Descending globes of hail impetuous fly;
High on the masts, with pale and livid rays,   420
Amid the gloom portentous meteors blaze;
The ethereal dome in mournful pomp array'd
Now buried lies beneath impervious shade;
Now, flashing round intolerable light,
Redoubles all the horror of the night——
Such terror Sinai's trembling hill o'erspread,
When Heaven's loud trumpet sounded o'er its head :
It seem'd, the wrathful Angel of the wind
Had all the horrors of the skies combined,

[1] ' Quarter : ' the quarter is the hinder part of a ship's side, or that part which is near the stern.

And here, to one ill-fated ship opposed,   43
At once the dreadful magazine disclosed;
And, lo! tremendous o'er the deep he springs,
The inflaming sulphur flashing from his wings;
Hark! his strong voice the dismal silence breaks,
Mad chaos from the chains of death awakes:
Loud, and more loud, the rolling peals enlarge,
And blue on deck the fiery tides discharge;
There all aghast the shivering wretches stood,
While chill suspense and fear congeal'd their blood;
Wide bursts in dazzling sheets the living flame,   44
And dread concussion rends the ethereal frame;
Sick earth convulsive groans from shore to shore,
And nature, shuddering, feels the horrid roar.
    Still the sad prospect rises on my sight,
Reveal'd in all its mournful shade and light;
Even now my ear with quick vibration feels
The explosion burst in strong rebounding peals;
Swift through my pulses glides the kindling fire,
As lightning glances on the electric wire:
Yet, ah! the languid colours vainly strive   45
To bid the scene in native hues revive.
    But, lo! at last, from tenfold darkness born,
Forth issues o'er the wave the weeping morn:
Hail, sacred vision! who, on orient wings,
The cheering dawn of light propitious brings;
All nature, smiling, hail'd the vivid ray
That gave her beauties to returning day—
All but our ship! which, groaning on the tide,
No kind relief, no gleam of hope descried;
For now in front her trembling inmates see   46
The hills of Greece emerging on the lee.
So the lost lover views that fatal morn,
On which, for ever from his bosom torn,

The maid, adored, resigns her blooming charms,   464
To bless with love some happier rival's arms.
So to Eliza[1] dawn'd that cruel day
That tore Æneas from her sight away,
That saw him parting, never to return,
Herself in funeral flames decreed to burn.
O yet in clouds, thou genial source of light !   470
Conceal thy radiant glories from our sight;
Go, with thy smile adorn the happy plain,
And gild the scenes where health and pleasure reign:
But let not here, in scorn, thy wanton beam
Insult the dreadful grandeur of my theme.
      While shoreward now the bounding vessel flies,
Full in her van St George's cliffs arise;
High o'er the rest a pointed crag is seen,
That hung projecting o'er a mossy green;
Huge breakers on the larboard bow appear,   480
And full a-head its eastern ledges bear:
To steer more eastward Albert still commands,
And shun, if possible, the fatal strands—
Nearer and nearer now the danger grows,
And all their skill relentless fates oppose;
For while more eastward they direct the prow,
Enormous waves the quivering deck o'erflow;
While, as she wheels, unable to subdue
Her sallies, still they dread her broaching-to:[2]
Alarming thought ! for now no more a-lee   490
Her trembling side could bear the mountain'd sea,
And if pursuing waves she scuds before,
Headlong she runs upon the frightful shore;

---

[1] 'Eliza:' or Dido. — [2] 'Broaching-to:' a sudden and involuntary movement in navigation, wherein a ship, whilst scudding or sailing before the wind, unexpectedly turns her side to windward.   It is generally occasioned by the difficulty of steering her, or by some disaster happening to the machinery of the helm.

A shore, where shelves and hidden rocks abound,　　494
Where death in secret ambush lurks around.
Not half so dreadful to Æneas' eyes
The straits of Sicily were seen to rise,
When Palinurus from the helm descried
The rocks of Scylla on his eastern side;
While in the west, with hideous yawn disclosed,　　500
His onward path Charybdis' gulf opposed:
The double danger he alternate view'd,
And cautiously his arduous track pursued.
Thus, while to right and left destruction lies,
Between the extremes the daring vessel flies;
With terrible irruption bursting o'er
The marble cliffs, tremendous surges roar;
Hoarse through each winding creek the tempest raves,
And hollow rocks repeat the groan of waves.
Should once the bottom strike this cruel shore,　　510
The parting ship that instant is no more!
Nor she alone, but with her all the crew
Beyond relief are doom'd to perish too:
But haply she escapes the dreadful strand,
Though scarce her length in distance from the land:
Swift as the weapon quits the Scythian bow,
She cleaves the burning billows with her prow,
And forward hurrying with impetuous haste,
Borne on the tempest's wings the isle she past:
With longing eyes, and agony of mind,　　520
The sailors view this refuge left behind;
Happy to bribe with India's richest ore
A safe accession to that barren shore.
When in the dark Peruvian mine confined,
Lost to the cheerful commerce of mankind,
The groaning captive wastes his life away,
For ever exiled from the realms of day,

Not half such pangs his bosom agonize   528
When up to distant light he rolls his eyes!
Where the broad sun, in his diurnal way
Imparts to all beside his vivid ray;
While, all forlorn, the victim pines in vain
For scenes he never shall possess again.
   V. But now Athenian mountains they descry,
And o'er the surge Colonna frowns on high;
Where marble columns, long by time defaced,
Moss-cover'd on the lofty Cape are placed:
There rear'd by fair devotion to sustain,
In elder times, Tritonia's sacred fane;
The circling beach in murderous form appears,   540
Decisive goal of all their hopes and fears:
The seamen now in wild amazement see
The scene of ruin rise beneath their lee;
Swift from their minds elapsed all dangers past,
As dumb with terror they behold the last.
And now, while wing'd with ruin from on high,
Through the rent cloud the ragged lightnings fly,
A flash, quick glancing on the nerves of light,
Struck the pale helmsman with eternal night:
Rodmond, who heard a piteous groan behind,   550
Touch'd with compassion, gazed upon the blind;
And, while around his sad companions crowd,
He guides the unhappy victim to the shroud:
" Hie thee aloft, my gallant friend!" he cries;
" Thy only succour on the mast relies."
The helm, bereft of half its vital force,
Now scarce subdued the wild unbridled course;
Quick to the abandon'd wheel Arion came,
The ship's tempestuous sallies to reclaim:
The vessel, while the dread event draws nigh,   560
Seems more impatient o'er the waves to fly;

Fate spurs her on !—Thus, issuing from afar,   5
Advances to the sun some blazing star,
And, as it feels attraction's kindling force,
Springs onward with accelerated course.
    The moment fraught with fate approaches fast !
While thronging sailors climb each quivering mast,
The ship no longer now must stem the land,
And, Hard a starboard ! is the last command:
While every suppliant voice to Heaven applies,   5
The prow, swift wheeling, to the westward flies;
Twelve sailors, on the fore-mast who depend,
High on the platform of the top ascend—
Fatal retreat ! for, while the plunging prow
Immerges headlong in the wave below,
Down prest by watery weight the bowsprit bends,
And from above the stem deep-crashing rends:
Beneath her bow the floating ruins lie;
The fore-mast totters, unsustain'd on high;
And now the ship, forelifted by the sea,   5
Hurls the tall fabric backward o'er her lee;
While, in the general wreck, the faithful stay
Drags the main top-mast by the cap away:
Flung from the mast, the seamen strive in vain,
Through hostile floods, their vessel to regain;
Weak hope, alas ! they buffet long the wave,
And grasp at life though sinking in the grave;
Till all exhausted, and bereft of strength,
O'erpower'd they yield to cruel fate at length;
The burying waters close around their head—   5
They sink ! for ever number'd with the dead.
    Those who remain the weather shrouds embrace,
Nor longer mourn their lost companions' case:
Transfix'd with terror at the approaching doom,
Self-pity in their breasts alone has room.

Albert, and Rodmond, and Palemon, near,   596
With young Arion, on the mast appear:
Even they, amid the unspeakable distress,
In every look distracting thoughts confess;
In every vein the refluent blood congeals,
And every bosom mortal terror feels;
Begirt with all the horrors of the main,
They view'd the adjacent shore, but view'd in vain.
Such torments in the drear abodes of hell,
Where sad despair laments with rueful yell,—
Such torments agonize the damned breast,
That sees remote the mansions of the blest.
    It comes! the dire catastrophe draws near,
Lash'd furious on by destiny severe:
The ship hangs hovering on the verge of death,   610
Hell yawns, rocks rise, and breakers roar beneath!
O yet confirm my heart, ye powers above!
This last tremendous shock of fate to prove;
The tottering frame of reason yet sustain,
Nor let this total havoc whirl my brain;
Since I, all trembling in extreme distress,
Must still the horrible result express.
    In vain, alas! the sacred shades of yore
Would arm the mind with philosophic lore;
In vain they'd teach us, at the latest breath   620
To smile serene amid the pangs of death:
Immortal Zeno's self would trembling see
Inexorable fate beneath the lee;
And Epictetus, at the sight, in vain
Attempt his Stoic firmness to retain:
Had Socrates, for godlike virtue famed,
And wisest of the sons of men proclaim'd,
Spectator of such various horrors been,
Even he had stagger'd at this dreadful scene.

In vain the cords and axes were prepared,   630
For every wave now smites the quivering yard ;
High o'er the ship they throw a dreadful shade,
Then on her burst in terrible cascade ;
Across the founder'd deck o'erwhelming roar,
And foaming, swelling, bound upon the shore.
Swift up the mounting billow now she flies,
Her shatter'd top half-buried in the skies ;
Borne o'er a latent reef the hull impends,
Then thundering on the marble crags descends :
Her ponderous bulk the dire concussion feels,   640
And o'er upheaving surges wounded reels.
Again she plunges ! hark ! a second shock
Bilges the splitting vessel on the rock :
Down on the vale of death, with dismal cries,
The fated victims shuddering cast their eyes
In wild despair ; while yet another stroke
With strong convulsion rends the solid oak :
Ah, Heaven !—behold her crashing ribs divide !
She loosens, parts, and spreads in ruin o'er the tide.
    Oh, were it mine with sacred Maro's art,   650
To wake to sympathy the feeling heart ;
Like him, the smooth and mournful verse to dress
In all the pomp of exquisite distress ;
Then, too severely taught by cruel fate,
To share in all the perils I relate,
Then might I, with unrivall'd strains, deplore
The impervious horrors of a leeward shore.
    As o'er the surf the bending mainmast hung,
Still on the rigging thirty seamen clung :
Some on a broken crag were struggling cast,   660
And there by oozy tangles grappled fast ;
Awhile they bore the o'erwhelming billows' rage,
Unequal combat with their fate to wage ;

Till all benumb'd and feeble they forego   664
Their slippery hold, and sink to shades below :
Some, from the main yard-arm impetuous thrown
On marble ridges, die without a groan :
Three, with Palemon, on their skill depend,
And from the wreck on oars and rafts descend ;
Now on the mountain-wave on high they ride,   670
Then downward plunge beneath the involving tide ;
Till one, who seems in agony to strive,
The whirling breakers heave on shore alive :
The rest a speedier end of anguish knew,
And press'd the stony beach——a lifeless crew !
    Next, O unhappy chief ! the eternal doom
Of Heaven decreed thee to the briny tomb :
What scenes of misery torment thy view !
What painful struggles of thy dying crew !
Thy perish'd hopes all buried in the flood   680
O'erspread with corses, red with human blood !——
So, pierced with anguish, hoary Priam gazed,
When Troy's imperial domes in ruin blazed ;
While he, severest sorrow doom'd to feel,
Expired beneath the victor's murdering steel——
Thus with his helpless partners to the last,
Sad refuge ! Albert grasps the floating mast :
His soul could yet sustain this mortal blow,
But droops, alas ! beneath superior woe ;
For now strong nature's sympathetic chain   690
Tugs at his yearning heart with powerful strain :
His faithful wife, for ever doom'd to mourn
For him, alas ! who never shall return,
To black adversity's approach exposed,
With want and hardships unforeseen enclosed ;
His lovely daughter, left without a friend
Her innocence to succour and defend,

                    R

By youth and indigence set forth a prey   69
To lawless guilt, that flatters to betray—
While these reflections rack his feeling mind,
Rodmond, who hung beside, his grasp resign'd ;
And, as the tumbling waters o'er him roll'd,
His outstretch'd arms the master's legs enfold.
Sad Albert feels their dissolution near,
And strives in vain his fetter'd limbs to clear,
For death bids every clenching joint adhere.
All faint, to Heaven he throws his dying eyes,
And, O protect my wife and child ! he cries—
The gushing streams roll back the unfinish'd sound,
He gasps ! and sinks amid the vast profound.   71
 Five only left of all the shipwreck'd throng
Yet ride the mast which shoreward drives along ;
With these Arion still his hold secures,
And all assaults of hostile waves endures ;
O'er the dire prospect as for life he strives,
He looks if poor Palemon yet survives—
" Ah ! wherefore, trusting to unequal art,
Didst thou, incautious ! from the wreck depart ?
Alas ! these rocks all human skill defy ;   7:
Who strikes them once, beyond relief must die :
And now sore wounded, thou perhaps art tost
On these, or in some oozy cavern lost!"
Thus thought Arion ; anxious gazing round
In vain, his eyes no more Palemon found.
The demons of destruction hover nigh,
And thick their mortal shafts commission'd fly ;
When now a breaking surge, with forceful sway,
Two, next Arion, furious tears away :
Hurl'd on the crags, behold they gasp, they bleed !   7
And, groaning, cling upon the elusive weed ;

Another billow bursts in boundless roar !   732
Arion sinks ! and Memory views no more.
 Ha ! total night and horror here preside,
My stunn'd ear tingles to the whizzing tide ;
It is their funeral knell ! and, gliding near,
Methinks the phantoms of the dead appear :
But, lo ! emerging from the watery grave,
Again they float incumbent on the wave ;
Again the dismal prospect opens round,—   740
The wreck, the shore, the dying and the drown'd !
And see ! enfeebled by repeated shocks,
Those two, who scramble on the adjacent rocks,
Their faithless hold no longer can retain,
They sink o'erwhelm'd ! and never rise again.
 Two with Arion yet the mast upbore,
That now above the ridges reach'd the shore :
Still trembling to descend, they downward gaze
With horror pale, and torpid with amaze.
The floods recoil ! the ground appears below !   750
And life's faint embers now rekindling glow ;
Awhile they wait the exhausted waves' retreat,
Then climb slow up the beach with hands and feet.
O Heaven ! deliver'd by whose sovereign hand
Still on destruction's brink they shuddering stand,
Receive the languid incense they bestow,
That, damp with death, appears not yet to glow :
To thee each soul the warm oblation pays
With trembling ardour of unequal praise ;
In every heart dismay with wonder strives,   760
And hope the sicken'd spark of life revives ;
Her magic powers their exiled health restore,
Till horror and despair are felt no more.
 Roused by the blustering tempest of the night,
A troop of Grecians mount Colonna's height ;

When, gazing down with horror on the flood,   766
Full to their view the scene of ruin stood—
The surf with mangled bodies strew'd around,
And those yet breathing on the sea-wash'd ground :
Though lost to science and the nobler arts,
Yet nature's lore inform'd their feeling hearts ;
Straight down the vale with hastening steps they hied,
The unhappy sufferers to assist and guide.
  Meanwhile those three escaped beneath explore
The first adventurous youth who reach'd the shore.
Panting, with eyes averted from the day,
Prone, helpless, on the tangly beach he lay.
It is Palemon ! oh, what tumults roll
With hope and terror in Arion's soul !—
" If yet unhurt he lives again to view   780
His friend, and this sole remnant of our crew,
With us to travel through this foreign zone,
And share the future good or ill unknown ?"
Arion thus ; but ah, sad doom of fate !
That bleeding memory sorrows to relate ;
While yet afloat, on some resisting rock
His ribs were dash'd, and fractured with the shock :
Heart-piercing sight ! those cheeks so late array'd
In beauty's bloom, are pale with mortal shade ;
Distilling blood his lovely breast o'erspread,   790
And clogg'd the golden tresses of his head ;
Nor yet the lungs by this pernicious stroke
Were wounded, or the vocal organs broke.
Down from his neck, with blazing gems array'd,
Thy image, lovely Anna ! hung portray'd ;
The unconscious figure, smiling all serene,
Suspended in a golden chain was seen.
Hadst thou, soft maiden ! in this hour of woe
Beheld him writhing from the deadly blow,

What force of art, what language could express   800
Thine agony, thine exquisite distress ?
But thou, alas ! art doom'd to weep in vain
For him thine eyes shall never see again.
With dumb amazement pale, Arion gazed,
And cautiously the wounded youth upraised :
Palemon then, with equal pangs oppress'd,
In faltering accents thus his friend address'd :
" O rescued from destruction late so nigh,
Beneath whose fatal influence doom'd I lie ;
Are we, then, exiled to this last retreat   810
Of life, unhappy ! thus decreed to meet ?
Ah ! how unlike what yester-morn enjoy'd,
Enchanting hopes ! for ever now destroy'd ;
For wounded, far beyond all healing power,
Palemon dies, and this his final hour :
By those fell breakers, where in vain I strove,
At once cut off from fortune, life, and love !
Far other scenes must soon present my sight,
That lie deep-buried yet in tenfold night—
Ah ! wretched father of a wretched son,   820
Whom thy paternal prudence has undone ;
How will remembrance of this blinded care
Bend down thy head with anguish and despair !
Such dire effects from avarice arise,
That, deaf to nature's voice, and vainly wise,
With force severe endeavours to control
The noblest passions that inspire the soul.
But, O thou sacred power ! whose law connects
The eternal chain of causes and effects,
Let not thy chastening ministers of rage
Afflict with sharp remorse his feeble age !   830
And you, Arion ! who with these the last
Of all our crew survive the shipwreck past—

Ah! cease to mourn, those friendly tears restrain,   833
Nor give my dying moments keener pain!
Since Heaven may soon thy wandering steps restore,
When parted hence, to England's distant shore.
Shouldst thou, the unwilling messenger of fate,
To him the tragic story first relate;
Oh! friendship's generous ardour then suppress,
Nor hint the fatal cause of my distress;   840
Nor let each horrid incident sustain
The lengthen'd tale to aggravate his pain:
Ah! then remember well my last request
For her who reigns for ever in my breast;
Yet let him prove a father and a friend,
The helpless maid to succour and defend—
Say, I this suit implored with parting breath,
So Heaven befriend him at his hour of death!
But, oh! to lovely Anna shouldst thou tell
What dire untimely end thy friend befell;   850
Draw o'er the dismal scene soft pity's veil,
And lightly touch the lamentable tale:
Say that my love, inviolably true,
No change, no diminution ever knew:
Lo! her bright image, pendent on my neck,
Is all Palemon rescued from the wreck:
Take it! and say, when panting in the wave
I struggled life and this alone to save.
  " My soul, that fluttering hastens to be free,
Would yet a train of thoughts impart to thee,   860
But strives in vain; the chilling ice of death
Congeals my blood, and chokes the stream of breath:
Resign'd, she quits her comfortless abode
To course that long, unknown, eternal road—
O sacred source of ever-living light!
Conduct the weary wanderer in her flight;

Direct her onward to that peaceful shore,   867
Where peril, pain, and death prevail no more.
   " When thou some tale of hapless love shalt hear,
That steals from pity's eye the melting tear ;
Of two chaste hearts, by mutual passion join'd,
To absence, sorrow, and despair consign'd ;
Oh ! then, to swell the tides of social woe
That heal the afflicted bosom they o'erflow,
While memory dictates, this sad shipwreck tell,
And what distress thy wretched friend befell :
Then, while in streams of soft compassion drown'd,
The swains lament, and maidens weeps around ;
While lisping children, touch'd with infant fear,
With wonder gaze, and drop the unconscious tear ;   880
Oh ! then this moral bid their souls retain,
All thoughts of happiness on earth are vain ! "[1]
   The last faint accents trembled on his tongue,
That now inactive to the palate clung ;
His bosom heaves a mortal groan—he dies !
And shades eternal sink upon his eyes.
   As thus defaced in death Palemon lay,
Arion gazed upon the lifeless clay ;
Transfix'd he stood, with awful terror fill'd,
While down his cheek the silent drops distill'd :   890
   " O ill-starr'd votary of unspotted truth !
Untimely perish'd in the bloom of youth ;
Should e'er thy friend arrive on Albion's land,
He will obey, though painful, thy command ;
His tongue the dreadful story shall display,
And all the horrors of this dismal day :

[1] ——————————— sed scilicet ultima semper
Expectanda dies homini ; *dicique beatus*
Ante obitum nemo supremaque funera debet.
                                        OVID, Metam. lib. iii.

Disastrous day! what ruin hast thou bred,   897
.What anguish to the living and the dead!
How hast thou left the widow all forlorn ;
And ever doom'd the orphan child to mourn,
Through life's sad journey hopeless to complain !
Can sacred justice these events ordain ?
But, O my soul ! avoid that wondrous maze,
Where reason, lost in endless error, strays ;
As through this thorny vale of life we run,
Great Cause of all effects, thy will be done ! "
    Now had the Grecians on the beach arrived,
To aid the helpless few who yet survived :
While passing, they behold the waves o'erspread
With shatter'd rafts and corses of the dead ;   910
Three still alive, benumb'd and faint they find,
In mournful silence on a rock reclined :
The generous natives, moved with social pain,
The feeble strangers in their arms sustain ;
With pitying sighs their hapless lot deplore,
And lead them trembling from the fatal shore.

———

OCCASIONAL ELEGY,

IN WHICH THE PRECEDING NARRATIVE IS CONCLUDED.

1   THE scene of death is closed ! the mournful strains
        Dissolve in dying languor on the ear ;
    Yet pity weeps, yet sympathy complains,
        And dumb suspense awaits o'erwhelm'd with fear

———

2 But the sad Muses with prophetic eye
    At once the future and the past explore ;
  Their harps oblivion's influence can defy,
    And waft the spirit to the eternal shore—

3 Then, O Palemon ! if thy shade can hear
    The voice of friendship still lament thy doom,
  Yet to the sad oblations bend thine ear,
    That rise in vocal incense o'er thy tomb.

4 From young Arion first the news received
    With terror, pale unhappy Anna read ;
  With inconsolable distress she grieved,
    And from her cheek the rose of beauty fled :

5 In vain, alas ! the gentle virgin wept,
    Corrosive anguish nipt her vital bloom ;
  O'er her soft frame diseases sternly crept,
    And gave the lovely victim to the tomb.

6 A longer date of woe, the widow'd wife
    Her lamentable lot afflicted bore ;
  Yet both were rescued from the chains of life
    Before Arion reach'd his native shore !

7 The father unrelenting phrenzy stung,
    Untaught in virtue's school distress to bear ;
  Severe remorse his tortured bosom wrung,
    He languish'd, groan'd, and perish'd in despair.

8 Ye lost companions of distress, adieu !
    Your toils, and pains, and dangers are no more ;
  The tempest now shall howl unheard by you,
    While ocean smites in vain the trembling shore :

9　On you the blast, surcharged with rain and snow,
　　In winter's dismal nights no more shall beat ;
　Unfelt by you the vertic sun may glow,
　　And scorch the panting earth with baneful heat ;

10　No more the joyful maid, with sprightly strain,
　　Shall wake the dance to give you welcome home ;
　Nor hopeless love impart undying pain,
　　When far from scenes of social joy you roam :

11　No more on yon wide watery waste you stray,
　　While hunger and disease your life consume—
　While parching thirst, that burns without allay,
　　Forbids the blasted rose of health to bloom :

12　No more you feel contagion's mortal breath
　　That taints the realms with misery severe,
　No more behold pale famine, scattering death,
　　With cruel ravage desolate the year.

13　The thundering drum, the trumpet's swelling strain,
　　Unheard, shall form the long embattled line :
　Unheard, the deep foundations of the main
　　Shall tremble, when the hostile squadrons join.

14　Since grief, fatigue, and hazards still molest
　　The wandering vassals of the faithless deep ;
　Oh ! happier now escaped to endless rest,
　　Than we who still survive to wake and weep.

15　What though no funeral pomp, no borrow'd tear,
　　Your hour of death to gazing crowds shall tell ;
　Nor weeping friends attend your sable bier,
　　Who sadly listen to the passing bell ;

16 The tutor'd sigh, the vain parade of woe,
    No real anguish to the soul impart ;
  And oft, alas ! the tear that friends bestow
    Belies the latent feelings of the heart.

17 What though no sculptured pile your name displays,
    Like those who perish in their country's cause ?
  What though no epic Muse in living lays
    Records your dreadful daring with applause ?—

18 Full oft the flattering marble bids renown
    With blazon'd trophies deck the spotted name ;
  And oft, too oft, the venal Muses crown
    The slaves of vice with never-dying fame.

19 Yet shall remembrance from oblivion's veil
    Relieve your scene, and sigh with grief sincere ;
  And soft compassion at your tragic tale
    In silent tribute pay her kindred tear.

MISCELLANEOUS POEMS.

THE DEMAGOGUE. [1]

BOLD is the attempt, in these licentious times,
When with such towering strides sedition climbs,
With sense or satire to confront her power,
And charge her in the great decisive hour.
Bold is the man, who, on her conquering day,
Stands in the pass of fate to bar her way :
Whose heart, by frowning arrogance unawed,
Or the deep-lurking snares of specious fraud,
The threats of giant-faction can deride,
And stem with stubborn arm her roaring tide.　　　10
For him unnumber'd brooding ills await,
Scorn, malice, insolence, reproach, and hate :
At him, who dares this legion to defy,
A thousand mortal shafts in secret fly :
Revenge, exulting with malignant joy,
Pursues the incautious victim to destroy :
And slander strives, with unrelenting aim,
To spit her blasting venom on his name :

[1] This poem was intended by the author to be a political satire on Lord Chatham, Wilkes, and Churchill, and to refute the opinions expressed in the poems of Churchill.

Around him faction's harpies flap their wings,   1!
And rhyming vermin dart their feeble stings :
In vain the wretch retreats, while in full cry
Fierce on his throat the hungry bloodhounds fly.
Enclosed with perils, thus the conscious Muse,
Alarm'd, though undismay'd, her danger views.
Nor shall unmanly Terror now control
The strong resentment struggling in her soul.
While Indignation, with resistless strain,
Pours her full deluge through each swelling vein ;
By the vile fear that chills the coward breast,
By sordid caution is her voice suppress'd.   s
While Arrogance, with big theatric rage,
Audacious struts on power's imperial stage ;
While o'er our country, at her dread command,
Black Discord, screaming, shakes her fatal brand ;
While, in defiance of maternal laws,
The sacrilegious sword rebellion draws :
Shall she at this important hour retire,
And quench in Lethe's wave her genuine fire ?
Honour forbid ! she fears no threat'ning foe,
When conscious justice bids her bosom glow :   4
And while she kindles the reluctant flame,
Let not the prudent voice of friendship blame !
She feels the sting of keen resentment goad,
Though guiltless yet of satire's thorny road.
Let other Quixotes, frantic with renown,
Plant on their brows a tawdry paper crown !
While fools adore, and vassal-bards obey,
Let the great monarch ass through Gotham bray !
Our poet brandishes no mimic sword,
To rule a realm of dunces self-explored ;   l
No bleeding victims curse his iron sway ;
Nor murder'd reputation marks his way.

True to herself, unarm'd, the fearless Muse   53
Through reason's path her steady course pursues:
True to herself advances, undeterr'd
By the rude clamours of the savage herd.
As some bold surgeon, with inserted steel,
Probes deep the putrid sore, intent to heal;
So the rank ulcers that our patriot load,
Shall she with caustic's healing fires corrode.   60
    Yet ere from patient slumber satire wakes,
And brandishes the avenging scourge of snakes;
Yet ere her eyes, with lightning's vivid ray,
The dark recesses of his heart display;
Let candour own the undaunted pilot's power,
Felt in severest danger's trying hour!
Let truth consenting, with the trump of fame,
His glory, in auspicious strains, proclaim!
He bade the tempest of the battle roar,
That thunder'd o'er the deep from shore to shore.   70
How oft, amid the horrors of the war,
Chain'd to the bloody wheels of danger's car,
How oft my bosom at thy name has glow'd,
And from my beating heart applause bestow'd;
Applause, that, genuine as the blush of youth
Unknown to guile, was sanctified by truth!
How oft I blest the patriot's honest rage,
That greatly dared to lash the guilty age;
That, rapt with zeal, pathetic, bold, and strong,
Roll'd the full tide of eloquence along;   8
That power's big torrent braved with manly pride,
And all corruption's venal arts defied!
When from afar those penetrating eyes
Beheld each secret hostile scheme arise;
Watch'd every motion of the faithless foe,
Each plot o'erturned, and baffled every blow:

A fond enthusiast, kindling at thy name,   87
I glow'd in secret with congenial flame;
While my young bosom, to deceit unknown,
Believed all real virtue thine alone.
    Such then he seem'd, and such indeed might be,
If truth with error ever could agree!
Sure satire never with a fairer hand
Portray'd the object she design'd to brand.
Alas! that virtue should so soon decay,
And faction's wild applause thy heart betray!
The Muse with secret sympathy relents,
And human failings, as a friend, laments:
But when those dangerous errors, big with fate,
Spread discord and distraction through the state,   100
Reason should then exert her utmost power
To guard our passions in that fatal hour.
    There was a time, ere yet his conscious heart
Durst from the hardy path of truth depart;
While yet with generous sentiment it glow'd,
A stranger to corruption's slippery road;
There was a time our patriot durst avow
Those honest maxims he despises now.
How did he then his country's wounds bewail,
And at the insatiate German vulture rail!   110
Whose cruel talons Albion's entrails tore,
.Whose hungry maw was glutted with her gore!
The mists of error, that in darkness held
Our reason, like the sun, his voice dispell'd.
And lo! exhausted, with no power to save,
We view Britannia panting on the wave:
Hung round her neck, a millstone's pond'rous weight
Drags down the struggling victim to her fate!
While horror at the thought our bosom feels,
We bless the man this horror who reveals.   120

But what alarming thoughts the heart amaze,   12
When on this Janus' other face we gaze!
For, lo, possess'd of power's imperial reins,
Our chief those visionary ills disdains!
Alas, how soon the steady patriot turns!
In vain this change astonish'd England mourns!
Her vital blood, that pour'd from every vein,
So late, to fill the accursed Westphalian drain,
Then ceased to flow; the vulture now no more
With unrelenting rage her bowels tore.   13
His magic rod transforms the bird of prey!
The millstone feels the touch, and melts away!
And, strange to tell, still stranger to believe,
What eyes ne'er saw, and heart could ne'er conceive,
At once, transplanted by the sorcerer's wand,
Columbian hills in distant Austria stand!
America, with pangs before unknown,
Now with Westphalia utters groan for groan:
By sympathy she fevers with her fires,
Burns as she burns, and as she dies expires.   14
    From maxims long adopted thus he flew,
For ever changing, yet for ever true:
Swoln with success, and with applause imflamed,
He scorn'd all caution, all advice disclaim'd:
Arm'd with war's thunder, he embraced no more
Those patriot principles maintain'd before.
Perverse, inconstant, obstinate, and proud,
Drunk with ambition, turbulent and loud,
He wrecks us headlong on that dreadful strand
He once devoted all his powers to brand!   15
    Our hapless country views with weeping eyes,
On every side, o'erwhelming horrors rise;
Drain'd of her wealth, exhausted of her power,
And agonized as in the mortal hour;

Her armies, wasted with incessant toils,   15
Or doom'd to perish in contagious soils,
To guard some needy royal plunderer's throne,
And sent to fall in battles not their own.
The enormous debt at home, though long o'ercharged,
With grievous burdens annually enlarged: 16
Crush'd with increasing taxes to the ground,
That suck, like vampires, every bleeding wound:
Ground with severe distress the industrious poor
Driven by the ruthless landlord to the door.
    While thus our land her hapless fate bemoans
In secret, and with inward sorrow groans;
Though deck'd with tinsel trophies of renown,
All gash'd with sores, with anguish bending down ;
Can yet some impious parricide appear,
Who strives to make this anguish more severe ?   17
Can one exist, so much his country's foe,
To bid her wounds with fresh effusion flow ?
There can ; to him in vain she lifts her eyes,
His soul relentless hears her piercing sighs !
Shameless of front, impatient of control,
He spurs her onward to destruction's goal !
Nor yet content on curst Westphalia's shore
With mad profusion to exhaust her store,
Still peace his pompous fulminations brand,
As pirates tremble at the sight of land :   18
Still to new wars the public eye he turns,
Defies all peril, and at reason spurns;
Till press'd with danger, by distress assail'd,
That baffled courage, and o'er skill prevail'd ;
Till foundering in the storm himself had brew'd,
He strives at last its horrors to elude.
Some wretched shift must still protect his name,
And to the guiltless head transfer his shame:

Then hearing modest diffidence oppose   189
His rash advice, that golden time he chose;
And while big surges threaten'd to o'erwhelm
The ship, ingloriously forsook the helm.
   But all the events collected to relate,
Let us his actions recapitulate.
   He first assumed, by mean perfidious art,
Those patriot tenets foreign to his heart:
Next, by his country's fond applauses swell'd,
Thrust himself forward into power, and held
The reins on principles which he alone,
Grown drunk and wanton with success, could own;   200
Betray'd her interest and abused her trust;
Then, deaf to prayers, forsook her in disgust;
With tragic mummery, and most vile grimace,
Rode through the city with a woful face,
As in distress, a patriot out of place!
Insults his generous prince, and in the day
Of trouble skulks, because he cannot sway!
In foreign climes embroils him with allies,
And bids at home the flames of discord rise!
   She comes! from hell the exulting fury springs,   210
With grim destruction sailing on her wings!
Around her scream a hundred harpies fell!
A hundred demons shriek with hideous yell!
From where, in mortal venom dipt on high,
Full-drawn the deadliest shafts of satire fly;
Where Churchill brandishes his clumsy club,
And Wilkes unloads his excremental tub,
Down to where Entick, awkward and unclean,
Crawls on his native dust, a worm obscene!
While with unnumber'd wings from van to rear   220
Myriads of nameless buzzing drones appear:

From their dark cells the angry insects swarm, 222
And every little sting attempt to arm.
Here Chaplains, Privileges, moulder round,
And feeble Scourges,[1] rot upon the ground:
Here hungry Kenrick strives, with fruitless aim,
With Grub-street slander to extend his name:
At Bruin flies the slavering, snarling cur,
But only fills his famish'd jaws with fur.
Here Baldwin spreads the assassinating cloak, 230
Where lurking rancour gives the secret stroke;
While gorged with filth, around this senseless block,
A swarm of spider-bards obsequious flock:
While his demure Welch goat, with lifted hoof,
In Poet's corner hangs each flimsy woof;
And frisky grown, attempts, with awkward prance,
On wit's gay theatre to bleat and dance.
Here, seized with iliac passion, mouthing Leech,
Too low, alas! for satire's whip to reach,
From his black entrails, faction's common sewer, 240
Disgorges all her excremental store.
    With equal pity and regret the Muse
The thundering storms that rage around her views;
Impartial views the tides of discord blend,
Where lordly rogues for power and place contend;
Were not her patriot-heart with anguish torn,
Would eye the opposing chiefs with equal scorn.
Let freedom's deadliest foes for freedom bawl,
Alike to her who govern or who fall!
Aloof she stands, all unconcern'd and mute, 250
While the rude rabble bellow, "Down with Bute!"
While villany the scourge of justice bilks,
Howl on, ye ruffians! "Liberty and Wilkes."

---

[1] 'Chaplains,' 'Privileges,' 'Scourges:' certain poems intended to be very satirical.

Let some soft mummy of a peer, who stains 254
His rank, some sodden lump of ass's brains,
To that abandon'd wretch his sanction give;
Support his slander, and his wants relieve!
Let the great hydra roar aloud for Pitt,
And power and wisdom all to him submit!
Let proud ambition's sons, with hearts severe, 260
Like parricides, their mother's bowels tear!
Sedition her triumphant flag display,
And in embodied ranks her troops array!
While coward justice, trembling on her seat,
Like a vile slave descends to lick her feet!
Nor here let censure draw her awful blade,
If from her theme the wayward Muse has stray'd!
Sometimes the impetuous torrent, o'er its mounds
Redundant bursting, swamps the adjacent grounds;
But rapid, and impatient of delay, 270
Through the deep channel still pursues its way.
   Our pilot now retired, no pleasure knows,
But every man and measure to oppose;
Like Æsop's cur, still snarling and perverse,
Bloated with envy, to mankind a curse,
No more at council his advice will lend,
But with all others who advise contend:
He bids distraction o'er his country blaze,
Then, swelter'd with revenge, retreats to Hayes:
Swallows the pension; but, aware of blame, 280
Transfers the proffer'd peerage to his dame.
The felon thus of old, his name to save,
His pilfer'd mutton to a brother gave.
   But should some frantic wretch whom all men know
To nature and humanity a foe,
Deaf to the widow's moan and orphan's cry,
And dead to shame and friendship's social tie;

Should such a miscreant, at the hour of death, 288
To thee his fortunes and domains bequeath;
With cruel rancour wresting from his heirs
What nature taught them to expect as theirs;
Wouldst thou with this detested robber join,
Their legal wealth to plunder and purloin?
Forbid it, Heaven! thou canst not be so base,
To blast thy name with infamous disgrace!
The Muse who wakes, yet triumphs o'er thy hate,
Dares not so black a thought anticipate:
By Heaven, the Muse her ignorance betrays;
For while a thousand eyes with wonder gaze,
Though gorged and glutted with his country's store, 300
The vulture pounces on the shining ore;
In his strong talons gripes the golden prey,
And from the weeping orphan bears away.

The great, the alarming deed is yet to come,
That, big with fate, strikes expectation dumb.
Oh, patient, injured England, yet unveil
Thy eyes, and listen to the Muse's tale,
That true as honour, unadorn'd with art,
Thy wrongs in fair succession shall impart!

Ere yet the desolating god of war 310
Had crush'd pale Europe with his iron car,
Had shook her shores with terrible alarms,
And thunder'd o'er the trembling deep, "To arms!"
In climes remote, beyond the setting sun,
Beyond the Atlantic wave, his rage begun.
Alas! poor country, how with pangs unknown
To Britain did thy filial bosom groan!
What savage armies did thy realms invade,
Unarm'd, and distant from maternal aid!
Thy cottages with cruel flames consumed, 320
And the sad owner to destruction doom'd;

Mangled with wounds, with pungent anguish torn,   322
Or left to perish naked and forlorn!
What carnage reek'd upon thy ruin'd plain!
What infants bled! what virgins shriek'd in vain!
In every look distraction seem'd to glare,
Each heart was rack'd with horror and despair.
To Albion then, with groans and piercing cries,
America lift up her dying eyes;
To generous Albion pour'd forth all her pain,   330
To whom the wretched never wept in vain.
She heard, and instant to relieve her flew,
Her arm the gleaming sword of vengeance drew;
Far o'er the ocean wave her voice was known,
That shook the deep abyss from zone to zone:
She bade the thunder of the battle glow,
And pour'd the storm of lightning on the foe;
Nor ceased till, crown'd with victory complete,
Pale Spain and France lay trembling at her feet.

Her fears dispell'd, and all her foes removed,   340
Her fertile grounds industriously improved,
Her towns with trade, with fleets her harbours crown'd,
And plenty smiling on her plains around:
Thus blest with all that commerce could supply,
America regards with jealous eye,
And canker'd heart, the parent, who so late
Had snatch'd her gasping from the jaws of fate;
Who now, with wars for her begun, relax'd,
With grievous aggravated burthens tax'd,
Her treasures wasted by a hungry brood   350
Of cormorants, that suck her vital blood;
Who now of her demands that tribute due,
For whom alone the avenging sword she drew.

Scarce had America the just request
Received, when, kindling in her faithless breast,

Resentment glows, enraged sedition burns,   85
And, lo! the mandate of our laws she spurns!
Her secret hate, incapable of shame
Or gratitude, incenses to a flame,
Derides our power, bids insurrection rise,   86
Insults our honour, and our laws defies ;
O'er all her coasts is heard the audacious roar,
" England shall rule America no more !"
    Soon as on Britain's shore the alarm was heard,
Stern indignation in her look appear'd ;
Yet, loth to punish, she her scourge withheld
From her perfidious sons who thus rebell'd ;
Now stung with anguish, now with rage assail'd,
Till pity in her soul at last prevail'd,
Determined not to draw her penal steel   37
Till fair persuasion made her last appeal.
    And now the great decisive hour drew nigh,
She on her darling patriot cast her eye ;
His voice like thunder will support her cause,
Enforce her dictates, and sustain her laws ;
Rich with her spoils, his sanction will dismay,
And bid the insurgents tremble and obey.
    He comes !——but where, the amazing theme to hit,
Discover language or ideas fit ?
Splay-footed words, that hector, bounce, and swagger, 38
The sense to puzzle, and the brain to stagger ?
Our patriot comes ! with frenzy fired, the Muse
With allegoric eye his figure views !
Like the grim portress of hell-gate he stands,
Bellona's scourge hangs trembling in his hands !
Around him, fiercer than the ravenous shark,
" A cry of hell-hounds' never-ceasing bark ; "
And lo ! the enormous giant to bedeck,
A golden millstone hangs upon his neck !

On him ambition's vulture darts her claws,   390
And with voracious rage his liver gnaws.
Our patriot comes !——the buckles of whose shoes
Not Cromwell's self was worthy to unloose.
Repeat his name in thunder to the skies !
Ye hills fall prostrate, and ye vales arise !
Through faction's wilderness prepare the way !
Prepare, ye listening senates, to obey !
The idol of the mob, behold him stand,
The Alpha and Omega of the land !
    Methinks I hear the bellowing demagogue   400
Dumb-sounding declamations disembogue,
Expressions of immeasurable length,
Where pompous jargon fills the place of strength ;
Where fulminating, rumbling eloquence,
With loud theatric rage, bombards the sense ;
And words, deep rank'd in horrible array,
Exasperated metaphors convey !
With these auxiliaries, drawn up at large,
He bids enraged sedition beat the charge :
From England's sanguine hope his aid withdraws,   410
And lists to guide in insurrection's cause.
And lo ! where, in her sacrilegious hand,
The parricide lifts high her burning brand !
Go, while she yet suspends her impious aim,
With those infernal lungs arouse the flame !
Though England merits not her least regard,
Thy friendly voice gold boxes shall reward !
Arise, embark ! prepare thy martial car,
To lead her armies and provoke the war !
Rebellion wakes, impatient of delay,   420
The signal her black ensigns to display.

       *   *   *   *

To thee, whose soul, all steadfast and serene,   422
Beholds the tumults that distract our scene ;
And, in the calmer seats of wisdom placed,
Enjoys the sweets of sentiment and taste :
To thee, O Marius ! whom no factions sway,
The impartial Muse devotes her honest lay !
In her fond breast no prostituted aim,
Nor venal hope, assumes fair friendship's name :
Sooner shall Churchill's feeble meteor-ray,   430
That led our foundering demagogue astray,
Darkling to grope and flounce in Error's night,
Eclipse great Mansfield's strong meridian light,
Than shall the change of fortune, time, or place,
Thy generous friendship in my heart efface !
Oh ! whether wandering from thy country far,
And plunged amid the murdering scenes of war ;
Or in the blest retreat of virtue laid,
Where contemplation spreads her awful shade ;
If ever to forget thee I have power,   440
May Heaven desert me at my latest hour !
   Still satire bids my bosom beat to arms,
And throb with irresistible alarms.
Like some full river charged with falling showers,
Still o'er my breast her swelling deluge pours.
But rest and silence now, who wait beside,
With their strong flood-gates bar the impetuous tide.

A POEM,

SACRED TO THE MEMORY OF HIS ROYAL HIGHNESS
FREDERIC PRINCE OF WALES.

FROM the big horror of War's hoarse alarms,
And the tremendous clang of clashing arms,
Descend, my Muse! a deeper scene to draw
(A scene will hold the listening world in awe)
Is my intent : Melpomene inspire,
While, with sad notes, I strike the trembling lyre!
And may my lines with easy motion flow,
Melt as they move, and fill each heart with woe :
Big with the sorrow it describes, my song,
In solemn pomp, majestic, move along.   10
   O bear me to some awful silent glade,
Where cedars form an unremitting shade ;
Where never track of human feet was known ;
Where never cheerful light of Phœbus shone ;
Where chirping linnets warble tales of love,
And hoarser winds howl murmuring through the grove ;
Where some unhappy wretch aye mourns his doom,
Deep melancholy wandering through the gloom ;
Where solitude and meditation roam,
And where no dawning glimpse of hope can come !   20
Place me in such an unfrequented shade,
To speak to none but with the mighty dead ;
To assist the pouring rains with brimful eyes,
And aid hoarse howling Boreas with my sighs.
   When Winter's horrors left Britannia's isle,
And Spring in blooming vendure 'gan to smile ;

When rills, unbound, began to purl along,   2
And warbling larks renew'd the vernal song;
When sprouting roses, deck'd in crimson dye,
Began to bloom, ...   3
Hard fate! then, noble Frederic, didst thou die:
Doom'd by inexorable fate's decree,
The approaching summer ne'er on earth to see:
In thy parch'd vitals burning fevers rage,
Whose flame the virtue of no herbs assuage;
No cooling medicine can its heat allay,
Relentless destiny cries, "No delay!"
Ye powers! and must a prince so noble die?
(Whose equal breathes not under the ambient sky:)
Ah! must he die, then, in youth's full-blown prime,   4
Cut by the scythe of all-devouring Time?
Yes, fate has doom'd! his soul now leaves its weight,
And all are under the decree of fate;
The irrevocable doom of destiny
Pronounced, "All mortals must submissive die."
The princes wait around with weeping eyes,
And the dome echoes all with piercing cries:
With doleful noise the matrons scream around,
With female shrieks the vaulted roofs rebound:
A dismal noise! Now one promiscuous roar   5
Cries, "Ah! the noble Frederic is no more!"
The chief reluctant yields his latest breath;
His eye-lids settle in the shades of death;
Dark sable shades present before each eye,
And the deep vast abyss, Eternity!
Through perpetuity's expanse he springs;
And o'er the vast profound he shoots on wings;
The soul to distant regions steers her flight,
And sails incumbent on inferior night:

With vast celerity she shoots away,   60
And meets the regions of eternal day,
To shine for ever in the heavenly birth,
And leave the body here to rot on earth.
The melancholy patriots round it wait,
And mourn the royal hero's timeless fate.
Disconsolate they move, a mournful band!
In solemn pomp they march along the strand:
The noble chief, interr'd in youthful bloom,
Lies in the dreary regions of the tomb.
   Adown Augusta's pallid visage flow   70
The living pearls with unaffected woe:
Disconsolate, hapless, see pale Britain mourn,
Abandon'd isle! forsaken and forlorn!
With desperate hands her bleeding breast she beats;
While o'er her, frowning, grim destruction threats.
She mourns with heart-felt grief, she rends her hair,
And fills with piercing cries the echoing air.
Well mayst thou mourn thy patriot's timeless end,
Thy Muse's patron, and thy merchant's friend!
What heart shall pity thy full-flowing grief?   80
What hand now deign to give thy poor relief?
To encourage arts, whose bounty now shall flow,
And learned science to promote, bestow?
Who now protect thee from the hostile frown,
And to the injured just return his own?
From usury and oppression who shall guard
The helpless, and the threatening ruin ward?
Alas! the truly noble Briton's gone,
And left us here in ceaseless woe to moan!
Impending desolation hangs around,   90
And ruin hovers o'er the trembling ground:
The blooming spring droops her enamell'd head,
Her glories wither, and her flowers all fade:

The sprouting leaves already drop away; 94
Languish the living herbs with pale decay:
The bowing trees, see! o'er the blasted heath,
Depending, bend beneath the weight of death:
Wrapp'd in the expansive gloom, the lightnings play,
Hoarse thunder mutters through the aërial way:
All Nature feels the pangs, the storms renew, 100
And sprouts, with fatal haste, the baleful yew.
   Some power avert the threatening horrid weight,
And, godlike, prop Britannia's sinking state!
Minerva, hover o'er young George's soul;
May sacred wisdom all his deeds control!
Exalted grandeur in each action shine,
His conduct all declare the youth divine!
   Methinks I see him shine a glorious star,
Gentle in peace, but terrible in war!
Methinks each region does his praise resound, 110
And nations tremble at his name around!
His fame, through every distant kingdom rung,
Proclaims him of the race from whence he sprung:
So sable smoke in volumes curls on high;
Heaps roll on heaps, and blacken all the sky:
Already so, his fame, methinks, is hurl'd
Around the admiring, venerating world.
So the benighted wanderer, on his way,
Laments the absence of all-cheering day;
Far distant from his friends and native home, 120
And not one glimpse does glimmer through the gloom:
In thought he breathes, each sigh his latest breath,
Present, each meditation, pits of death:
Irregular, wild chimeras fill his soul,
And death, and dying, every step control.
Till from the east there breaks a purple gleam,
His fears then vanish as a fleeting dream:

Hid in a cloud the sun first shoots his ray, 128
Then breaks effulgent on the illumined day ;
We see no spot then in the flaming rays,
Confused and lost within the excessive blaze.

ODE ON THE DUKE OF YORK'S SECOND DEPARTURE FROM ENGLAND AS REAR-ADMIRAL.

WRITTEN ABOARD THE ROYAL GEORGE.

AGAIN the royal streamers play,
  To glory Edward hastes away ;
Adieu, ye happy silvan bowers,
  Where pleasure's sprightly throng await !
Ye domes, where regal grandeur towers
  In purple ornaments of state !
  Ye scenes where virtue's sacred strain
  Bids the tragic Muse complain !
  Where satire treads the comic stage,
  To scourge and mend a venal age ; 10
Where music pours the soft, melodious lay,
And melting symphonies congenial play :
Ye silken sons of ease, who dwell
In flowery vales of peace, farewell !
In vain the goddess of the myrtle grove
  Her charms ineffable displays ;
In vain she calls to happier realms of love,
  Which Spring's unfading bloom arrays ;
In vain her living roses blow,
And ever-vernal pleasures grow ; 20

The gentle sports of youth no more   21
    Allure him to the peaceful shore ;
Arcadian ease no longer charms,
    For war and fame alone can please :
His throbbing bosom beats to arms,
To war the hero moves, through storms and wintry seas.

CHORUS.

The gentle sports of youth no more
Allure him to the peaceful shore,
For war and fame alone can please :
To war the hero moves, through storms and wintry seas.

Though danger's hostile train appears   31
To thwart the course that honour steers ;
Unmoved he leads the rugged way,
Despising peril and dismay.
His country calls ; to guard her laws,
Lo ! every joy the gallant youth resigns ;
The avenging naval sword he draws,
And o'er the waves conducts her martial lines :
Hark ! his sprightly clarions play ;
Follow where he leads the way !   40
The piercing fife, the sounding drum,
Tell the deeps their master's come.

CHORUS.

Hark ! his sprightly clarions play,
Follow where he leads the way !
The piercing fife, the sounding drum,
Tell the deeps their master's come.

Thus Alcmena's warlike son
The thorny course of virtue run,

When, taught by her unerring voice,
    He made the glorious choice :
Severe, indeed, the attempt he knew,
Youth's genial ardours to subdue :
For pleasure, Venus' lovely form assumed ;
    Her glowing charms, divinely bright,
In all the pride of beauty bloom'd,
    And struck his ravish'd sight.
        Transfix'd, amazed,
        Alcides gazed :
        Enchanting grace
        Adorn'd her face,
And all his changing looks confess'd
The alternate passions in his breast :
Her swelling bosom half reveal'd,
    Her eyes that kindling raptures fired,
A thousand tender pains instill'd,
    A thousand flattering thoughts inspired :
Persuasion's sweetest language hung
In melting accent on her tongue :
Deep in his heart the winning tale
    Infused a magic power ;
She press'd him to the rosy vale,
    And show'd the Elysian bower :
Her hand that trembling ardours move,
Conducts him blushing to the blest alcove :
    Ah ! see, o'erpower'd by beauty's charms,
    And won by love's resistless arms,
The captive yields to nature's soft alarms !

CHORUS.

    Ah ! see, o'erpower'd by beauty's charms,
    And won by love's resistless arms,
The captive yields to nature's soft alarms !

Assist, ye guardian powers above !   8
From ruin save the son of Jove !
By heavenly mandate virtue came,
   And check'd the fatal flame :
Swift as the quivering needle wheels,
Whose point the magnet's influence feels,
     Inspired with awe,
     He, turning, saw
     The nymph divine
     Transcendent shine ;   9
And, while he view'd the godlike maid,
His heart a sacred impulse sway'd :
His eyes with ardent motion roll,
And love, regret, and hope, divide his soul.
   But soon her words his pain destroy,
    And all the numbers of his heart,
    Return'd by her celestial art,
Now swell'd to strains of nobler joy.
Instructed thus by virtue's lore,
His happy steps the realms explore,   10
   Where guilt and error are no more :
The clouds that veil'd his intellectual ray,
Before his breath dispelling, melt away :
Broke loose from pleasure's glittering chain,
He scorn'd her soft inglorious reign :
Convinced, resolved, to virtue then he turn'd,
And in his breast paternal glory burn'd.

CHORUS.

Broke loose from pleasure's glittering chain,
He scorn'd her soft inglorious reign :
Convinced, resolved, to virtue then he turn'd,   11
And in his breast paternal glory burn'd.
              T

So when on Britain's other hope she shone,   112
   Like him the royal youth she won :
Thus taught, he bids his fleet advance
To curb the power of Spain and France :
Aloft his martial ensigns flow,
And hark ! his brazen trumpets blow !
    The watery profound,
    Awaked by the sound,
    All trembles around :   120
While Edward o'er the azure fields
   Fraternal wonder wields :
High on the deck behold he stands,
And views around his floating bands
   In awful order join :
They, while the warlike trumpet's strain,
Deep sounding, swells along the main,
   Extend the embattled line.
Then Britain triumphantly saw
   His armament ride   130
   Supreme on the tide,
And o'er the vast ocean give law.

CHORUS.

Then Britain triumphantly saw
   His armament ride,
   Supreme on the tide,
And o'er the vast ocean give law.

   Now with shouting peals of joy,
   The ships their horrid tubes display,
Tier over tier in terrible array,
   And wait the signal to destroy.   140
The sailors all burn to engage :
   Hark ! hark ! their shouts arise,

And shake the vaulted skies ! 143
Exulting with bacchanal rage.
Then, Neptune, the hero revere,
  Whose power is superior to. thine !
And, when his proud squadrons appear,
  The trident and chariot resign !

CHORUS.

Then, Neptune, the hero revere,
  Whose power is superior to thine ! 150
And, when his proud squadrons appear,
  The trident and chariot resign!

Albion, wake thy grateful voice !
Let thy hills and vales rejoice !
O'er remotest hostile regions
  Thy victorious flags are known ;
Thy resistless martial legions
  Dreadful move from zone to zone.
Thy flaming bolts unerring roll,
And all the trembling globe control : 160
Thy seamen, invincibly true,
No menace, no fraud, can subdue :
  To thy great trust
  Severely just,
All dissonant strife they disclaim :
  To meet the foe,
  Their bosoms glow ;
Who only are rivals in fame.

CHORUS.

Thy seamen, invincibly true,
No menace, no fraud, can subdue : 170
All dissonant strife they disclaim,
And only are rivals in fame.

For Edward tune your harps, ye Nine!   173
    Triumphant strike each living string ;
For him, in ecstasy divine,
    Your choral Io Pæans sing !
For him your festive concerts breathe !
For him your flowery garlands wreath !
    Wake ! O wake the joyful song !
      Ye Fauns of the woods,   180
      Ye Nymphs of the floods,
    The musical current prolong !
Ye Silvans, that dance on the plain,
    To swell the grand chorus accord !
Ye Tritons, that sport on the main,
    Exulting, acknowledge your lord !
Till all the wild numbers combined,
    That floating proclaim
    Our Admiral's name,
In symphony roll on the wind !   190

CHORUS.

    Wake ! O wake the joyful song !
    Ye Silvans, that dance on the plain,
    Ye Tritons, that sport on the main,
    The musical current prolong !

Oh, while consenting Britons praise,
    These votive measures deign to hear !
For thee my Muse awakes her lays,
For thee the unequal viol plays,
    The tribute of a soul sincere.
Nor thou, illustrious chief, refuse   200
    The incense of a nautic Muse !
For ah ! to whom shall Neptune's sons complain,
But him whose arms unrivall'd rule the main ?

Deep on my grateful breast 204
Thy favour is imprest :
No happy son of wealth or fame
To court a royal patron came !
A hapless youth, whose vital page
Was one sad lengthen'd tale of woe ;
Where ruthless fate, impelling tides of rage, 210
Bade wave on wave in dire succession flow ;
To glittering stars and titled names unknown,
Preferr'd his suit to thee alone.
The tale your sacred pity moved ;
You felt, consented, and approved.
Then touch my strings, ye blest Pierian choir !
Exalt to rapture every happy line ;
My bosom kindle with Promethean fire ;
And swell each note with energy divine !
No more to plaintive sounds of woe 220
Let the vocal numbers flow !
Perhaps the chief to whom I sing
May yet ordain auspicious days,
To wake the lyre with nobler lays,
And tune to war the nervous string.
For who, untaught in Neptune's school,
Though all the powers of genius he possess,
Though disciplined by classic rule,
With daring pencil can display
The fight that thunders on the watery way ; 230
And all its horrid incidents express ?
To him, my Muse, these warlike strains belong ;
Source of thy hope, and patron of thy song !

CHORUS.

To him, my Muse, these warlike strains belong ;
Source of thy hope, and patron of thy song !

THE FOND LOVER.

A BALLAD.

1 A NYMPH of every charm possess'd,
    That native virtue gives,
Within my bosom all confess'd,
    In bright idea lives.
For her my trembling numbers play
    Along the pathless deep,
While, sadly social with my lay,
    The winds in concert weep.

2 If beauty's sacred influence charms
    The rage of adverse fate;
Say why the pleasing soft alarms
    Such cruel pangs create?
Since all her thoughts by sense refined,
    Unartful truth express;
Say wherefore sense and truth are join'd
    To give my soul distress?

3 If when her blooming lips I press,
    Which vernal fragrance fills,
Through all my veins the sweet excess
    In trembling motion thrills;
Say whence this secret anguish grows,
    Congenial with my joy?
And why the touch, where pleasure glows,
    Should vital peace destroy?

4 If, when my fair, in melting song,
    Awakes the vocal lay,

Not all your notes, ye Phocian throng,
  Such pleasing sounds convey;
Thus wrapt all o'er with fondest love,
  Why heaves this broken sigh?
For then my blood forgets to move,
  I gaze, adore, and die.

5 Accept, my charming maid, the strain
  Which you alone inspire;
To thee the dying strings complain
  That quiver on my lyre.
 · O give this bleeding bosom ease,
  That knows no joy but thee;
Teach me thy happy art to please,
  Or deign to love like me.

ON THE UNCOMMON SCARCITY OF POETRY

IN THE GENTLEMAN'S MAGAZINE FOR DECEMBER LAST,

1755, BY I. W., A SAILOR.

THE springs of Helicon can winter bind,
And chill the fervour of a poet's mind?
What though the lowering skies and driving storm
The scenes of nature wide around deform,
The birds no longer sing, nor roses blow,
And all the landscape lies conceal'd in snow;
Yet rigid Winter still is known to spare
The brighter beauties of the lovely fair:
Ye lovely fair, your sacred influence bring,
And with your smiles anticipate the Spring!   10

Yet what avail the smiles of lovely maids,
Or vernal suns that glad the flowery glades ?
The wood's green foliage, or the varying scene
Of fields and lawns, and gliding streams between ?
What, to the wretch whom harder fates ordain
Through the long year to plough the stormy main ?
No murmuring streams, no sound of distant sheep,
Or song of birds invite his eyes to sleep.
By toil exhausted, when he sinks to rest,
Beneath his sun-burnt head no flowers are prest:
Down on the deck his fainting limbs are laid,
No spreading trees dispense their cooling shade,
No zephyrs round his aching temples play,
No fragrant breezes noxious heats allay.
The rude, rough wind which stern Æolus sends,
Drives on in blasts, and while it cools, offends.
He wakes, but hears no music from the grove;
No varied landscape courts his eye to rove.
O'er the wide main he looks to distant skies,
Where nought but waves on rolling waves arise;
The boundless view fatigues his aching sight,
Nor yields his eye one object of delight.
No " female face divine," with cheering smiles,
The lingering hours of dangerous toil beguiles.
Yet distant beauty oft his genius fires,
And oft with love of sacred song inspires.
Even I, the least of all the tuneful train,
On the rough ocean try this artless strain :
Rouse then, ye bards, who happier fortunes prove,
And tune the lyre to Nature or to Love !

DESCRIPTION OF A NINETY-GUN SHIP.

FROM THE GENTLEMAN'S MAGAZINE, MAY 1759.

AMIDST a wood of oaks with canvas leaves,
Which form'd a floating forest on the waves,
There stood a tower, whose vast stupendous size
Rear'd its huge mast, and seem'd to gore the skies,
From which a bloody pendant stretch'd afar
Its comet-tail, denouncing ample war :
Two younger giants,[1] of inferior height,
Display'd their sporting streamers to the sight :
The base below, another island rose,
To pour Britannia's thunder on her foes :   10
With bulk immense, like Ætna, she surveys
Above the rest, the lesser Cyclades :
Profuse of gold, in lustre like the sun,
Splendid with regal luxury she shone,
Lavish in wealth, luxuriant in her pride,
Behold the gilded mass exulting ride !
Her curious prow divides the silver waves,
In the salt ooze her radiant sides she laves ;
From stem to stern, her wondrous length survey,
Rising a beauteous Venus from the sea :   20
Her stem, with naval drapery engraved,
Show'd mimic warriors, who the tempest braved ;
Whose visage fierce defied the lashing surge,
Of Gallic pride the emblematic scourge.
Tremendous figures, lo ! her stern displays,
And holds a Pharos[2] of distinguish'd blaze :

---

[1] 'Younger giants :' fore and mizen masts.—[2] 'Pharos :' her poop lanthorn.

U

By night it shines a star of brightest form,   2'
To point her way, and light her through the storm :
See dread engagements pictured to the life,
See admirals maintain the glorious strife :
Here breathing images in painted ire,
Seem for their country's freedom to expire :
Victorious fleets the flying fleets pursue—
Here strikes a ship, and there exults a crew :
A frigate here blows up with hideous glare,
And adds fresh terrors to the bleeding war.
But leaving feigned ornaments, behold !
Eight hundred youths, of heart and sinew bold,
Mount up her shrouds, or to her tops ascend,
Some haul her braces, some her foresail bend ;   4
Full ninety brazen guns her port-holes fill,
Ready with nitrous magazines to kill ;
From dread embrazures formidably peep,
And seem to threaten ruin to the deep :
On pivots fix'd, the well-ranged swivels lie,
Or to point downward, or to brave the sky ;
While peteraroes swell with infant rage,
Prepared, though small, with fury to engage.
Thus arm'd, may Britain long her state maintain,
And with triumphant navies rule the main !   5

THE END.

BALLANTYNE, PRINTER, EDINBURGH.

Check Out More Titles From HardPress Classics Series In this collection we are offering thousands of classic and hard to find books. This series spans a vast array of subjects – so you are bound to find something of interest to enjoy reading and learning about.

Subjects:
Architecture
Art
Biography & Autobiography
Body, Mind &Spirit
Children & Young Adult
Dramas
Education
Fiction
History
Language Arts & Disciplines
Law
Literary Collections
Music
Poetry
Psychology
Science
…and many more.

Visit us at www.hardpress.net

CPSIA information can be obtained
at www.ICGtesting.com
Printed in the USA
BVHW091904220819
556561BV00021B/4846/P

9 781407 636504